UNDER HITLER'S BANNER

Edmund Blandford

UNDER HITLER'S BANNER

Serving The Third Reich

Motorbooks International
Publishers & Wholesalers ®

This edition first published in 1996 by Motorbooks International,
Publishers & Wholesalers, 729 Prospect Avenue, PO Box 1,
Osceola, WI 54020, USA.

Previously published by Airlife Publishing Ltd, Shrewsbury, England.

Library of Congress Cataloging-in-Publication Data available

ISBN 0-7603-0268-5

Printed and bound in Great Britain.

CONTENTS

INTRODUCTION

I must record my thanks to the late Betti Brockhaus for her great assistance in helping me to assemble these personal accounts of life under the Hitler regime. These Germans were caught up in the Third Reich that the Nazis believed would last for a thousand years, and while a few really embraced the notion of a Europe dominated by the 'New Order', most looked only to a better everyday life. If Hitler seemed to offer a way out of difficulties then they voted for him, and whatever dismay they may have felt when war came they were for the best part ready to fight for their country.

It is difficult for nations used to a free Press to appreciate just how completely opinion is moulded by propaganda and the great lie as so expertly dispensed by the Nazi Minister of Propaganda and Public Enlightenment Dr Paul Josef Goebbels. Yet for all the Nazi deceptions faith in Hitler declined rapidly when the crunch came, for as always the great majority longed for peace and an end to suffering.

Perhaps it is only a dwindling handful of ex-Nazis and a few blinkered youths of the present generation who still believe Hitler was right.

Edmund L. Blandford 1995

Each one of the following thirteen accounts is prefaced by additional material relevant to some aspect of it. This is intended to help set the scene not only for the purpose of added interest but to enable the reader to gain a more complete picture of the whole.

CHAPTER I

Heidi Brendler

ollowing Hitler's 'accession' to power on 30 January 1933 the Nazis set about organising the National Socialist State which finally put paid to the old system whereby each 'county' of Germany was responsible for its own organisations. From 1933 the Central Government, as embodied by the National Socialist German Workers Party, or NSDAP, imposed its own organisational structure on the new Reich, so that fresh areas of administration were instituted based on the 'Gau' (region) and 'Kreis' (district), and so on right down to the 'block', in theory a perfect pyramid of disciplined command into which was poured a new army of Nazi bosses with the power to hire and fire on the spot. This they did, employing a grand scheme of 'jobs for the boys' which either squeezed new posts into the existing administration or sacked old hands who were considered unsympathetic or alien to the new regime. Above all, Jews, Freemasons and non-Nazi socialists of the democratic sort were ruthlessly ousted or arrested. A gigantic new bureaucracy took shape, for the existing civil service needed to be supervised and ideologically inspired to carry through Hitler's programme of completely Nazifying the 'home front' before he turned his gaze on the armed forces.

Along with the already existing Nazi paramilitary organisations, which as a result of lax laws had been allowed to grow into virtually a 'state within a state', came yet more which took over the duty of overseeing every aspect of the German citizen's life 'from the cradle to the grave' in an even more comprehensive fashion than the British Labour Party's interpretation of that phrase, and certainly way beyond that of the Communist regime of Stalin's USSR.

The Deutsche Arbeits Front (German Labour Front), or DAF, took over the workers' interests on behalf of the nation, for the trade unions were abolished. The DAF was yet another uniformed organisation set up along the usual lines, complete with its ranks and banners and songs, in fact all the trappings of Nazi militaristic order, though its duties lay basically on the factory floor in assessing hours and wages, conditions and arbitration; this on the face of it was its chief raison d'être, but in reality its function lay in keeping the German labour force in line and totally amenable to the Führer's will.

However, the imposition of a revamped national welfare service could be seen in a more favourable light, even if its ultimate aim was the ensuring of a healthy, cosseted nation that would regard the Nazi State as its great benefactor. The National Sozialistische Volkswohlfahrt (National Socialist People's Welfare), or NSV, began life a year before the Nazis took office, to 'become the main and if possible exclusive provider of faith, hope and charity for the German people'. Its leader was Oberfehlsleiter Erich Hilgenfeld who stated: 'It seemed to the founders that the German people had fallen into demoralisation as a result of the political parties', which is most likely true, in view of the multiplicity of such parties and the comments of those around at the time. It is said that the SA brownshirts formed the first objects of the NSV's care for very many of these men were unemployed and in need, so what was more natural than that an organisation set up by their own Party should assist them? Yet it cannot be denied that the NSV did its utmost to care for the community as a whole (within limits) over the coming years of the Nazi regime, especially during the war years and air raids when the mobile soup kitchens toured the streets dispensing soup and National Socialist slogans.

NSV directorates were set up in each of the thirty-two Gaus, 705 in the Kreis and a further 21,624 in local offices, and director Hilgenfeld's grand titles were added to when he was also made head of the Winterhilfswerk (Winter Relief) help organisation which in part relied on SA brownshirt street collectors for its funds. The NSV membership numbered but a few hundred in 1933, but by the year's end had risen to 112,000, by 1934 3,721,000, and to over five million in the following year. In 1937 it had climbed to 7,942,000 and by 1942 had reached a staggering sixteen million. The reason for such enthusiastic socialism is not hard to find, for the Nazis made sure that such responsibilities were brought home to everyone. Indeed, the Reich Labour Court had the power to dismiss any official who declined to take on such work. It has to be borne in mind that near compulsion existed under the Nazis to join 'voluntary' organisations; the NSV was the final refuge of any who were unqualified to enlist or to be dragooned into other groups. A good example of the population's 'enthusiasm' is the case of Austria, where the pattern was set after its incorporation into the Greater Reich in 1938, for the country was at once afforded the full benefits of National Socialism on the Nazi pattern, so that every one person in four was enrolled in the NSV. Not that such a great programme of welfare benefit could survive on charity, for such is impossible in any country maintaining the money system. The Winter Relief scheme had to be funded by an extra ten per cent on income tax.

The head of the NSV was not by previous employment especially qualified to command such a huge organisation; not that this particularly mattered, for as with other governments top administrators were chosen for organising abilities and drive and the Nazis were no exception in that sense, though mistakes in selection were made, for no amount of Nazi zeal and loyalty to the Führer could make up for incompetence. The other aspect of course was that the Nazis could not tolerate any other charitable organisations any more than they could abide political opponents.

However, the parameters set by the NSV did not include the mentally disabled and other 'worthless elements', so these were left to the churches to care for until such time as the crackpot theorists such as Himmler and others found it necessary to set about 'cleansing' the nation of its impurities and sanctioned euthanasia and the concentration camp as the final cure. Otherwise, health was part of the NSV care programme which also took over kindergartens which numbered around 15,000 before the war, containing half a million children under school age.

The Nazis set high store by motherhood, not only awarding medals for the most successful women in this field but setting up and taking over rest and convalescent homes for pregnant women and new mothers. The NSV administered the NS-Gemeindeschwestern or nursing service for sick families etc, as well as funding the so-called 'Hitler Freiplatz-Spende' by which old campaigners of the Nazis' 'days of struggle' (Kampfzeit) were provided with free hotel beds and recreation. In some other countries this would have amounted to a scandalous misuse of public money, the paying off and care of old political comrades from money raised by taxes and charity collecting. But since all other political parties had been abolished the Nazis had free rein and saw such activities as a State duty, quite apart from the 'old pals act'.

The funds of the NSV, raised from street collections and taxes, were also swelled by membership dues which ran from one to twelve Reichsmarks and were increasingly swollen by the Winter Relief collections, which operated not only in public streets but at home and in the factory where refusal to contribute could bring dismissal on the spot by the Nazi work boss. The NSV also took under its wing (in a manner of speaking) the layabouts, drunks and tramps; this department was called the 'Wandererfürsorge'. Ostensibly, such folk were to be assisted into health and a home of some sort prior to work, but later on the Nazis saw no sense in wasting funds in such a manner, finding the concentration camp the best place for the workshy. A citizen who was shy of taking on duties for the welfare or contributing to party funds was considered 'hostile to folk community' or 'contrary to factory fealty', so again in this sense the Nazi regime was much akin to that of the Communists with its absurd jingoistic sloganising to cover every aspect of life.

From 1933 the NSV began monopolising the charity scene, crowding out the older established collections of the church etc, even refusing them permission to continue, or generally making street collecting difficult, rather like a gangster mob crowding out the opposition in the American days of Capone when various collecting rackets were rife. In time the NSV ran over a dozen charities, having taken over some existing ones, and not all of these were for the collecting of money: household scraps were collected to feed the pigs of some local authorities.

It has been estimated that vast sums were coerced from the German people under the guise of charity, some 600m RM annually or around £51m in sterling at mid-1939 value, which can in turn be reassessed at today's prices, and it is supposed that of these large amounts of money a proportion was siphoned off for more dubious purposes. For example, the German clothing industry had never had it so good, for the NSDAP were continually dreaming up ever new branches for the family tree, every one of which seemed to require its own distinctive uniform. A spokesman for the German tailoring industry stated in 1939 that every third German was dolled out in a uniform of one kind or another. Apart from the Party organisations with their plethora of coverings, the armed forces themselves soaked up vast amounts of uniform cloth in a way unequalled by any other military group in the world, even the Americans. The money for all this extravagance, apart from its armaments which were increasing at a galloping pace, came from the Treasury which of course was one of the very first offices the Nazis plundered, and it is a safe bet that those in power felt free to siphon off monies from any one of the Party's many sources of revenue and redirect them wherever they pleased.

The Winter Relief fund assisted 253 out of every 1,000 persons in the 1933–34 period, but by 1936–37 this had been reduced to 161 per 1,000, and one observer commented that when Germany's fortunes ebbed the quality of help was progressively reduced.

When war came further tasks were handed over to the NSV: schoolgirls numbering 17,000 were taken as volunteer nursing assistants, and when the air raids became bad special evacuee trains had to organised which required a meal service and aid en route to safer destinations and the arranging of shelter on arrival. The issuing of gas masks was also undertaken by the organisation in conjunction with the Reichs Luft Bund air raid protection service.

As Heidi Brendler relates, being married to a member of the SS brought esteem and in some instances favoured treatment. The vast proportion of men in the wartime Waffen-SS fought as combat troops and took no part in the running of concentration camps or as members of extermination squads.* This is not the

*see *Hitler's Second Army: the Waffen-SS* (Airlife, 1994)

place to enter into a detailed discussion on the combat SS, but the simple defini-
tion made is necessary in view of the wild inaccuracies still maintained in the
popular media today.

Heidi Brendler's husband appears to have joined the Waffen-SS at a fairly
early stage; this new army did not take the title 'Waffen-SS' until late 1940, following its comparatively small participation in the Polish and Western campaigns. Its leaders did their utmost to instil a new kind of spirit and tactics into
these units which resulted at its best in an élite force noted for its great reliability and *esprit de corps* in combat. SS troops believed themselves superior to all
others, as belonging to a 'crack outfit', and the 'classical' German SS divisions
became noted for their dash and daring, but certain events involving a minority
perhaps bred a legend of atrocity among them which it must be said has been
fostered by certain parts of the media outside Germany ever since.

To belong to the SS was to members akin to Britons or Americans owing allegiance to the Paras or Marines, though it is doubtful if even these élite forces
ever maintained the camaraderie and absolute loyalty of a strain comparable to
Freemasons. Every commander engaged in trying to create something special
in a combat unit does his best to drum into his men their superiority over all
other soldiers; in this way the SS, Paras and Marines assumed an arrogance and
total belief in themselves.

However, by the mid-war years the rigid policy of selection instilled by
Reichsführer Himmler and the Waffen-SS leaders was so diluted that many
thousands of non-Germans were allowed into its hitherto exclusive ranks,
which led not only to a drastic fall in combat reliability but also to a rise in
atrocities.

The NSV, in common with other civilian women's organisations, was taken
over by the National Socialist Frauenschaft in about 1940, this body assuming
overall responsibility for activities and welfare.

"I was born and brought up in Dresden and remember the terrible days following Germany's defeat in the Great War. Things were very bad, food was scarce,
and the rationing system which had begun well in 1914 had collapsed because of
the English blockade and our lack of good allies. By 1918 starvation was a real
threat: if you knew somebody in the country then it was like God's gift of life, for
you could go and visit them and hopefully buy or barter goods for food. I recall
that my mother had an aunt who owned a small farm to the east of the city and we
used to go there by train to see what we could obtain. I had two brothers and my
father was away in the Army and things got so bad that my mother wanted to
send us away to live with the aunt. But the woman did not care for this idea as
she had no children and did not know (as she told us) how to care for them.

UNDER HITLER'S BANNER

So although we managed to obtain a few things from her in our visits, mostly potatoes and turnips, we never did very well out of it. I believe she had her local friends to help and was not I think all that well disposed towards us. I'm afraid it's not always a case of relatives helping each other, at least that is what we found in those awful days when we went so hungry.

After the Armistice things got worse because of all the soldiers returning from the Front; until then I believe they did a lot of living off the land in France and Belgium. My father had survived but was wounded and told us of his shame at the great defeat and of his terrible experiences at the Front. We were quite shocked at some of the language he used and could see that he felt very bitter. I suppose we did not fully understand all they had been through, the terrible sacrifices made over four years; it was the same for the Allies, and for what?

As the 1920s came so did things improve slightly, but the money became more and more useless so we had terrible inflation. My father raged at the incompetence of the politicians and financiers which caused us such hardship, although privately I think he realised by then that the Kaiser should never have led us into that stupid war. I'm sure he was mad.

My father managed to get a job through an old Army friend; it was not much, just digging ditches and drains and that sort of thing. He was a good skilled carpenter but there were about six million unemployed at least and so many chasing jobs, which were very few. Our poor country was completely disorganised and bankrupt, many factories had closed down and there were beggars everywhere, most of them ex-servicemen including many wounded and I'm afraid a lot of these simply died. It was a very sad and depressing time, but we did not give up hope that somehow someone would come along and pick up the pieces. I'm afraid we had little faith in those leaders or politicians who did try their best to pull the country together. They were not very effective.

I suppose it was in the late 1920s when I first saw Hitler, and then only by chance. He was doing his best to pick himself up after the Munich putsch and a spell in prison. We heard something about that affair, but you see in Germany then it was all very local down in Bavaria and did not affect the country as a whole. I had just left school and was earning a few pfennigs running errands for neighbours while my two brothers were also looking for work as they were about a year or so older than myself. Hitler made one of his flying visits to try and organise a local party and made a speech in the street which was where I saw him. I was too young to be very interested and went past on my bicycle. I heard him shouting and waving his fist in a crowd but could not hear much of what he said.

When I got home that day from my little jobs one of my brothers was talking about Hitler and said that he seemed to know what he was talking about. I did

14

not listen much as it was about politics and the enemy and the Jews etc, but I believe my brothers were quite interested; they were both around sixteen at the time. But my mother had too many worries at the time about food and such things to take much notice. As for my father, he said little; he seemed to be so exhausted by his labours and brooded a lot.

Time went by and I managed to get a little job in a store and both my brothers went away to a technical training school in a factory making machinery and were paid a small wage. So somehow we survived the worst days that followed when the big depression came, around 1929–31 I believe. By that time there were frequent street battles all over Germany between Hitler's brownshirts and the Reds who were very strong and well organised. I saw a lot of street parades by both these parties and heard that in some places the Bolsheviks, as we called them, had actually taken over. Although I was young I could see by all my parents said that they were worried as these people seemed bent on destroying the old system and I may say in killing off anyone they felt as of the wrong blood, by which I mean the intelligentsia and upper classes.

Things got a lot more hectic with speeches and elections everywhere and more parades and we wondered how it would all end. There was more street fighting and murders everywhere and at times the police seemed powerless to keep order. I believe the Government of the day were under threat so they mobilised the Army. Things were very serious.

As you know, our old Chancellor Hindenburg was dying and finally sent for Hitler who by then had won over a lot of people. I myself was still not very interested because of normal girlish instincts, by which I mean I had found a boyfriend and was very taken up with him, so much so that I was very keen to get married. This was quite against my mother's wishes at the time although she relented later.

When Adolf Hitler came to power there was a great feeling of relief in most people because whatever happened next we knew that at least order was restored and we could go to bed at night without fear of a Bolshevik revolution. That I believe was the general feeling. You must realise that Hitler had played on our fears for a long time and people had become convinced of the truth of his warnings by actual events in some parts of Germany. As I said, I was not old enough or interested enough to follow all of this, but later I came to realise that the Red menace had been very real and in a way that other countries such as England never experienced.

It was not long before my new boyfriend told me that he had joined the SS and I did not fully understand what this entailed, except that he would be in uniform as some sort of policeman. He told me that it would be a very good thing as he would be paid and could help to rebuild Germany. It meant that he had to go away at times for training and various duties, but when he was at home in Dresden I was very proud to walk with him as he looked so smart. He met my parents who did not quite see him as I did but there were no problems. My brothers were not so indifferent and I could see that they were quite impressed. But while Karl was fully engrossed in his training to become a machinist Otto was, I found, more inclined to the military and it was he who showed most interest in my boyfriend.

I will describe how the Nazi Party programme affected our family.

First, all young people were expected to join one of their organisations, either the boys' or girls' youth, or if older one of the uniformed welfare groups, though for the men there was the SA brownshirts or the motor troops (NSKK) or air corps (NSFK) or the Party [which was itself a uniformed organisation with its own rank hierarchy]. There were so many. My father already belonged to one of the war veterans societies but all these were taken over later by the Nazis. Everyone in those various groups was expected to contribute to Party funds, 'for the good of the nation' as they used to say. In my case I had passed the age of the girls' youth groups but was eligible for other things. I will explain that at this time such things were not compulsory, but pressure was exerted in various ways, and when we saw so many friends enrolled it became almost expected of one. So I joined the Nazi womens' welfare group in Dresden which meant regular duties and these were wholly directed to assisting the sick and elderly.

In sickness everyone was entitled to benefit providing of course you were a German citizen and registered with the local welfare office which paid out a decent amount to keep one in food and board so long as the illness persisted. But there could be no abuse of the system, they were very strict and had the staff to check up; woe betide anyone who tried to milk the Nazi State!

There had always been a welfare system but it had suffered much during the bad years and had to be completely reshaped and reorganised under the Nazis. I myself had various duties both in the administration and calling on people and found it quite interesting. Of course, uniforms, meals etc were all paid for by the State, for the Nazis had taken over everything including the Treasury.

Before Hitler took over there had been some improvements, though the depression hardly helped. But after 1933 things did get a lot better because everyone – or most of us – felt that now we could get on with our lives without fear of revolution, although even the Nazis liked to boast of revolutionising everything. In fact little changed in everyday life: we still ate the same food and hoped for a holiday as always. But because the Nazis took steps to bring everything under their control there was I suppose a greater central organisation to drive everything along in the proper direction. Things seemed to get better and we had no thoughts at all of war, only that our country was getting back on to its feet again, whatever we thought of Hitler, and some thought he was a funny man! But he did seem to succeed in getting things done, so we did not worry about the outside world.

You see, even though I had joined this welfare organisation as a young woman my experience was in a way quite apart from all the business of politics and international affairs. I was too bound up with my everyday life and duties; I did not attend rallies and Party meetings at all. I suppose you could say that we were just some kind of civil servants in uniform. My mother was pleased that I was doing something useful and my father too, I felt, approved. As for my brothers, Otto was so impressed with my man friend that he too applied to join the SS, but was turned down as he was too short. In those early days they were very strict about that and had all sorts of crazy ideas about 'non-Aryan' qualities. Karl completed his training and went into the factory.

When 1935 came conscription started but my brothers were not too worried as to them it seemed a bit of an adventure, though I believe Karl was by then getting a little bored in the factory and was already looking for a change. Otto had been very hurt to be turned down by the SS, but when he eventually went into the Luftwaffe he decided that it had been a good thing after all.

In 1934 the big sensation had been the killing of Ernst Röhm and his gang. That was the way the Nazis referred to them, a 'gang of plotters and traitors', and a lot of other bad names. Hitler explained that they had plotted to take over and ruin all his plans for the new Germany and were so dangerous and armed that they had to be executed. It all caused a big sensation, but then most people thought, 'Well, we're better off without them.' We got on with our lives and I got married to my man in a rather quiet wedding and at first we were happy. Ludwig was now a junior officer and was one of the first to join the armed SS battalion in Dresden, which meant that he had to be away a great deal on duties and training; so when our first child, a little girl we called Marie, was born he saw little of her. At first we lived in a room in his parents' house, but soon found an apartment and all went well. I had of course left my work and would not return to it, for under the Nazis motherhood was almost a sacred duty and everything possible was done to ensure that babies and children were reared in the best circumstances. The fact that my Ludwig was in the SS was a help as everyone was that more anxious to be of assistance.

I can tell you that in those early days I had very little knowledge of what the SS really meant. All I knew was that they were a kind of protective State police and later on a sort of second 'Party' army and that my husband was an officer with good prospects of promotion. He sent me all I needed in wages for my care and the baby and I was satisfied though it was not good that he should be away so much.

Life in Germany under Hitler in the later 1930s was quite good, and as I grew a little older I began to take more notice of what was happening in the outside world and I did come to realise that we had enemies. At least, according to our papers there were those who did not care for the new German Government and I must admit that today, looking back, that man Hitler did make a lot of bellicose speeches about how he would bring every German outside the Reich home again whatever the cost, insisting that the German minorities must be protected, if necessary by force. But these years were so full of bluster I usually paid little attention. I was young and proud and my baby took up all my time and I was a happy mother. I liked to show off my little girl to everyone who stopped to speak in the streets of Dresden. It was really a nice time for me and when my Ludwig came home we would walk in the park and hold hands and everything seemed perfect.

Of course, when 1938 came and Mr Chamberlain visited Hitler we realised that things were quite serious and that some compromises would have to be made on both sides. I did not know anything at all about Czechoslovakia and could not understand what all the fuss was about. Perhaps I was stupid, but looking back I realise how we all were in the main and had no idea of the true state of affairs. My parents seemed quite worried, I believe; they did not want another war, for they were very concerned should their sons have to go through such an ordeal. By that time both Otto and Karl were in the Luftwaffe; Karl had become a pilot, much to our surprise as he was always more interested in mechanical things. Otto was in some kind of ground job but quite happy I believe; he had a fiancée and was very keen to get married before any war came.

I was still of a mind to have more children but my husband told me to wait a while and when war came I agreed with him.

The whole business came as a terrible shock for we all thought right to the last that the politicians would see sense and war would be avoided. I know I suddenly realised that both my husband and brother would be in danger and grew very worried. It was a difficult time as the fighting in Poland began and my husband was alerted to join his unit and be ready to go. But fortunately he was not sent and in a few weeks it was all over. Neither of my brothers was involved though Karl was in the reserve of a fighter squadron and would have gone if it had lasted longer.

Everyone was deliriously happy when it all ended. Many of the men came home and we celebrated with some of them from our town. We thought, what is the point of going on with this stupid war now that Poland has been defeated? The English and French just sat in their trenches opposite our troops on the Western Front and it all seemed so pointless. We were surprised and very disappointed when the war went on. But life continued as normal, though we had to know the air raid drill and were issued with gas masks. We had a good cellar in our home and when Ludwig was on leave he fitted it out with a bed and some furniture and light and it was quite comfortable. Not that I really expected to have to use it.

Then Ludwig went off to the Western Front in the spring of 1940 for training and it was not long before we heard the news of the great German attack which surprised most of us. I grew very worried as my husband's letters came less and less frequently and we knew that heavy battles were in progress. Both my brothers were involved in this attack though only Karl was in any danger; he told us about it later, but made it sound all very easy and we gathered that he saw very little action at all. As for Otto, he simply advanced behind the Army and did not receive a scratch.

When the war started everyone was issued with ration cards and at first everything seemed well organised: there were no shortages. We heard tales from the Allied side that Germany was in all sorts of difficulties as a result of the English and French blockade; I know our papers under Dr Goebbels used to make fun of such things. It is a fact that no real shortages occurred for some time, though there were people who missed luxuries such as we never had. The basic foodstuffs were never in short supply until about 1943.

After the great victory in France the atmosphere was unbelievable in Germany. Everyone was delirious with joy. I know my father got quite drunk when the end of the fighting was announced. It seemed impossible to believe that France had collapsed and England was beaten back across the Channel; I know we were terribly relieved when our men came home safely. Ludwig had been in some fighting but had not, he claimed, been in any great danger. He was of course delighted to be back with his wife and daughter and we had a good time celebrating.

It was then that my bad time began. The start of the air war across the Channel came as a great shock to us all. One moment it seemed we were all in such good spirits, and then it was seen that England was not going to give up. I never had any hatred for the English and neither did my family. I know there were some who felt differently, but for most Germans the 'Tommies' were rather like us, good workers and good soldiers and it was a great shame that we were at war with them. That I believe was the general feeling and I don't think it was very different over there in England. Of course there were very good reasons later for dislike and even hatred as the terrible air raids came and, of course, the awful crimes of the Nazis. But in the summer of 1940 we would sit around the table at home both with Ludwig's parents and my own and talk about this in a way we had never done before. As I have said, I was never politically minded, only the reality of the war had forced me to take more interest;

this was inevitable as soon as my Ludwig and two brothers became involved.

I remember my father telling me that he had met some Tommies in the war in France and talked with them and found them good men. Ludwig too said that he had seen many English prisoners and been quite impressed and did not understand why we were fighting them. Of course we were all under the influence of propaganda and most Germans only knew what Dr Goebbels wanted them to know. I knew that some people listened to the BBC radio news and dance bands, but most didn't because it was dangerous and forbidden. In any case some of the German radios were made so that you could only receive our own stations!

Well, our great disappointment came in 1940 and then we received the worst possible news: our dear Karl had been killed in the Channel battle. It was a cruel blow as he was such a dear boy, always serious but ready for a joke on special occasions. He had a certain way with him and was, I believe, a favourite with the ladies, but never got seriously involved with any girl before his death. We had a short letter from his Commanding Officer that Karl had been flying over the Channel and had become involved with some English fighters who 'overwhelmed' him, that was the word he used. We were terribly shocked and when Otto came home on special leave I could see that he was very shaken. My parents wept as I did and Ludwig cursed the war; it was the first time I had heard him speak that way. I can't say if he or we thought it a 'just' war, I only know that from that time on we cursed it and seriously. That is what happens when bereavement comes.

Of course we never received Karl's body; it was lost for ever in the Channel. My husband went off again for yet more training and received promotion; Otto was also away most of the time in France.

Then came the dreadful time in 1941 when the war in the East began. I will never forget that day. I was out shopping with my little girl and heard the news from a shopkeeper: 'Germany has attacked Russia'. Until then we had become so used to German victories and in any case I had got rather inured to it all, ever since Karl died. The Channel battle had not been of such importance – or so I thought. I did not realise what a big thing it was. And then the business in the Balkans and then Rommel in Africa. I wondered where it would ever stop. But the start of the war in Russia was the end. We knew there were such huge numbers of Russians, but the Soviet colossus the Nazis said would collapse in no time. I just shook my head and prayed as my Ludwig was one of the first to go and then die.

I last saw my husband in May 1941 before he went back to his unit. He was by then in the tank division of the SS and he told me he was going to Poland. He had never been there and said it might be interesting, that was all. We said goodbye at the station and I will never forget the look on his face as he kissed our child. Then the train left and I never saw him again. I never knew the details, but so many died in that awful war that it was often just a case of 'missing in action'. All I did learn later from a sergeant was that Ludwig was cut off and not seen again. This was I believe early in that war in Russia. It seemed so terribly pointless and amazing really as there were huge victories from the start and we had only a few casualties.

This second blow finished me. From that time on I was like a robot, I seemed to live from day to day hardly knowing what was happening outside at all. My parents did their best, but then my father fell ill and died. There seemed nothing but misfortune for us. I did my best to live and Ludwig's parents were very good to me but they too were suffering for they had lost their only son.

But the worst was to come in a way for when the air raids began it seemed as if God had forsaken us. It was indescribable. So many thousands were killed, I cannot speak of it. It seemed to us that the Allies had gone mad. We were terrified of the Russians, but the raids finished us and our beautiful old city. By the time the Russkis arrived they had nothing but huge heaps of rubble to occupy. Thank God I had escaped as so many women both young and old were mistreated by those devils. I can understand how they felt after the ruination of their country by Hitler's armies. I was one of the last refugees to get away in a cart pulled by a farm horse; my mother came with me. Otto survived the war thank God to rejoin us in Western Germany in 1946.**

CHAPTER 2

Paul Stresemann

𝕴 n the British Army Paul Stresemann would have been called a 'sapper', a term derived from an earlier era when it became the practice to 'sap' or undermine the enemy's trench or fortification system as a prelude to planting explosives. The term was current in World War I as applied to army engineers, and to a lesser extent in the later war, but has since died out. In the American Army the role was that of 'combat engineer', and certainly this term adequately describes the job that Stresemann and those like him undertook.

In the German Army engineers were called 'pioniere', though this word is not equitable with the 'pioneer' of the British Army, for such troops were of the Pioneer Corps and known as somewhat unskilled labourers. The engineer was something else, a trained specialist, especially in bridge building.

When an army advances it encounters obstacles and, if streams or broad rivers, the bridging units are hurried forward to lay down usable crossing points, often under enemy fire. Before the age of great technology such bridges were often rather flimsy affairs constructed of timber lengths flung and lashed over wooden pontoons, flat-bottomed boat-shaped sections, the whole being very susceptible to shell and mortar fire.

Infantry assigned to ford a river and establish a bridgehead on the far bank in enemy territory could expect casualties, both in attempting to cross the river and on arrival on the far bank. It was their job to hold on to the ground won until heavier weapons could arrive in support, and for this purpose engineer units equipped with suitable materials would be hard on the heels of the leading platoons, their job to fling over a bridge strong enough to take more troops carrying heavier weapons. Ideally, such bridgeheads would be sufficiently secured to enable the engineers to carry out their work undisturbed, but in a battle area where such crossings were contested this would be rare. It was the norm for the bridge builders themselves to be under fire from either an enemy directly sighting on them or mortar or artillerymen who had previously zeroed in on fixed lines. Obviously, the task of the bridging engineer units was dangerous or even suicidal.

In the case of existing bridges which had been blown up, heavier equipment and more time would be required to effect repairs, though it sometimes became possible to make a temporary link sufficient to take infantry until such time as proper repairs could be completed to enable tanks and other vehicles to cross over. Stone or brick bridges can be very thoroughly destroyed by a retreating enemy, but steel girder constructions can prove more difficult. The famous bridge at Remagen offers a case in point which when finally blown was far from being totally unusable. The destructive competence of engineers varies from army to army, and in any case in a fluid battle troops are sometimes prevented from carrying out a thorough job. Very many sizeable bridge structures were, however, destroyed on the many battle fronts in World War II; yet again, in some cases, such as in the German invasion in the West in 1940, bridges were taken intact in daring attacks by paratroops. In all cases bridge points are vital and care is taken by the attackers if possible to avoid damage, while in some complex situations, such as at Arnhem in 1944, both sides had good reason for wanting to keep the vital bridge intact.

In the advances by the German Army in Poland, the Western Front and in Russia, the terrain was often such that bridging engineers were exposed to great danger in trying to ford river obstacles. Once the leading infantry had effected their own crossing in rubber boats it was the job of the combat engineers to plunge into the water carrying pontoons and lines, often working from small rubber dinghies, attempting to span the river while shells and bullets cut into them and the surrounding area. If the fire was too heavy then the attempts might have to be abandoned, with men and materials expended for no result. Perhaps a fresh effort would be made later, when the enemy fire had been dampened, or else tried elsewhere. Then too in an age of air power such work could be neutralised by a single bomb or even by the weather: a heavy downpour could bring a swollen river and fierce currents to wash away temporary structures.

At the beginning of World War II a fair amount of old C-type bridging material was still in use by the German Army, small wooden pontoons with a superstructure capable of carrying only a five-ton load. But this equipment was soon augmented by types B and K, the latter becoming the standard pattern and utilising a box or bow girder capable of taking sixteen tons, while the B-type used a flatbed superstructure on undecked steel pontoons with a maximum load capacity of twenty tons. A lighter pattern (D) was adopted by infantry engineer units with a top loading of nine tons. All forward engineer units carried a supply of timber for light bridging tasks as described by Paul Stresemann, but heavier structures were built by GHQ units using S-type equipment or even the adopted Czech 'Herbert' bridge, both being capable of taking a load of twenty-four tons.

All vehicles of Germany Army bridging units were marked with the letter appropriate to the equipment carried – B, C, D, K and S.

The great innovation on the Allied side was of course the British Bailey bridge, named after its inventor, a prefabricated structure that could be simply bolted together in a comparatively short time, almost like a giant Meccano set.

"I was born in Berlin in 1911. I had an older sister by five years and my father earned quite good money as a bricklayer. We were never short of food and my mother seemed content. Berlin I remember as a beautiful city in many ways: there was so much to see and do and I remember as a boy I used to go to the zoo to watch the animals which fascinated me. I could also go to the parks and swim in the big lakes; I had learned to swim at school and this came in very useful later on.

When the Great War came my father went into the Reserve Army and was never in any fighting as he was employed continuously in the transporting of supplies to the Front. Later on he would tell us lots of stories of the things he had seen, but of course he did not suffer very much as did millions of others. When the war ended things were very bad and young as I was I could see that we were in all sorts of difficulties. But when one is young it all passes into memory without any kind of trauma and I began to enjoy the life of a schoolboy. Even the big depression did not upset me as I believe we were used to going without many things; it just came and went and then things began to get a little better.

As a boy I did see a lot of trouble in the streets with men marching and shouting but I never knew exactly what was going on although my parents used to speak of it and friends would visit us and discussions and arguments would take place.

Eventually we heard that the man called Adolf Hitler was the new head of Germany and that everything would turn out for the best. By that time my father was no longer a bricklayer but had his own small building firm and took me into it as he saw a great future in that business. I was interested and willing to learn as I did like to watch buildings going up and everything being fitted inside. There was a great deal to learn about construction work as well as the business side of it as my father wanted me to succeed him eventually.

My sister Greta worked as a secretary and seemed quite content with life, so all round we were a contented family. I remember a few incidents in the early 1930s just after Hitler came to power.

One day I was on my way to work when I saw a column of brownshirt Nazis break up a shop and loot the contents; they even tried to give away some goods to passers-by. It was of course a Jewish concern and I was shocked but went on my way to work. By that time Josef Goebbels was the Nazi Gauleiter of our city though we never saw any sign of him. The Minister of Propaganda was very busy with his world of the media and films.

On another occasion we were listening to some music on the radio when the programme was interrupted for a special announcement – the Führer was going to speak that evening on a very important matter concerning Germany's future in the world. So we listened and were amazed when he began ranting and raving against this country and that who he said were trying to encircle Germany. He had especially bitter words for those to the east of us in Czechoslovakia who he called rude names, and also the politicians of the West. Well, we did not know what to make of this man. I can tell you we had no connection with politics, we were not too amused by the Nazis' antics and all those funny capers and parades all of the time. I suppose they had their points and most Germans thought Hitler had saved Germany from the Bolshevik menace which had been real enough, though I myself did not take too much notice of such things. It is true to say, however, that after they came to power we had to stand up and be counted: you were either for them or against them, and things could be a little difficult as we had by then come to realise their strength and above all the police and Gestapo who were anxious to round up all the 'enemies of the Reich', which could involve a lot of people. We were just not a political family; we only wanted to get on with our lives and have nothing to do with such nonsense. But one had to be careful what one said to an increasing extent. We lived in a villa, but even in an ordinary street the police and Gestapo had their informers; the trouble was you could never be sure just who they were. We knew our neighbours and always spoke to them in the street of our suburb in the way of saying good morning etc, but we just did not know after 1934 who was a secret police spy. Things in that respect had changed greatly, although otherwise life went on as usual.

I myself had no interest in joining anything at all and my parents never tried to persuade me; there was always pressure of some kind to enrol in the Nazi Party organisations. A man came into our company who was a rabid Nazi, because they soon infiltrated everywhere, and it was impossible for my father to say no, there is no job for you here! He was forced I believe to take him on. It was as if a member of the Mafia had threatened him with dire penalties if he did not. So that was the situation. I believe the man worked in the office, something to do with the accounts, but one naturally assumed from my father's remarks that he was a stooge of the Party so we had to tread warily.

I did well enough in my job as my father thoughtfully put me through the mill so to speak of learning the construction side of it all before introducing me to the business angle. I enjoyed the first part best as I did not relish sitting about in an office, especially as I had to come into contact with the Nazis. But there were some nice girls there so it was not so bad.

Everything went along quite smoothly until 1935 when the bombshell of conscription was introduced. I was aghast as I had no interest in leaving my home and job, but after a while I was called up into the Army which was increasing in size by leaps and bounds. Then we had a new air force and I began to wake up to what was happening, not that I could do anything.

I remember very well the day I reported to the barracks in Berlin Lichterfelde. It was a cold and rainy day and I felt very miserable. We were shown into a barrack room and given a lecture by a sergeant-major before being issued with our equipment. It was a dreadful time and I felt very miserable. Worse was to come, for in no time we were taken out in the rain to learn drill and how to carry a rifle. The food was not bad but among my companions were some very rough types indeed who used foul language such as I had never heard before. I suppose it is the same everywhere, but when you come from a decent home and family it is hard, but I soon settled down and got used to all that.

Very soon we left the barracks and went off to training areas. I remember one at Doberitz where we learned all sorts of fieldcraft and the like and I suppose I enjoyed it in a way, but I had but one thought all the time which was to return to my home and job; my parents knew this when I went home on leave. I had hoped that in a year or so I would be released, but this did not happen. My sergeant decided that I was officer material and although I resisted strongly he bullied me into becoming an officer cadet and the die was cast. He tempted me with all the soft options I would have as an officer but I was not impressed as I knew perfectly well that it was the officers who would suffer the worst casualties in war, at least if they were in the infantry, and that appeared to be my lot.

My parents suggested I try to get out of the Army, in fact my father asked the Nazi in his firm to try and pull a few strings, but this proved impossible. The firm was functioning well enough without me. I was soon finished with the usual recruit training and bundled off to an officer cadet school, and it was there that I tried to get myself switched into a construction battalion, as I thought that if I was bound to stay in the Army then at least I could try to make the best of it by a transfer into my own kind of trade. This did not work at first as we had to learn to become officers, but after the course several of us were taken out to train in specialist groups and I succeeded in being sent to a pioneer school. This was much more interesting as I could try to put my great interest in constructing things to good use. We chiefly learned how to construct bridges but also all kinds of fieldworks and fortifications which, although interesting at first, soon became routine and I began to get bored.

By about 1937–38 I was forced like all young officers to take political indoctrination classes and I listened to a lot of claptrap about the Aryan race by some jumped-up Nazi official. I don't think we were over-impressed but had learned to say little in case we got into trouble. I went home a full lieutenant and my parents and sister seemed proud of me, and when I called at the office one of the girls called Helene seemed happy to go out with me. Certainly the wearing of a uniform can work wonders in some directions!

But as you know by 1938 Germany had occupied Austria, which became part of the Greater Fatherland, and then the Czech business came up and we wondered where it would all end. We were kept very busy on manoeuvres, but did not take part in those operations. By the following year Hitler had taken an even greater gamble by occupying the whole of Czechoslovakia on some pretext and breaking the treaty signed with the Allies. He then began his campaign of lies against Poland, though at the time we only knew what we were told by the Nazi-controlled media, so we had no way of knowing whether the Poles were murdering our people inside the border areas or not. It made no difference, because in no time we were ordered eastwards and found we were part of a large force poised on the border with Poland. I was very alarmed and said goodbye to my parents and girlfriend just before the war started.

This was my first experience of danger and it was very frightening even though we had great superiority in all arms. The Poles fought hard and fired back with all they had. In our first day we were part of a bridging column and moved forward just behind the infantry. The noise was terrific as our artillery and panzers and Stukas went into action. I had never experienced such noise, even in manoeuvres. We heard all kinds of rumour but knew little except that we were slowly advancing. Then we saw the first bloody, wounded men being brought back and I was sick and frightened. We moved on under sporadic fire but not in any great danger until the infantry and tanks were held up by a river obstacle. This was the moment I had dreaded, but as an officer I had no option but to lead our men forward in the dangerous task of attempting to build a crossing.

We ran forward with our rubber boats and timbers with all kinds of shellfire coming at us. It was absolutely terrifying, even though our own people were firing over at the Poles who were concealed in a wood and the ruins of a village. The dust from explosions was flying over us as we ran straight into the river and began assembling the rubber rafts and timbers with lashings of rope as a temporary crossing. We had to get our infantry across and then make a stronger bridge for the tanks. But as soon as we floated out into deeper water we came under terrible fire from a machine-gun and the man nearest me was killed. I saw him fall off into the water and float away but I could do nothing for him. We jumped into the water and clung to the sides of the rubber boats which in some cases were being holed and becoming useless. I don't know how long this went on, but I was so frightened I could hardly speak and the noise was tremendous.

I think our Stukas must have dealt with the opposition because the enemy fire became much less and at last we were able to make some progress and get a bridge across. The infantrymen were splendid and rushed across almost as soon as we had the last timber in place. It was then that I was able to look around and found that our commander had vanished along with several more men. These assault crossings were always very hard on the engineer units.

We returned to the far bank of the river and collapsed exhausted. It was my first battle and a gruelling experience. Yet we were given no respite for in no time we were ordered onto trucks and rushed across the same flimsy bridge we had made which was no use for the tanks, which had found another place to cross. We had to go forward and bridge a mined road; it was an easy task after the river crossing. I next saw many Polish wounded and prisoners and they looked quite terrible, bloody and bandaged and exhausted. I felt very sorry for them but we were given no respite, the advance had to continue. That night we had a short sleep in the ruins of a village but by dawn we were again on the march with our vehicles and bridging materials, just behind the forward troops and it all began again. The noise of the bombardment from artillery, tanks and Stukas was deafening, and I thought my nerves would snap. We tried to eat but it was useless for every time we settled down a lot of Polish fire came over and we had to dive for cover. The Poles fought hard but were continually outflanked and captured in large numbers.

But after a week of this we could see that their army was in retreat everywhere and we began to hope it was all over. Yet it must have been another two weeks before we heard that they had surrendered and the war was over. I never saw Warsaw which I believe was destroyed anyway; instead we began to pack up everything and make our way back to Germany. I personally had seen enough of war, but my fate was not in my hands.

There were great celebrations at home and I was very relieved to get back in one piece to be with my parents and my girlfriend. I was awarded the Iron Cross 2nd Class and had the red, white and black ribbon sewn on my tunic front, so I must admit I felt rather proud but did my best not to show how frightened I had really been. My father wanted to know about my experiences, but I didn't tell him all that much, though I think he guessed what I had seen and had enough. Like everyone we could see no reason for the war continuing and I was hoping that I would be allowed to return home as a civilian. But it was not to be.

After that grand leave in Berlin I was sent with my unit to West Germany where we began exercises and had a very hard time in that severe winter of 1939–40. We heard that there was to be a big offensive, but this was only a rumour. I was filled with dread as I could not see how I could survive many more actions like those in Poland. Eventually spring came and everything turned green again and I went home on leave to Berlin and got engaged to my lady friend. But on my return the worst happened: we were called to a big meeting and told of the impending German attack in the West. I will always remember that day.

I stood at the back of a crowd of our officers and NCOs while our CO told us the plan. My heart dropped into my boots and I wondered if I should report sick. You see, I was not really a warlike person at all; I was no soldier, I had no dislike of our 'enemies' and no desire at all to harm them. I just wanted to build things, not knock them down! But we were an indispensable part of the forward units and I could not escape my fate.

Before long we had moved up by night into the assembly areas and awaited the dawn in fear and unease. When the shelling started up it all began again and I was in turmoil. We advanced in column and crossed the border into France and the battle was joined. The noise was terrible, even worse than in Poland as our artillery and planes seemed to be stronger. I will never forget the first dead man I saw in that battle. He was one of the infantry sergeants attached to us and had been shot in the head so that his face was a bloody pulp. It was sickening and I wished I had turned away. He was only the first of many corpses I was to see.

We moved on through ruined villages and then deployed into the fields as the battle grew fiercer and more complex. And then we were ordered to ford a small river with rubber boats. This proved an easy task as there was no opposition, but we soon came to a much broader river and a very fierce battle ensued in which I was wounded. One moment I was helping my men to assemble our bridging equipment into the water, the next thing I knew I was lying down with my boots off being tended by a medic. I was bewildered and had no idea what had happened at all. The medic told me it was not serious, and then the shock wore off and I realised I had a sharp pain in my right leg. In fact I then felt the blood oozing out all over my foot, but this was soon stopped by the orderly who gave me a tablet and in no time I felt myself lifted up into a truck and taken to the rear. There was a farmhouse full of wounded and here I was given an injection while my wound was properly dressed. I was still in a state of amazement as it had all happened so quickly and despite my pessimism I had been taken by surprise. In fact I still have no idea what hit me – a bullet or shell splinter.

But that was the end for me so far as the French campaign was concerned, as after a short time I was sent back in a hospital train full of wounded to Germany and into a military hospital where the care was excellent. In a week or two I was able to hobble about and, having written to my parents, I soon began to receive some comforts including a letter and some sweets from my fiancée; she also sent me a large photo which became the envy of my comrades.

A month later I was allowed home on leave, by which time the war in France was in its closing stages, so once again I hoped I might escape back to civilian life. I can tell you the celebrations and relief in Germany were very great because we all thought the war was over and I believe a few thousand men were sent home, released from the Wehrmacht. But this may have been a propaganda exercise; I never met anyone myself who had been released.

When England refused Hitler's offer it seemed incredible, and I must admit it took my breath away, for although we had no great love for our dictator he had been proved right in the eyes of many Germans and had brought huge victories, so now far fewer people doubted him. But we were in any case terribly disappointed when the Channel battle started and we knew that we were taking losses again. Although I was not fully fit I was returned to my unit in Germany. I had some torn muscles and these needed time to heal. I was given a desk job and this suited me and I began to hope that whatever happened I would see the war out in a non-combat status.

This hope too was dashed, for in a few months, after the Channel battle had concluded, I was medically examined and pronounced one hundred per cent fit for active service. I was very disappointed but unable to fool the doctor.

But life was fairly easy. I had a splendid Christmas in Berlin and fixed a date for my wedding to Helene which was to be in February. A lot of people were invited including of course her parents and friends and quite a few colleagues from the old firm. By the middle of February I had managed to obtain leave and got married; the party was rather a special one much enjoyed by all. At that time there were no shortages despite the war so nothing was missing in that direction at our celebration. After we managed to get away we went for our honeymoon to a little cottage near the Baltic coast. It was very cold but we were much in love so the weather did not worry us. We had a few trips and then it was all over and we returned to Berlin where we had arranged a small apartment through one of my father's contacts in the business and furnished it quite comfortably. I was now a married man and very reluctant to return to the Army, but I had to go.

When I returned to my unit I was struck dumb by a rather terrible rumour which was circulating in a rather subdued manner; this concerned some big operations in the East. I could hardly believe my ears and once more grew frightened. Yet weeks went by and nothing happened so I began to hope that it had all been a false alarm. But then the fighting began as we invaded Yugoslavia and Greece and Crete, and before we knew it everyone was packing up and moving through Poland. I was in the utmost gloom as it had all happened very suddenly, even though we realised later that the plans and preparations must have been going on for some time.

We passed through the areas of the 'General Government', as they were called, and it was pitiful to see so much of the devastation of the 1939 campaign and how poverty-stricken the poor Poles looked. Many Germans had closed their hearts to such sights but I could never get over these sights of suffering. If I had known the rest of it – the mass shootings and deportations etc which we only heard rumours of, though not seeing any evidence – I think I would have run away. I can say that in all my army service I never saw a single atrocity, although of course when so many prisoners are taken as in Russia there is bound to be some chaos in feeding etc, for everything was in a terrible mess. Again, I had no idea that many of these poor devils would end up starving or dead in the West after they had been marched away in vast columns many, many miles long.

But on that quiet and terrible day when the Führer's proclamation was read to us before dawn in the East I just wanted to curl up somewhere and escape it all.* I can tell you that not one among us showed any bravado or 'get up and go' spirit. They did their job but with no joy, even when the victories came. We were a unit of builders and never – or rarely – took up arms unless we were directly attacked by enemy infantry. So we had a long, hard march forward, some on foot, some in vehicles, until we reached the first river obstacle and were rushed forward to do our job.

I remember my amazement on seeing the vast fields and plains in Russia, the hovels called houses and little villages which in some cases were burnt to the

---

*Hitler's order of the day to his troops was read out to them before the huge offensive began at dawn on 22 June 1941, some men hearing it at dusk the evening before, some later:

'Soldiers of the Eastern Front! Weighed down for many months by grave anxieties, compelled to keep silent, I can at last speak openly to you, my soldiers. About 160 Russian divisions are lined up along our frontier. For weeks this frontier has been violated continually – not only the frontier with Germany but also in the far north and in Romania . . . At this moment, soldiers of the Eastern Front, a build-up is in progress which has no equal in world history, either in extent or in number. Allied with Finnish divisions, our comrades are standing side by side with the victor of Narvik [General Dietl] on the Arctic Sea in the north . . . You are standing on the Eastern Front. In Romania, on the banks of the Prut, on the Danube, down to the shores of the Black Sea, German and Romanian troops are standing side by side, united under Head of State Antonescu. If this greatest Front in world history is now going into action, then it does so not only in order to create the necessary conditions for the final conclusion of this great war, or to protect the countries threatened at the moment, but in order to save the whole of European civilisation and culture.

German soldiers! You are about to join battle, a hard and crucial battle. The destiny of Europe, the future of the German Reich, the existence of our nation, now lie in your hands alone.'

ground. The poor peasants and children suffered terribly. It was all very cruel but we were always in movement and unable to settle down for very long; we took only short rests. It was always forward! forward! forward!

One day I was approached by a rather grubby Russian boy about six years old or so who asked me for a 'zigareet', but instead I gave him a piece of bread which he snatched and ran off with, disappearing behind a cottage. In a very few moments he had reappeared, this time leading a little girl not much bigger than himself. My comrades were asleep so these two children came over to see me and an amazing thing happened. The boy grinned at the little girl who was quite pretty in a childish fashion; she at once lifted up her shabby dress to disclose that she wore no underwear. They both grinned at me and then the boy said again, 'zigareet?' and pointed at the girl's private parts, both of them now grinning hugely. I was so amazed I just stood there gaping for a moment before giving them a piece of chocolate and making a swipe at them, sending them running.

We always found that there were some poor Russian civilians who were anxious to work for us, and in the case of the women who were invariably dirty they were literally willing to do anything for cigarettes or rations etc. I am sure that in some cases where discipline was slack they did succeed in their quest to become barrack-room whores, travelling concealed in some wagon for the soldiers' use. It happens in all armies but we ourselves never indulged in such things.

Then came the day when I was again wounded. It was inevitable, for sooner or later we would have a tough time fording a river and the Russians were always very good with artillery and mortars, if poor in other ways.

On this particular morning we had arrived forward just short of a built-up locality and under fire, to bridge a fair-sized stream which was deep enough to be considered an obstacle. We had just begun to master the job when a rain of shells began to fall about us and we were scattered. I was in my usual state of terror and had reached the far bank behind us when I felt something hit me in the back and was knocked flat by it. I was more winded at first, but then felt a terrible pain and cried out. There was an immediate lull so some of my men picked me up and carried me to one of our vehicles, laid me on the ground and tore off my tunic. I had caught a splinter in my lower left back, but it looked worse than it really was. I was bandaged up and taken to the rear and a better place for tending my wound. It was a barn set up as a dressing station and it already contained some stretcher cases. The doctor took a glance at me, probed about, which was very painful, but apparently did not see it as a serious wound, but I yelled out and passed into a faint. I next came to lying in a truck which was bumping along on one of those terrible Russian roads. I believe I ended up in a hospital in Kiev in one of the few buildings left standing and I was on my back for only two or three days before being allowed up. Once more I wondered if I could get out of the damned war – but no! My wound was considered superficial and in a week or less I was back at the Front and it began all over again.

I had become resigned to losing my life, but amazingly I did not. In fact the German advances continued right into that awful winter and I became inured to it all and quite expected to be left behind in the snows of Russia. The winter had come early and we were resting in one of the ruined cottages. The mud period had turned to snow and there we were in uniforms only fit for mild weather. We froze and froze and thank God the advance now ground to a halt, otherwise we would never have survived. Imagine trying to cross frozen rivers in the terrible cold of a Russian winter. Admittedly the ice would grow metres thick, but that came later; initially we were just smitten by an 'ordinary' cold snap without winter gear.

But then it got very much worse and I did not see how we could survive the cold which was hell. We sat around shivering in our hovel for days on end, unable to go anywhere, short of food and blankets, wondering what was happening. Even the Russian counter-offensive did not seem to affect our sector very much. We merely withdrew a few miles and settled down again to freeze. The first winter clothing arrived but there was not enough to go round and some of us still froze. The casualties from frostbite and sickness grew alarmingly. I was one of those and this too was a day I remember.

It was an awful, dark grey winter's day in November, I believe. I had been out on my rounds to inspect guards and equipment as usual as one never knew when thieving Russians or guerrillas might infiltrate our positions. I felt a bad chill coming on and by next day had gone down in a fever. I had pneumonia and was taken to the rear where the doctors found I was in a dangerous condition. I had little recollection of all this as I was unconscious; it was not really the fate I had expected.

It must have been at least two weeks before I awoke sufficiently to find that I was in a comfortable bed. When I was able to look around and take proper notice I found that I was in Germany and the nurses were a Godsend. Oh! how overjoyed I was to escape that Russian hell! A few days later my dear wife and parents came to see me and we had a wonderful reunion, though I began to worry when they told me about the air raids. However, it was early days in that kind of war as those raids were then only pinpricks. My people brought me some good things and I at once began to recover. But as I did so I began to realise what a terrible future I had in returning to the Front where things were not going well. The stupidity and enormity of that war was really coming home to me, but I could see no way out. I could not desert, so what hope was there? I felt trapped, as did millions of my comrades.

Sure enough, about a month later I was declared fit enough to leave the hospital, but to my great surprise I was not destined for the Russian front but sent to a depot in Berlin itself. This was amazing luck, and there I learned that I would be posted as an instructor to an engineer school, which was incredible. Apparently, despite all my terrors at the Front I had made a good impression and, of course, having been in the Polish and French campaigns and wearing a medal ribbon helped.

My people were also overjoyed, for it meant that I could get home to see them fairly frequently. The only blot on the horizon came when I learned that there was a rota system in use at the school: there was no question of any permanent staff, everyone had to take their turn at the Front, I was told, and that included me. I thought I had done enough in combat, but apparently not. But I tried to put the thought of it out of my mind. I would have a few months to enjoy the new life at least and I intended making the most of it.

My days were filled with talking, talking, talking, and this I grew sick of, even though I realised it was far, far better than the frozen hell of Russia where I knew my comrades were suffering. I had to lecture the new recruits in the techniques of bridge-building and construction of fortifications, using models and all I had learnt in practice. It really did become very boring as it was all so repetitive.

And then my wife gave birth to our son who we called Mark, and that was a wonderful tonic for me. I heard too that 'our Nazi' at the firm had been called into the Army so I was overjoyed at that also! I spent some very happy times at home in Berlin. Things had changed little there; we could still get reasonable rations, though not so many cafés were open. I was so overjoyed with my son that I tended to forget all about the cursed war. The air raids were not bad and so far nobody had been bombed out in our families or anything worse, so I was not especially worried.

However, when the air raids did become worse – and I recall the very big attack on Cologne – I felt that Germany was doomed. Russia would never be conquered, no matter how many of them we killed or captured, and now they had powerful allies. I felt, as did many others, that the war would be lost by us.

In the end I was called before my CO who told me that I must go back to the Front where I was needed. He himself was too old he said, but he wished he could accompany me! I nearly laughed at him, the old fool. I was very, very downhearted, and in a last leave told my parents that they should leave Berlin if they could as I felt it would be attacked as Cologne was. But my father would not hear of it. Of course he had his business to attend to, so I could see his point. My fears were justified however, and in full measure.

I returned to the Front in the summer of 1942 in the middle of a huge German offensive which seemed to achieve all its objectives, but then ground to a halt.

No matter how much territory we took or how many Russkis we killed or captured, or the booty gained, there was always more. Only half a dozen of my old comrades were left and we had a big job crossing a river under heavy fire. I had been away too long; the noise was so bad I just wanted to dig myself into the ground and fall asleep, anything to escape. But we were forced to go on and plunged into the water with our equipment. The river was splattered with bursting shells and bullets, with shoals of earth and debris and splinters falling on us. I saw men falling and screaming and I trembled so much I was on the point of giving up. But we got the bridgework in position and lost a dozen men in the process. By some miracle I survived but I knew not how; it was terrible. While the infantry and tanks crossed I just collapsed on the ground in a heap, totally exhausted and soaked through.

Those Russian summer days were very, very hot, but far preferable to the cursed cold of winter.

That day we had triumphed, but on another disaster befell us.

We had been driving all day and were filthy, hot and very thirsty and hungry. At last we reached our bivouac area, but had only just settled down to eat some food when the Russian artillery hit us. We were caught by surprise, in the open really with very little shelter, and took casualties at once. The detonations were very loud and I saw men, horses and trucks go flying up into the air in all directions in the confusion. I fell into a large hole or crater and the shelling went on for some time.

When it stopped and I dared to look out of my hole I saw a scene of utter desolation. All the horses and trucks and equipment were wrecked and only here and there a surviving soldier, as dazed as I was. We tried to assemble and pick up the pieces, but it was no use. We were sent as survivors to the rear. It was the end of our old unit and, in fact, I was the only survivor of the original bunch of men who had started out in Poland.

It is very painful to tell the next point, for I broke down completely. It does happen in battle. Men under fire reach a point where their nerves break and it is impossible for them to function any longer. This is what happened to me.

We had marched as our own transport had been destroyed and had at last reached shelter, completely exhausted and demoralised. We found a barn or something, I forget exactly what, and an officer was trying to take down details and give us orders, paying particular attention to me. I must have cracked up at that point. It is hard to describe – I just raged and collapsed onto the ground in tears. I was completely done for, I cried and cried like a baby and only vaguely felt myself being lifted up on to, I believe, the officer's vehicle and taken to another base area in the rear. It must have been an aid station as I was given an injection and fell fast asleep.

I woke up and found a young doctor asking me how I felt. I told him, 'Nuts,' and he said, 'It's shock. I expect you'll get over it soon.' My thoughts about that I kept to myself. I began to feel that I could never go back to the Front, even if I had to fake illness. I knew I was in a bad way; my nerves were shattered. In a day or two I was allowed out of bed and walked with a stick, I felt so weak. I had no interest in anything, I could not even write home, I was completely useless. Strangely, I did not have bad dreams or nightmares of my experiences at the Front. In fact I believe I slept well, which is odd. But by day I was like a useless vegetable. I found eating difficult, I could hardly swallow, although drinking came easily.

I was inspected by the medics in every way and discussed and I know they were trying to decide if I was a shirker or not. But I did deteriorate without any effort on my part. I was wilting away and clearly in no state to be sent to the Front again. I was in a sort of limbo, half dead in a way yet in the land of the living. It was simply battle fatigue, the effects of shock on the mind which precluded my functioning in waking hours. In the end, after a couple of weeks they had to get rid of me as they needed the room, with so many casualties. I was sent back with many others to Germany into a rehabilitation ward, doubtless the hope being to return me to Russia as more cannon fodder, or even to one of the other Fronts. By then it was all up in Africa and we were expecting the invasion, though it was some way off. I was granted sick leave and I will never forget the look on my wife and parents' faces when they saw me. I must admit I was in a sorry state and quite surprised at my own face in the mirror.

But then the worst happened: our flat was bombed, though fortunately my wife and son were not there at the time. They survived and moved into my parents' home which was very roomy. I was in a replacement unit and unsure as to my fate. But then I was downgraded medically and could not see how I could ever return to the Front. Then a good thing happened: I was again posted to the instructing school and this was where I ended my career in the German Army.

Although I went home to Berlin regularly the air raids became so bad that I finally persuaded my wife to leave, and found her a good room near my depot. But soon afterwards my dear parents were killed in one of the air raids. They had gone down into the cellar as usual but the bomb blew everything down on to them and they could not be rescued in time. Luckily my sister was elsewhere and survived. It was a terrible setback to us and we were in a bad way for some time because my parents' remains were not discovered for some weeks. I became ill again and my wife and boy visited me in hospital. Then I was discharged as medically unfit so that severed my connections with active duty.

As the Americans came nearer so we made a great effort to escape the Russian advance, hard though this was, for the military, police and SS were very active and all men of military age were being stopped in the streets. In fact, despite my discharge I was almost taken into the Volkssturm (Home Guard). I was told to report to the local commander, but by then the Russians were not far away and entering the Berlin suburbs. By a great effort we managed to escape with the help of an old friend who pulled a few strings and had a car with petrol.

I will never forget my immense relief when we saw the first American tanks. I don't think those Yanks realised how relieved we were to see them."

CHAPTER 3

Helene Streibling

he tale that follows must be one of the little classics of World War II and has remained untold until now. It tells of what one can assume was a fairly 'plain cook' and the villains of the Gestapo, though not unnaturally here the agents are not shown in their worst colours. In fact, Nazi Germany's secret policemen rarely are depicted in the popular media all that accurately, more often than not being portrayed as black uniformed thugs of the SS.

The Gestapo of Nazi Germany originated in the Prussian political police, and there was nothing unusual in that since the police forces of all nations contain a branch dedicated to weeding out subversives and are usually a quite different department to military (counter) intelligence. In Britain we have the Special Branch and MI5, while in America the FBI handles not only interstate crime but espionage and any anti-American activities.

When the Nazis took power the Prussian police force fell into the greedy hands of General Göring who, although an ex-air ace, had taken very much to politics and Hitler and coveted the political arm of the state police. In due course one Rudolf Diels emerged as chief of the secret department and plans were made to extend its powers throughout a Nazified Germany, which as mentioned elsewhere had previously been split into separate states, each with its own police and prison system, somewhat as in Britain. But Diels was soon ousted, having fallen out of favour with Himmler, the new Reichsführer of police, displacing Göring who had more than enough on his plate in other directions.

The Prussian political police squad had comprised professional detectives, and this became the model for the national force; the personnel were not mere brownshirt revolutionaries who changed into brown felt hats and long leather raincoats. They were men skilled in detection, surveillance and interrogation, and in organisational terms had no direct connection with the SS which soon set up its own intelligence department, the Sicherheitdienst, or SD.

The ex-poultry farmer Heinrich Himmler showed great zeal in setting up the huge Nazi German 'Sipo' (abbreviation for Sicherheitspolizei, or Security Police) and despite his cranky traits into 'blood and soil' he did a very thorough job. The problem was that each arm of this police empire vied for greater power, with the result that yet another Nazi bureaucratic set-up began overreaching itself and poaching on other territory. Germany was indeed a highly policed state, the most so in history, with town and country police (two separate forces), the SS, Gestapo, the Military Police and its arm the Secret Field Police, which often worked in occupied territories with the SD, or even the long established secret service under Admiral Canaris, the Abwehr.

But of all these forces the Gestapo were the most feared everywhere since it was at all times a plain clothes force and employed a small army of informers who, as indicated elsewhere, could be the friendly neighbour or the apartment block janitor, anybody who lived and worked among the people and was thus on the face of it privy to their conversations, gossip and opinions. No one has yet been able to state exactly how many were bona fide Gestapo agents, as distinct from the hired help, the 'V' men or trusties. The Gestapo had its rank system based on the old plain clothes branch (Kommisar, Kriminalrat etc); the number has been variously quoted as from a few hundred to several thousand. One clue lies in a Gestapo identity disc held by the author, an oval brass plate bearing the legend 'Geheimestaatspolizei' on one side and an eagle and swastika on the reverse; it also bears the number 6483. Obviously, even a few thousand German agents had their powers increased enormously by the recruiting of informers and sub-agents.

Yet in this unusual tale we may have an example of one security agency overstepping the mark and reaching into the province of the Abwehr, or foreign intelligence, though there may well have been other ramifications not disclosed to Helene Streibling. It is however surprising that the Gestapo should recruit a small-time cook and transport her across Germany to try and entrap an ally.

"I was born in 1918 in Hanover and I had two sisters. My father owned a flour mill and bakery so when the bad times came we did not do too badly though things were difficult. Many people came to us for help and we did our best for them, but the great problem came when the currency became almost worthless.

As a girl I attended high school and wanted to become a nurse but changed my mind and decided to become a cook. My mother was a very good cook and did all she could to help me through my studies at the cookery classes which I attended after leaving high school. But jobs were hard to find and I was seventeen before I found a post in a college which needed someone to help the cook who was an old woman. I was taken on for a month's trial and did well, so then I received a proper wage and a chance to advance myself, for the old lady told me she wished to retire in a few years, so if I wanted her job it could be mine. But I was a little too young and would need much more experience.

The college was for the boys of wealthy parents and concentrated on science, mathematics and history, and was considered a good grounding for the military.

After three years' hard work the old lady told me she had had enough of the working life and wished to retire. When she told this to the head of the school he was not very pleased but agreed, providing she allowed me to take a trial as sole cook for the two hundred boys and staff for one month. This we both agreed to though I was very nervous at such a responsibility and felt I would certainly need assistance as the work was too much for one person.

However, I went ahead and did my best, but at the end of the month the old lady told the college head that I could not possibly do such a job alone and must have help. He was reluctant but finally agreed to hire a young assistant so that the old lady could leave in peace of mind. This was soon done and a young boy came to help me who was very conscientious and worked hard. Between us we managed the job, which was a heavy one and lasted all day and into the evening. My mother was worried about me because of all this hard work and the wages were not good. I decided I would carry on for a while but think about a different kind of work or even find another post.

The weeks went by in the period when the Nazis were taking over the country, and changes followed in some directions as they took over many institutions, and this included the college. I do not know how it happened, but the whole staff and curriculum were changed so that it became a Nazi school for young leaders and was no longer private. The Nazi officials inspected everything and asked me how I liked it there, so I boldly told them that unless I received more help I would have to leave. At this they laughed and said this was no problem and they would see to it that I received all the help I needed. What's more they asked me if there was anything else I needed, so I became even bolder and said 'a proper wage!' I can tell you that within a week or so I was given a very good raise in pay. This pleased me very much as I liked the place and those Nazis said 'Nothing is too good for our young boys, so do your best and feed them well, cook!'

So within a fortnight all the old faces had vanished and the big mansion became filled with boys of about fifteen to eighteen years of age, all in Hitler Youth uniforms and very smart and correct, and soon I got to know a lot of them. I took no interest in what they were taught and saw virtually nothing of that side of it at all. They would sometimes come downstairs to the basement where I did all the cooking in big ovens to make special requests such as on birthdays or at Christmas, and I was always happy to oblige. They used to give me small presents, flowers or a brooch or chocolates, which was nice.

I was of course still very young to be in such a position, but I believe the experience matured me a great deal. In fact while I was there I even received a proposal of marriage which was very funny as on that day I was covered in flour and other mess and the young instructor (he could not have been over twenty-five) told me he loved my cooking and needed a good and dutiful wife. I was very flattered but told him politely that I was much too young to marry. He was not too upset, he just shrugged his shoulders and went away smiling.

This job lasted for a long time, but by 1939 I was becoming a little bored with it all and decided to leave. I told them at the school of my intention and as before they were understanding and said that they would find a new cook but never so good as myself, which was very nice of them.

I began looking around and at last saw a job open in a large factory where I could see I would act in a supervisory capacity with much less effort in some ways and a better wage. I applied for this job and was accepted at once, but on trial as they felt I was a little young. The fact that I had worked for a Nazi Party organisation and had a very good reference carried some weight. I began work and the hours were quite long but I was in charge of three other cooks, one of them a man; they seemed quite happy to work under a girl who was younger and I think they respected my experience and ability, at least after I had been there a while, and it all went very smoothly. The factory was making chinaware and all sorts of crockery, including items to special order of quality, and employed about one hundred people, so in that sense the workload of preparing meals for them which they took in a canteen was less than at the Hitler Youth school.

When the war came it was a great shock and very sad and everyone was rather quiet. A lot of the older people remembered all the suffering of the Great War and here now was another which could be even worse. But we all carried on as usual though at home we had certain air raid precautions to attend to, especially as the local air raid protection squads called round all the houses checking and ensuring that all the work was done properly. At the factory we had no air raid shelter so the Party organisation told the manager he must build one. There were no cellars so the poor man decided he must have a concrete bunker built outside, but I don't believe he could afford it. The firm's orders fell and then the factory was forced to close down, which was a blow as I loved my job.

At that time there was not the direction of labour that came later, for although we were at war in Poland it was all quiet elsewhere so we had no 'total war' on the home front. Even so, the people were told that war meant sacrifices and we should all do our best for the sake of the Führer and the men at the Front. But

though there was rationing it was not severe; the only problem was my employment and when I tried the labour office they sent me to a Wehrmacht canteen as
an assistant, but all I had to do was wash dishes and this I felt was a waste. But I
was forced to do the job to get some wages while I looked for something better;
I almost wished I was back in the Hitler Youth school, and was on the point of
returning there to see if a job was available when one of my father's friends told
him of a high Nazi Party official who owned a big house with a wife who was
not very good at cooking. He liked to entertain important guests at home sometimes and felt that for this he needed a good cook who could easily cope with
such company, perhaps including even the Führer himself (which seemed
unlikely to me).

I was able to pass the word that I was free if he would give me a trial, and this
came about shortly afterwards. I was to attend for an interview at his home
which was in the evening, but when I arrived it was his wife who saw me. She
was dressed in a long gown and seemed rather flamboyant and questioned me
closely about my career so far. She told me that we would be entertaining very
important people and that I would be given all I needed and would have to serve
and cook the meals. I would not have a regular schedule but would be given my
own room and would have to be available whenever they needed me. I was
shown a rather nice self-contained bedroom and decided that I would accept
this post as the wage offered seemed better than I had earned so far. At least I
would see how things worked, and at least it would be a new experience for me.
The kitchen in the house was very adequate and it was obvious that no expense
had been spared, though I was not sure how long these people had lived in the
house. Not every Nazi bought or rented his own property; some were gifted to
them in a manner of speaking for 'services rendered', and in some cases had
been confiscated from some unfortunate owners.

I wondered when I could begin this new life and meet the boss of the house,
and was told to move into my room a week later. I was told to keep myself to
myself. Guests were not allowed, though I could receive mail and use the telephone. In this connection I was expected to take calls for the owners if they
were away and, I gathered, even act as a receptionist at times. I was quite agreeable but had no intention of being put upon no matter how important a man my
new boss turned out to be. I will not mention his name as it is not one that will
register as one beyond the locality, though he was important in his Party area.

I moved into my room a week later with my belongings in a suitcase and soon
afterwards the lady of the house called me down to meet her husband who was
in the study-lounge and at work at his desk. He was dressed in his brown Party
uniform and the usual swastika armband and stood up to greet me. He was a
large, red-faced man of heavy build and seemed pleasant enough. He said he

hoped I would be happy with them and carry out my duties well. I replied that I thought I could and returned to my room to sort out my things.

A little later the lady came up to tell me that they were going out and might return later for drinks and a snack. I was shown all the necessary wines and schnapps etc and glasses and told to stand by later in case they needed me. I had a little radio in my room that they had provided and sat down for a while to listen to some music, but as soon as they had left I went to inspect the house, and especially the kitchen. There was a large, well-furnished front room in which I assumed they entertained their guests, and a good dining room, apart from the lounge-cum-study. Upstairs were four bedrooms not including my own, a good bathroom and two toilets. The garden at the rear was a little untidy.

I returned to my room and sat reading a newspaper, and at about eleven p.m. heard the couple returning; they were laughing and joking and had several people with them. I opened my door as the lady came for me. She asked for a selection of drinks with glasses to be placed on a tray but that she would do the serving, and I should stand by in the kitchen in case they wanted sandwiches. I did as I was told and sat in the kitchen while a party started up in the front room, and after a while the lady came to the kitchen and asked me to prepare a few sandwiches of various kinds, so I got busy. When they were ready she had not reappeared so I picked up the tray and made my way to the front room, knocking on the door which was opened by my employer, the lady, who asked me to take the tray into the room and place it on a side table. There were at least six men and women in the room all sitting or standing about drinking; the men were all in uniform, including an SS officer. They glanced at me and one of the women remarked to my employer that she had found a 'maid' at last, being told that I was in fact the cook-housekeeper, which seemed to interest them. I returned to the kitchen, wondering if I should wait up to wash the dishes. Soon the lady came in with the empty tray and asked me to wait up a little longer as her husband wished to speak to me.

So I sat down to wait, and after about half an hour I heard the guests leaving, and after they had driven off in their cars the man of the house came in and asked me to go with him into his study. He told me to sit down, so it all seemed rather like another interview. He then told me that from the security viewpoint it was very important that I should never repeat anything I might overhear to anyone outside. He said that his SS friend had impressed this aspect upon him; there was a war on and I had already been vetted by them and found 'respectable'. In wartime he told me we could not afford to take chances so I must always be alert in this kind of thing and take no notice whatever of whoever I saw or happened to hear. I promised to do this and he dismissed me.

The very next day to my great surprise I had been to the shops for some groceries and was in the kitchen when a caller at the door in civilian clothes introduced himself and came inside although the owners were out. I was a little upset as I didn't know who he was, and as he stepped into the house I saw another man and a woman waiting in a car outside. He took me into the front room and pulled out a little badge. It was an oval disk and on it were the words 'Geheimestaatspolizei – the Gestapo! My legs went weak and he told me politely enough to sit down. I was then questioned closely as to the previous evening's events: who had come to the house, how many people, what were they wearing, what were they talking about, who did I think they were and so on. I replied as best I could; I had hardly noticed them at all as I was only in the room for a few seconds and the only remark I heard concerned my own status.

He then asked me about my previous work 'for the Party', if I had liked it, what did I think about the war etc, and did I listen to the radio, and if so what? I answered in this fashion: the war was bad, but I hoped it went well for us as we had had enough in the last one, though I was too young to know much about it, and I was not interested in politics. Yes, I had enjoyed working at the Hitler Youth school, I only left because I wanted a change and a little less footwork! He seemed satisfied with my answers and said thank you, now I could return to my room. 'Say nothing about this to anyone – *anyone*! Do you understand?'

I agreed and let him out of the house. I watched through the front window as the three drove away and returned to my room wondering what it was all about. I was nervous and thinking about what would happen next. I even wondered if they wanted me to spy on someone, even my employers. I was a bit daft I suppose, but you see I had no idea what it was all about so I had to assume it was all to do with the security business that the boss had talked about the previous evening.

I said nothing about this questioning to my employers, but when I saw my parents the next weekend (I had a few hours off each Sunday) I told them and they became concerned. My sister thought I must have been indiscreet but this was not so. I returned to my work and maintained a strict silence in every way though being as polite as I could. Several more occasions occurred when guests came, and during some of these I realised that my boss would take one or two of his male friends into his own study for more private conversations while the ladies remained in the front room, or even in the dining room where I served full meals. It was of no great importance to me and I was fairly happy in my work so long as I was not under any kind of surveillance. It occurred to me that my employers might be either more important people than I realised or enemy agents. This sounds ridiculous, but all kinds of possibilities came into my mind at that time. But in the end I could see that if my employer was an important Party man then certain aspects of his security had to be looked into.

Nothing much happened for the next few weeks; the war had ended in Poland and it was all quiet in the West. And then, to my great surprise, I had another visit from the Gestapo man and I was extremely frightened. He had his female companion with him, who was a very plain type of woman in a raincoat and hat; they took me into the front room again and told me to sit down. They were quite pleasant but looking me over all the time as if sizing me up and I felt very uncomfortable. After a few simple questions such as how did I like my job and living there etc, they asked me if I felt like a change of employment. I was very surprised, I didn't know, I was quite happy there, it all depended on why? The woman then asked me if I would like to work for the Government. I had no idea what she meant and did not know what to say at first. The man then said that it was every German's duty to help the war effort, did I not agree? Of course, I told him, but how could I be of help?

He said that they had it in mind for me to move on to something bigger; after all, my present work was not exactly of great importance, my employers could easily find another cook if they needed one. Did I not agree? Well, I suppose so, I told them, but what did it all mean? The woman then said that I could do similar work in places directed by them and that it would be very important work for the war effort and, above all, very, very confidential. Was I interested?

I was in a great state of surprise. I said yes, I suppose so. Could I stay in my own town, or would I have to go away? And was it dangerous? At this they laughed and said of course not, there was no danger involved. But I would inevitably be under orders and might have to leave home, but all would be in order; all I had to do was agree and I would receive instructions a little later. So I told them I was happy to go along with it, but what about my employers? Don't worry, they said, leave that to us. On the right day all I would need to do was pack my bag and go home and wait until they came for me.

I was so amazed I just sat there, open-mouthed. They stood up and shook hands in quite a friendly fashion and said that I would be hearing from them fairly soon. Once more they warned me not to speak to anyone of this matter and I agreed. I at once thought of my parents and if I should tell them, and then decided to say I had had a better offer.

A few days later the telephone rang when my employers were out of the house; it was the woman from the Gestapo and she told me that it was time for me to pack up and leave. I was to go home and tell my family that I had been directed with excellent references to a Government job, and that I was waiting to hear just where, or something like that. So I agreed to do this, went upstairs and packed my bag, left the house and arrived home not long afterwards. My parents were very surprised to see me. My father was there as he did not attend his mill and bakery every day but only called there occasionally to supervise and make sure all was in order. I told them that my employers had told me that I was needed in more important work for the war effort but that I would remain in my usual profession. This surprised them but they accepted it, and I told them that the local Party office would notify me when and where my new job was to be.

A week went by and then a telephone message came for me: I was to call back a certain number and they would be waiting for me. I did this and the same woman of the Gestapo told me to be round the corner with my packed bag in a few minutes. I told my mother who was in the house that my new job was ready, and that she was not to worry as I would let her know as soon as I had begun work.

Sure enough, as soon as I went into the next street the same car I had seen before came by and stopped and the Gestapo man ordered me to step inside. He said little except that he was so glad that I had decided to take up their offer. To my surprise we went to the police station but walked straight through the building out of a back door and into another car with the same woman sitting behind the wheel. It was all very mysterious and I wondered what could be going on. I felt I was either a prisoner or even some important agent being taken to do a dirty job!

They said nothing to me as we drove out of town for a very long way. I had no idea where we were going and did not like to ask. I wondered why they were taking all this time and trouble over me. Eventually I noticed that we were on the autobahn for Berlin and this excited me. I had only been there a couple of times on short holidays, but again it seemed a little crazy. What was I doing in this situation? Well, after a few miles the car was stopped so that the man could go somewhere to do his business, and while he was away I asked the woman where they were taking me and what it was all about. She told me that I must not worry as everything about my new job would be explained to me when we reached Berlin.

When we finally arrived in the city I felt hungry and sleepy; we had not stopped for anything at all. It was now dark and I was worried and mystified and wished I had never gone to work in that 'Party house'. I might still have been in my previous job instead of being 'kidnapped' and taken to Berlin.

I believe it was about April or May 1940 when we stopped outside a large house in the city which was not really blacked out at all: there were plenty of lights about; in fact the windows of this house were all lit up which surprised me. It would all change later of course. We entered the house and went into a small room and shortly the woman came in carrying some cups of coffee and bread rolls which I ate at once. I have always been a good eater, and if I do not get my regular meals I get rather unwell. The woman went off again and I heard voices as if people were discussing arrangements of some kind, and at last they came back into the room. The Gestapo man was carrying a piece of paper and he sat down opposite me and told me that owing to the nature of the job I had to swear an oath of secrecy to Adolf Hitler and Greater Germany. He wrote down a few details about me on the paper and then asked me to sign it. I signed it and then had to swear verbally another oath to Hitler that I would remain true and loyal and maintain secrecy etc, something like that. In all this I had to raise my hand as in a proper oath-taking ceremony and say 'I do' and 'Heil Hitler!' after them. They all smiled and the man left while the woman told me what my new job would entail.

They – the Gestapo – had to keep a very close eye on all foreigners because of the war and the certain fact that the enemy secret services would try hard to infiltrate our country in many ways to subvert the Reich. This could not be allowed to happen of course, but our security services were usually one step ahead of them. They had a way of guarding not only our secrets but important people in the Government, etc. But the vital thing was intelligence; it was very important to have eyes and ears everywhere, did I not agree? Otherwise the cunning enemies of the Reich would try to sneak in spies, saboteurs and agent provocateurs. We were not going to let that happen, and had already taken certain measures to ensure that it didn't, and this included the placing of our own agents in certain areas including foreign embassies and establishments, etc. This was where I would find my work, for they had secured me in a post in one of these as an assistant cook. It was apparently common to employ German labour in such places, so there would be nothing suspicious in it.

I listened to all this with interest and amazement and could see at once what they were driving at: I was being asked to spy on my new employers! It was all too fantastic; what did I know of such things? Absolutely nothing. I was too frightened to do anything of the sort, but I had no chance to protest as the woman told me that all I had to do was keep my eyes and ears open and report once a week to my superior who would be introduced to me. That was all, otherwise I would have my own quarters and do the usual chores. I realised at once that the new job could not be in the British or French embassies, so where could it be? Who were the other enemies of the Reich?

The woman then explained that all such places were used for spying, even the friendly ones, and especially in wartime. No matter who they were, they all wanted to know what Germany was doing or going to do next, and reported on all they found to their governments. So I asked her where I was being sent, and she said to the Italian embassy staff. I found this hard to believe as the Italians would have their own staff to supervise the cooks to prepare meals in their own style. But when I said this to the Gestapo woman she laughed and told me that although this was so, they did have a certain amount of 'friendly help' in various directions. After all, they were allies so it was up to the Germans to help them in every way.

Then the man returned and he had another with him who he introduced to me simply as 'Frank'. He said that from then on he would be able to look after me and all my needs and that I was to report to him. With that they said 'Heil Hitler!' and left me. Frank told me to follow him so I did. We left by another exit and got into his car. He told me that he had a room for me near the embassy and the hours of work were already arranged, and that apart from meeting him every Friday in the Tiergarten, which I would easily reach by tram, my time was my own. However, he warned me that on no account must I tell anyone where I worked or anything at all if possible. I could say I was a cook, but in a private house. If I felt lonely in the city he could arrange for some company and would be glad to do this, but it was essential that I remained aloof from new friends, especially men. I would be given a train ticket home every month plus pay and allowances.

It was all so amazing that I could find nothing to say as we drove off around the streets until we reached a large villa in a rather nice road and I was taken inside and shown a room upstairs. The landlady, I was told, was always paid in advance, and they said I could make friends with the other lodgers up to a point but should always remember that I was under an oath of secrecy.

I went to bed that night after having a little soup that my landlady gave me. She was an oldish woman and a widow who seemed glad of a little company. I could have breakfast and supper with her whenever I wished; she did not see much of her other tenants as they were all younger (as indeed I was). But she seemed to like me, especially when I told her I had come all the way from Hanover to work as a cook. When she asked me about my new job I said that I was to work in one of the many ministries.

Next morning the man Frank called for me and as we drove off he said he was in a hurry as he had 'other business', so he would take me to the embassy and introduce me to the supervisor who, it seemed, was a German woman of Italian extraction and spoke both languages fluently. We drove through the gates and into the yard and on round to the rear entrance. Frank seemed to know the way inside the house and asked me to wait while he found the overseer, who I assumed looked after all the cooking and general household duties including the cleaners who must have been German and handy as spies. When Frank returned he had the overseer with him, a thick-set, middle-aged woman who told me that I was highly recommended and that she hoped I would work well. Frank said goodbye and told me that he would be calling on me regarding 'arrangements'. The overseer then took me to a side room where I hung up my coat. Next to this was a large kitchen and storeroom and she began showing me everything and how the meals were prepared. I was dubious about this cooking arrangement and could not see how I could be of use as a spy as I did not expect to leave the lower floor. The woman told me that I had a certain amount of cleaning to do first before we began any cooking and all that would be explained in due course.

So I took up the materials and brushes and did as I was told. By now I was feeling less than pleased with my new situation which seemed a little crazy and to no good purpose, but I had no option other than to give it a try. I certainly could not run off back home again.

It was almost midday before the overseer came into the kitchen again with another woman, an Italian, I believe, as they were speaking volubly in that language. I was introduced and the day's menus were explained and what they would consist of; not all the staff were present every day and therefore the number of meals would vary, but they must always be in an Italian style. But I need not worry as everything would be explained and they had a lot of stuff flown in from home.

There were six meals to prepare in Italian style and I found no problems at all; in fact I was underemployed but could still see no useful purpose in my being there. But when the meals were ready the overseer gave me a smart apron and cap and told me that I would be serving them and that I was to load up one tray while she prepared another. We then went upstairs in a small lift and I was shown into a large dining room where the Italians were already waiting and talking and drinking wine. We served up the plates and they were most polite and some spoke in German to me and made little compliments. These were the first Italians I had seen, and as they spoke to the serving maid in her own language I at once realised that I might well be able to pick up some information. But I was not at all happy about it as I was no spy and could not agree with the morality of it as they were supposed to be allies, even if not yet in the war on our side.

I was never sure how much the overseer knew, but I felt fairly certain that she must have been in the pay of the Gestapo. That afternoon I was allowed out for some air and walked round the streets for an hour or so thinking it all over. I was no longer a simple cook but a paid Gestapo informer.

After a week had passed, Frank met me in the Tiergarten and gave me my wages in a plain brown envelope. He had sent me a note telling me where and at what time to meet him on the Friday and I tackled him as to what was expected of me. But all he said was, 'Patience! We have plenty of time.'

After a couple of weeks I had still heard and seen nothing, as whenever I was serving them meals or if they passed me while I was cleaning they spoke in

Italian. Because of this I grew impatient and told Frank that it all seemed point-less, yet he insisted that things were going according to plan, whatever that meant. And then one evening a lot of guests arrived and I had to help serve drinks and sandwiches, and I saw a lot of very important people from the foreign embassies and heard a lot of different languages, among them English, though not from Englishmen – it seemed to be a second language with some of the guests. I did my best to 'listen in', but only heard snatches of general conversation, and even then only that in German was comprehensible. I learned nothing, but as it was a Friday I was obliged to report later to Frank and he seemed quite happy that I was trying my best. Even so, it all seemed rather silly to me.

Later on I realised that he and his bosses were probably playing a waiting game and hoping that eventually, when the Italians got used to my face, they would perhaps become indiscreet, and I wondered if all the embassies had spies in them, and guessed they must have.

There was, I discovered, one Italian who was quite interested in me as he began smiling every time he saw me and was very polite. I just smiled and tried to be the same, but one evening I found him playing cards by himself in one of their large rooms where they usually drank together and he asked me in German how I liked the job. I told him I was quite happy there, and then he asked me to sit down and tell him about myself and my background, so I did and he seemed very interested. I gave him the drink he had asked for and he said goodnight, smiling broadly. The next evening I saw him on the stairs and he asked me to take a drink to his room, so I agreed. It was about seven o'clock and I had been about to leave for my billet, so I put my coat on and took the drinks along but found him in his dressing gown. He seemed surprised that I had my coat on and said, 'Oh, I thought you were going to join me?' I was surprised and rather nervous, at once realising the possibilities but afraid that if I got into the wrong kind of situation I could compromise myself.

I told him that it was time for me to go home as my work was finished, so he asked me what I did in my spare time. I said nothing very much as my home was far away, so he told me that in view of this he would be glad to show me the sights of the city; in fact he would be honoured to do so. He had a family and missed them terribly, but duty was duty and he had to finish his tour in Berlin, which he liked very much though he had no friends there. So if I wouldn't mind he would appreciate my company for a few outings until he returned home in a few months' time. I decided to accept but to be very careful and ask Frank to have us followed! This seemed ridiculous as the Italian seemed so very polite and harmless, and when I told Frank about this encounter he was very, very pleased and complimented me.

A few days later, as I was serving some meals, the Italian whispered in my ear that he would expect to meet me outside the embassy at seven o'clock that evening. He would, he said, have his car, and I was very flattered but in a whirl as I had no great attraction as a female; in fact I was rather plain, and certainly had nothing very smart to wear as I had left all my better clothes at home. But I thought I had better go through with it and see what happened. At least it would help me to get over my boredom.

This was in the summer of 1940 and the evenings were rather warm, but I had nothing to wear out except my usual workaday coat so I felt rather foolish in his company. At that time it was possible to stroll anywhere around the city including the parks and lakes, so I wondered if I was in for a romantic evening, or perhaps he would take me to a theatre and a meal afterwards. I'm afraid all sorts of silly ideas entered my head.

I waited outside the embassy, walking up and down, with the nearby policeman on duty beginning to wonder I'm sure just what I was up to. Then a black car drew up which I assumed had come from the rear, and there was the Italian. He called me over and jumped out to help me into the front seat next to him and we drove off. I must admit I was quite excited as I had not had a man friend before and had only been interested in my job, rightly or otherwise. And here I was being driven about Berlin by a foreign gentleman. I think at that moment I wondered why Frank and his masters had not chosen a more attractive girl, but realised of course that she had to look the part. And I did. A plain cook and housemaid, so that Italian may have been a little desperate for female company.

Not knowing the city well I had no idea where he was taking me. The first thing he said as we set off was to ask me my name, so I told him. He said he was called Giorgio and was from Naples, such a grand, beautiful city he told me, if only I could see it. Ah! it would make him so happy if I could see it – but! the war spoiled everything. I asked him where we were going, and he said, 'Why don't we visit your beautiful lake and see if we can hire a boat to sail?'

This took me by surprise and I felt very nervous as I'd never done anything like that before. So I said no, we could just drive around but I'd love to see the water. He seemed quite happy with this so we drove on and when we reached the lake he stopped the car and opened the windows. We sat there looking at the water and talking and he asked me again about my home and family and if I had anyone 'in the war', and how he would much rather be at home in Naples, but then quickly added that he was already feeling better being with me! I thought this might be the prelude to more Italian flattery and I don't know what. We then drove off and he said he knew a nice little café with an orchestra and would I kindly accompany him for a meal, yes? He was so terribly polite and gentlemanly I couldn't refuse.

I've no idea where the place was but it was somewhere near the city centre, and it did have a nice little orchestra that played light music and tangos that I enjoyed very much. We ate German food and I asked him if he enjoyed it; he laughed and said that Italian food was something special. Well, it may have been for him, but I didn't care for what I had seen and helped to prepare.

Giorgio told me that one day he hoped to become Vice-Consul and more and that the great Duce was always rewarding for good service, and who knows, he might even end up as a General in North Africa in one of their colonies.

At last I decided it was time I was returning to my billet, so he insisted on taking me home and said goodnight to me beside the car, bowing politely and even kissing my hand. It was all very romantic and amazing for me, and he told me that he would see me the next day, but had to go away for a day or two afterwards.

I had a couple of days in hand before seeing Frank and the next morning Giorgio sent for a snack which I prepared and took up for him on the overseer's directions. This time I got the shock of my life as he was outside the same room as before and in his dressing gown and told me to put the food on the table next to his bed. He closed the door and took my hand and told me that as he had to leave he was very sad as he loved me! This was so astonishing that I just stood there gaping at him and didn't know what to say. He asked me if I thought he was a 'good man' and a real friend. I said yes, I thought he was a nice gentleman, but I did not want to say more as I felt I must be careful. He took my hands and pulled me onto the bed and kissed me heartily. I was completely taken aback and did not know what to do; I just looked at him and laughed at him in embarrassment and ran out of the room. When I reached the kitchen the overseer was preparing some food. She took one look at me and told me to help her, in rather brusque tones.

I was in something of a quandary, as although I wanted to do what was expected of me I felt Giorgio might go too far and get us both into trouble. I reported all that had happened to Frank and he was absolutely amazed and delighted. He slapped me on the backside and said, 'My Helene! You have worked wonders! You really have. I'm very pleased with you. Now we can go forward from here. You must really cultivate this man and get him to talk as much as he wishes to. The Italians are all the same: once he starts you'll have trouble stopping him, believe me. But do not try to question him; all we are interested in is their ideas and politics and intentions. I'm sure that if you simply ask him about his job and how he likes it he will tell you everything you wish to know.' I made it plain that I did not want to be sexually compromised, I was not that kind of a girl at all and had to draw the line somewhere. But all Frank did was laugh and say, 'Helene, you must do as your conscience dictates, but do bear in mind that there are more important things at stake than a girl's virginity!'

I was shocked and said no more so he took me back to my billet where I found the old lady waiting for me. She said there was a letter from home for me and that I could eat with her. I was almost tempted to confide in her, but managed to keep quiet and speak only of mundane matters such as the weather and the war. At that time the Channel battle was raging and our radio and newspapers were full of the glorious deeds of our Luftwaffe. Also, of course, the Italians had entered the war on our side and this I thought might give Giorgio further cause to see us as 'close allies'.

There was no sign of Giorgio for two or three days but a lot of coming and going at the embassy. Then he reappeared and told me to bring some drinks to his room at seven o'clock. I did so but this time realised that the overseer was watching me closely. When I reached his room the door was slightly ajar and I went in to place the tray down on the table. The radio was playing music and I believe I heard an Italian singer. I did not at first see Giorgio, but then realised that he must have got behind me and was hiding behind the door. As soon as I put down the tray I felt his arms around me and he planted a kiss on my neck. I was taken by surprise and was quite shaken, but he held me firmly and told me he loved me. He then kissed me on the lips and before I could stop him had toppled us both onto the bed and was trying to pull up my dress. I was struggling and he kept on kissing me and telling me how wonderful I was, how much he loved me and with Germany and Italy as the 'Grand Axis' we must work even closer together.

I just did not know what to do but tried to keep calm, remembering my instructions. I told him that if he didn't behave himself I would leave at once and never come back; but if he did we could sit for a moment and talk, but not for long as my overseer was watching me as I was afraid for my job. I'm not sure if he fully understood all this, although his German was good, it was not perfect, and I could never claim to be well-spoken. But he sat back looking at me with his dark brown eyes and said, 'But I love you darling.' I said, 'Think of your family Giorgio, and think of my job. We don't want to get into trouble, do we?'

He stood up and paced about, thinking. Then he said he knew what to do: he would see to it that I got a little holiday with him. That was it. He would arrange for a weekend away and ask for a cook to go with him. I told him it sounded ridiculous and could never work. I had no desire to go away with him at all but could not think what to say. But he grabbed me again and kissed me and said that he would arrange everything. 'You will see,' he said. 'Go now, I will let you know later.'

The overseer saw me later and to my surprise warned me not to get too friendly with any of the Italians and to keep my place. She told me that if I did not I would have to leave. This was surprising as I had considered that she was also in the pay of the Gestapo. I did not know what to think so resolved to ask Frank for advice; Giorgio was becoming insistent and I thought I might need help urgently. On the other hand, I could always pretend I wanted to stay away from him and ask the supervisor to substitute someone else and leave me to kitchen work. As it was a few days short of my next meeting with Frank I decided to ask for time off work; I told the overseer that I did not feel well and must stay in bed for a few days. I don't think she believed me but she had no choice.

I stayed away from the embassy for the next three or four days and then met Frank and explained the situation and he was not at all pleased. He told me the overseer was a fool and should have been instructed not to interfere. But it seemed that his own authority was limited and I believe he had to ask for further instructions. As for myself, I refused to go away with Giorgio, I had decided on that; I also felt that I had got nowhere. Between this sex-starved Italian and the overseer I was in a difficult situation.

We drove around in Frank's car until he came to a decision. He told me to take a walk around the park and he would pick me up at the same place in an hour. So I walked around the edge of the park and while I was doing so the air raid sirens sounded and I didn't know what to do. I waited about at the rendezvous hoping that Frank would come earlier and he did so and drove us away. He said that he had consulted his superiors and been told what to do. I was to remain at the embassy and carry on as before, and by the time I got back there the overseer would have been 'dealt with'. I was horrified at this remark, but Frank told me not to worry; he said, 'We want her there. We'll simply tell her to stick to her own business and leave you alone and, above all, to be a loyal German.'

Well, when I got back to the embassy the woman gave me a peculiar look but said no more about the Italians. So I carried on as usual wondering what would happen next. And sure enough, as expected Giorgio invited me away for a weekend in the country. He told me he had leave and a nice cottage to visit and we would be very happy. I told him I had promised to go home again and that he was welcome to come with me if he wished. I had been neglecting my family and had to go. He was very disappointed and I believe angry and said it would not be the same. I could not really appreciate how he felt for me, and he said that as soon as I changed my mind I should let him know, as he was distraught. It was a very typical Italian performance and I left his room laughing and very amused by it all.

However, I was not there just to cook and wash dishes; I had to do something to keep Frank happy as he felt I was in a very good position. It may have been that they simply did not trust the Italians and wanted to get wind of any defection to the Allies. I knew the Americans were in Berlin and always very charming, but they too made their reports back on everything they saw and heard. I had seen them at the embassy and they certainly kept watch on the Italians and all other allies of the Germans.

I wondered if I was being foolish. A weekend away would be fun and I was old enough to take care of myself and could perhaps learn something of real value. I had by then overcome my moral scruples and found the situation of no great importance. I felt it was rather like a foolish and pointless game. I even had the notion of confiding in Giorgio so that he could invent some stories that I could pass on to Frank, or else try to get him to work for us. I did not believe that he would do this, but my bosses had gone over all the angles, as you might say, and had something rather cunning in mind – blackmail. Of course it was all standard spy trickery later and probably even then, but it was all a new experience for me. I had been home twice and naturally my parents wanted to know what I was doing and if I had seen any famous people. I told them I was simply a cook and general help in a foreign embassy and they should not ask me any more as it was government service and secret. I think they thought it all rather silly, but had to respect my position.

Then the trap was sprung. I was given my orders and in no uncertain manner. Frank told me that I must now agree to Giorgio's request and go away with him for a weekend. We would be watched and all would be well. That was all he said, except that I must agree to whatever arrangements the Italian made and leave the rest to him.

Well, I was at home in my billet one evening and had not seen Giorgio for a few days when my landlady came to me and said there was a man at the door. It was Frank and he told me that I had to go with him at once and take my coat. I wondered what was happening. He said we were going for a little outing and I would soon see. He drove me back to the embassy and let me in through a side door and left me alone; there was no sign of the overseer or other staff. Then Frank returned and said that Giorgio was alone in his room and that I must go to him and agree to his proposal and he would attend to everything else. He then left me.

I was very nervous as I went up to Giorgio's door and knocked. He answered and seemed very surprised and delighted to see me. In fact he took hold of me and kissed me and pulled me into his room. 'At last!' he said, 'At last!' and all sorts of other romantic phrases. 'I knew you would come back to me, I have been missing you terribly! My love, you have come to say you will go away with me, yes?'

I told him that I would, but not as his wife. He said not to worry, he understood perfectly, and he knew I would have a very happy time with him. It was then the middle of the week and he said he would arrange to go away for the following weekend and that he would expect me to leave Friday night with him, that he did not care a fig for the overseer and would have her dismissed if she caused any trouble. He then kissed me again and I managed to leave, telling him that I would be ready after work on Friday. Giorgio said that I was making him very happy and he would buy me lots of nice clothes and anything else I wanted.

When Friday came I finished work by seven-thirty and already had my suitcase with me with a few things packed for the weekend. The overseer said, 'Going home again? You are not due for more leave yet, surely?' I told her she was right but no more, so she was left guessing.

I left the embassy and saw the same policeman watching me as I waited for Giorgio who arrived on foot and took me to his car which was parked elsewhere. We drove off into the darkness and I had no idea where we were going, but Giorgio said he had managed to borrow a cottage from one of the older staff for the weekend, from one of the officials with an understanding nature, I gathered. It was all very amazing and as we left the city I wondered if we were being followed, but could not see out of the back of the car.

We stopped at a little café for some cakes and coffee and then drove on into the countryside outside eastern Berlin. To my surprise we did not go far, only a very few miles, before we reached a lake and then the cottage nearby. It was a small isolated house among trees and looked rather dull and gloomy. Giorgio said he had arranged everything and removed his own and my suitcase from the boot of the car and we entered the house. It was quite attractive inside and complete with radiogram and records, flowers in the rooms with two good bedrooms upstairs all made up ready as if for each of us. I was agreeably surprised. The kitchen was adequate and Giorgio asked me to prepare some omelettes as he had brought some supplies. I found all I needed and set to work while he went upstairs to unpack his personal belongings.

Naturally as a fairly young girl I was nervous and had no intention of compromising myself if I could help it. I was also very conscious of the fact that we were, I assumed, being watched! I did not relish any lovemaking scenes with the Gestapo looking on. However, it was all very unusual for me and I was in a bit of a daze.

When Giorgio came downstairs again he said it was perfect, he had arranged everything, I could inspect it all when we had eaten. While I made the omelettes and some coffee he went into one of the rooms and started trying to get a fire going. The materials were there but he was unsuccessful so he gave up, sat down and switched on the radio, twiddling the dial and looking for some music. I served up the meal and pulled the curtains and, of course, wondered how many pairs of eyes were outside. I also wondered as we began eating if it was worth all this trouble. I could not see what importance Giorgio could be at all. If he had been a British agent then it would have been simple and understandable, yet when I thought of this it occurred to me that perhaps he was!

When we had finished our meal we sat on two armchairs in front of the electric fire listening to the radio, and then Giorgio twiddled the dial again and listened to the BBC news in Italian! I was very surprised but did not realise at first what it was until he told me. He seemed very interested but then changed over to some music on another station. By then it was getting quite late and I felt tired so I took the dishes to the kitchen and went to the bathroom, intending to go to bed. I heard Giorgio come upstairs and go into one of the bedrooms singing heartily and I couldn't help being amused.

When I came out of the bathroom and went into what I thought was my bedroom I found all my things laid out on the bed, plus a box of chocolates and some beautiful flowers with a loving message pinned to them. It was all very sweet and in different circumstances I would have been thrilled by that as a woman. But I was growing very apprehensive and felt that we were nearing the climax of this fantasy. I went into Giorgio's room to thank him for his gifts most sincerely, after knocking of course. He was already in his dressing gown and he began singing to me in Italian which I found very embarrassing, apart from which I thought if the Gestapo were listening in then they must be having a good laugh at his romantic antics.

I then turned away, saying goodnight, but he leapt forward and took me in his arms, removing the flowers and chocolates and placing my hands about his neck. We stayed like this for some moments and I could sense his passion rising so I tried to struggle free and reminded him of our agreement.

'How can I forget! I am only interested in making love to you and having you as my wife. My love! I am desolate, my heart bleeds –' he said, and a lot more which was very theatrical. Frankly, I was not sure how far he was putting it on or how far he intended trying to go with me. But I told him that I was very tired and had been working hard all day and walked back to my bedroom. But he simply followed me and closed the door. He then switched off the main light, leaving the bedside lamp on, and I could see that I was in a difficult situation. He took me in his arms once more and bore me back onto the bed, crushing the flowers which I had put down there. I was most uncomfortable and not the least bit amorous and hoped that if there was to be any intervention it would come right then. But he kept me pinned there and I tried to tell him that he was a representative of his country and should behave like a gentleman. But there was no stopping him and he was really carried away. As much as I struggled I could not escape from him and in the end we were in a highly compromising situation. He was very heavily perfumed and had on a fancy shirt that he had opened underneath his dressing gown, and he wore nothing else below that which was a completely new situation for me.

I was wondering what to do in desperation, whether to give in and have done with it and then go back to Hanover, or fight him with all I had. But this seemed unlikely as I am never a violent person even in the most provocative circumstances. I had never been in such a situation with a man and frankly was at a loss.

However, just as I found I had missed my chance to escape there was a loud bang and we both fell to the floor. The main light came on and to our astonishment and great embarrassment we saw three men and a woman standing there laughing at us. I leapt up and rearranged my clothing. Giorgio was absolutely speechless with amazement and then rage; he was furious and stood up, his face red and embarrassed at his compromised condition. The man who was nearest and probably in charge told me to leave the room, and as I did the woman took me downstairs and was very sympathetic and kind which surprised me. She said that all had been arranged and they had done their best to intervene at what they hoped was the right moment and that it was no longer my concern. Giorgio would now be thoroughly interrogated and charges would be threatened, but it was no concern of mine. He was of course a friendly foreign assistant attaché and would be allowed to go but not without certain arrangements being made. I was told to collect my things and when I went upstairs I could hear the men talking, but there was no sign of Giorgio. I suddenly felt terribly sorry for him as he was basically harmless, but I believe there was more to it than I realised. I was told very little.

I had to go outside with the woman and wait in the back seat of their car. Some time later Giorgio was brought out with two of the men and put into his own car. Then the third man joined us and we drove back to Berlin in silence. When we reached the city the agents told me not to go back to the embassy and that new instructions would reach me shortly. So I was dropped off at my billet and went to bed but had great difficulty in sleeping.

Next day I told the landlady I had the day off and in the evening Frank came and told me I could now return to Hanover and that I would be contacted later regarding further employment. He gave me some wages and a train ticket and saw me off at the station, saying goodbye and thanking me for my service in our cause.

It was a very strange feeling to get home again in those circumstances. At times I could hardly believe that the adventure had happened to me. My parents were very curious and wondered if I had been dismissed, but I told them that staff changes due to the war had made me redundant, but that I would be re-employed locally. A little later I was on my way home from shopping when a car drew up and I saw the same men and woman of the Gestapo who had first recruited me. They told me that they knew I had been of great service to the Reich and this was appreciated, but that from then on I was free to go my own way and could choose any employment I wished, though I might be directed as a cook to some post later to help the war effort. I must never speak of my experiences to anyone, did I understand?

I never heard from the Gestapo again or learned what had become of Giorgio. Not long afterwards I found a new job as a cook in a large household for the elderly and ended the war there.**"**

CHAPTER 4

Herbert Kranzler

I n World War II the war at sea was nowhere more prolonged or bitter than in the Atlantic Ocean. The Allies, but especially the British, had learned severe lessons in the earlier war, and it was Britain that had most to gain or lose because of its tremendous dependence on world trade for which it needed its sea lanes. It was therefore the British Government and Admiralty which, noting increasing German truculence under Hitler, sought to come to an agreement on naval parity in the 1930s.

Germany had become Britain's greatest trade rival in the era of Bismarck, when German goods had begun to flood a world market previously dominated by Britain, which had become the greatest industrial power in the Victorian age. The war that followed in 1914 was really as much about trade as German militarism and the invasion of Belgium, which hardly threatened to upset Britain's traditional foreign policy stance of never allowing any single power to dominate Europe.

By the mid-1930s Nazi Germany had begun openly violating the Treaty of Versailles, but sought an accommodation with Britain, for Hitler was intent on avoiding a war in the West, though he allowed it as a possibility by 1944 by which time he reckoned he would be well ready for it.

The Anglo-German Naval Agreement signed in 1935 stipulated that the Reichsmarine (soon to be redesignated the Kriegsmarine) would not exceed one third the strength of the Royal Navy, with Germany, in defiance of the Versailles Treaty, permitted to build submarines to sixty per cent of British strength. This go-it-alone policy on the part of the British ignored international treaties and was concluded without consulting the French. For their part the Germans gave the spurious undertaking that U-boats would never be used against merchant shipping, even offering to do away with this category of warship altogether. According to Winston Churchill, the Germans made this offer only because they knew perfectly well that no other nation would agree to it.

So anxious were the British to come to terms with Nazi Germany that they laid down a programme of naval construction that was far greater than they could possibly entertain, which was especially galling to the Scandinavians who had just protested to Germany on its introduction of conscription. But the predictable failure of the 'no submarines' clause meant that the new Kriegsmarine could enthusiastically begin a programme of U-boat construction, with the result that between 1935 and 1945 no less than 1,170 U-boats were built. It would be wrong to suggest however that a huge fleet of German subs came into being before the outbreak of war; that this did not happen was due to various factors connected with naval policy and materials. There were a few in the German Navy who saw the submarine as a war-winning weapon, while others of more traditional stance looked to the heavy surface warship, as did many in other navies.

On 19 August 1939 twenty-one German U-boats were already in position in the North Sea and north-west Atlantic, prepared for a war with Britain, the outbreak of which would surprise not only the Führer but the Kriegsmarine's naval staff. The proportion of submarines sent to their action stations was eighty per cent, higher than would ever be equalled later.

During the evening of the first day of the war, 3 September 1939, U-30, under the command of Lieutenant Fritz-Julius Lemp, torpedoed and sank the British liner *Athenia* (13,581 tons) carrying 1,400 passengers of whom 112 were lost, and these included some children. World headlines of a decidedly hostile nature resulted, forcing Germany to deny responsibility. Lieutenant Lemp maintained radio silence, but if guilty he had contravened his orders which may have seemed vague or even stupid to U-boat commanders and were certainly restrictive since they stated that they were to operate against enemy shipping in the following manner: they were to stop vessels, board them and inspect cargo and papers and, if justified, sink them after the crew had been allowed to board the lifeboats.

Merchantmen in convoy, armed merchant cruisers and warships were excepted, and within hours of the BBC announcement of the sinking Hitler himself had ordered that the existing orders to U-boat commanders were to be repeated, emphasising that no passenger ships were to be attacked until further notice. As soon as Lieutenant Lemp reached port his log was confiscated and altered.

Shortly afterwards, on 17 September, U-29, under Lieutenant Otto Schuhart, sank the 22,000-ton aircraft carrier *Courageous* in the north-west Atlantic, and in the following month in a brilliant operation Lieutenant Gunther Prien took his U-47 into the seemingly impregnable Royal Navy base at Scapa Flow to sink the old battleship *Royal Oak*, which went down with eight hundred sailors on board.

Obviously, the war at sea was far from being a 'phoney' one, yet Hitler being a landlubber, and despite such victories by the Kriegsmarine, seemed to pin greater hopes on the Luftwaffe, possibly because Göring was an old croney and had the Führer's ear to a much greater extent than Grand Admiral Raeder. During a visit to Naval HQ the then Commodore Dönitz told Hitler that in his opinion three hundred U-boats could bring Britain to its knees, but the Führer stayed silent for a while, remarking later that the Luftwaffe would chase the Royal Navy around the coasts of Britain. This comment was prompted by some Luftwaffe attempts to bomb the Royal Navy at Scapa and in the Firth of Forth, the result of which had been to force the Admiralty to remove their Home Fleet to the greater safety of north-west Scotland.

Later on, after the war had intensified and the RAF was making constant raids on Germany, a Nazi Press cartoon depicted Britain's air force as gripping Germany by the wrist (but only just), while Germany's U-boats had Britain by the throat. This was not far short of the truth, for Dönitz's sea wolves were indeed strangling Britain's sea lanes. By February 1943 the daily average of U-boats in the Atlantic was an amazing 116, of which forty-eight were actually in operational zones, the rest being either en route to them or returning to base. Yet the Atlantic is a vast area of water for less than fifty submarines to cover. But the main convoy routes lay in the north from Halifax (Nova Scotia) to Liverpool, so it was along these lanes that the German submarines lay in wait, by the mid-war years operating in packs, and until 1943 having it mainly their own way so that Allied ships were being sunk far quicker than they could be replaced. An acute shortage of escort ships prevented proper protection: the Royal Navy had been disappointed on the outbreak of war to discover that its 'winning' anti-U-boat weapon, the 'Asdic' apparatus, had not been as effective as hoped; too many U-boats escaped destruction.

But it was the extreme lack of air cover over the convoys that had proved the chief benefit to the enemy; the 'Atlantic gap' would not begin to be covered until a huge number of ships and valuable cargoes had been lost. Long-range patrol planes, coupled with the forming of hunter-killer groups of warships, would sound the death knell for U-boat operations. Heavy bombing of the all but impregnable U-boat bases in western France proved ineffective, smashing up the French towns but leaving the twelve-foot-thick concrete pens virtually unscathed. Air patrols, mines and even British submarines in the Bay of Biscay were a great menace, however, to the passing U-boats, apart from the existing fact that the Royal Navy had captured valuable German code books from the disabled U-570, and was able to plot the course and position of U-boats almost everywhere.

The life of a submarine crew at sea was a very hazardous one, little compensated for in some navies by a small extra amount of danger money. Not until the showing of the very successful German TV serial *The Boat* was an approximation of the realities of life in a U-boat in World War II known by the general public.

The respective need and usage of submarines in the war by the German and British Navies can be gauged from the losses sustained: the Germans 968, the British about sixty. Even allowing for Allied unpreparedness, in the nine months from September 1939 German losses in submarines were heavy, and not all were due to Allied warship action: some U-boats simply vanished, probably lost to mines, especially in the English Channel. Yet the figure of twenty-three lost pales beside the losses incurred later, for in the year June 1944 to May 1945 no less than 167 were lost. Of the 55,000 seamen who served aboard German submarines in the ten years between 1935 and 1945, 27,491 were killed.

The principal German U-boat of the Atlantic battles was the Type VII of various forms with a crew of about forty-four and a submerged displacement of 983 tons, of which 650 were built. German U-boats carried out some three thousand operations in World War II, during which they sank 2,840 ships (including 150 warships) to a total of 14 million tons.

"I was born into a military family in Potsdam, and I had three brothers, two of whom were to become Army officers, like my father who was a Colonel at the end of World War I. But as I grew up to boyhood I had no leanings at all in that direction. I attended high school and left with some honours in the mid-thirties but was obliged to join the Labour Corps in the Hitler regime.

The Labour Corps was designed to give youth a toughening-up and disciplinary training before entering the Wehrmacht; that was the primary aim – it was not really designed as a social project. In fact, of course, militarisation began in the Hitler Youth and even before in the Jungvolk, so by the time a lad reached seventeen or eighteen he was already able to march in step and salute and shout 'Heil Hitler' on every conceivable occasion. Since this was the norm for all boys I was unable to escape so was taken into the Labour service when I was sixteen-and-a-half and did two years training which was hardening. We were marched and drilled as in the Wehrmacht and often without spades. Of course we had uniforms and jackboots and often went on marches singing our corps songs. In actual labouring we were engaged in all sorts of things from digging ditches to helping to construct bridges and even houses and buildings, tree felling, and in fact anything that involved manual labour in a drive to toughen up and militarise German youth. There was the Nazi creed of 'back to the soil', chiefly instigated by Himmler.

I believe this service did me some good physically as it was bound to, but in terms of a career it was no help at all, and in fact I had no prospect at all of civilian employment for no sooner had I finished my RAD stint than I was taken into the Navy. I was given that small choice which was against my father's wishes; he never gave up hope that I would go into the Army but I had no interest in it at all. My only reason for going into the Navy was a love of the sea, or at least the idea of it. I had only been to the coast once and enjoyed it immensely, though I don't believe the Prussians had any great love of the ocean; that side of things came from places like Hamburg and Kiel.

I was sent to Wilhelmshaven as a recruit seaman and had to do more marching and all the rest of it, receiving lectures on German naval tradition and all the great engagements at sea. We learnt about the famous sea battles of history including Trafalgar, Copenhagen, and the Russian defeat at the hands of the Japanese. We did a lot of physical training and became even fitter and then began going out in small boats over the bay. Sometimes we had to row, and on other occasions we went in small motor boats and were taught how to handle such craft. We also sailed in small dinghies and this was excellent sport. Naturally, we had parades and inspections and overall it was not a bad time.

Next we were split up into specialised classes according to which branch of the service we had been designated for. I had volunteered for the U-boat arm because I was fascinated at the idea of sailing beneath the ocean, this from the point of view of experience and not, I may add, because I had any interest in going to war. I had a great hope that I would complete my training and be released into civilian life and find some job of a technical kind. In fact this spell helped to foster a great interest in ships and I had an idea that I might take up ship design and construction. It would mean an apprenticeship in draughtsmanship, but I was confident that my technical drawing was good enough. I'm afraid that none of these aspirations was fulfilled; the madman Hitler saw to that! The international situation seemed to grow worse by the month.

I must mention that we were always encouraged to hold political discussions in that training period, but always under supervision. In fact the man in charge was a political officer and he saw to it that the Nazi viewpoint was put before anything and in such a way that all counter-argument was stilled. There were no debates as such in the democratic style. For example, this officer, who was in fact a senior NCO, just put forward a series of political tenets that were impossible to refute, and woe betide you if you tried to do so! He was most likely a political appointee, and would turn on you and ridicule you as if you were a poor fool, a dolt, and hold you up before the assembly as naive and ignorant.

'Was the Treaty of Versailles fair?' he would ask. Of course everyone knew that it was not.

'Was it right that the victor (so-called) should steal our overseas colonies?' No, we did not think so.

'Why did these democracies have such large overseas possessions when they had smaller populations than we had?'

Why indeed!

And so on and so on, and one was not permitted to start up any alternative lines of enquiry. In other words, these so called 'discussions' became mere Nazi monologues. I cannot claim that these young men had any political sense; all these lectures had to do was appeal to our usual national instincts, and he had won us over. We were not really dyed-in-the-wool Nazis, though of course some were. We were not fools, it was just that the Nazis were very good at propaganda and forbade any counter-organisations, and counter-argument was considered anti-German, Bolshevist and subversive. You were either with them or against them. So it was easier to swim with the tide than against it.

In my case I very soon decided to keep quiet at such meetings, which I saw later were designed only to strengthen our belief and resolve in the Nazi German cause as they had formulated it. Not that they did not have some truth on their side, but how they used it was another matter.

The U-boat training areas were concentrated mainly in the Baltic, but the actual bases were at Kiel, Wilhelmshaven, Flushing and some smaller places. There were technical training schools which of course included the theory of U-boat warfare, fleet actions with submarines and the latest ideas in tactics and weapons, plus counter-measures against the submarine. In my case I was most interested in the handling side so elected to be trained as a helmsman which was a very important job and would keep me close to the commander and his foremost officers. At first I attended a mock-up U-boat control tower with other men and we were instructed in the rudiments of handling. Then we were taken down into a submarine with many other tradesmen and inspected it from stem to stern. It was all very fascinating and I was very interested in the design and structure of the boat. Then we did our first sea trials just off the coast in quite shallow water and were shown the various 'attitudes' adopted in manoeuvring the boat, both on the surface and below. I will never forget our first dive which was exciting but a little nerve-racking. The captain was of course instructing us with the help of a training crew including competent NCOs who had served in U-boats in the earlier war. The boat was only a small coastal type used for training and not nearly as big as the later sort used by us in the Atlantic.

We took turns at the helm under the watchful and sometimes scornful eye of an NCO and tried to follow his orders; especially difficult they were too when we dived below the surface. It was all a question of buoyancy and it required a very expert touch and experience to balance the tankage so that the boat remained in control in a particular attitude for manoeuvring. The captain had great patience and he needed it.

This training included the torpedo and engine room personnel, and later a deck gun crew were trained, first on land and then at sea. But this was not until we had achieved some competence and then assembled as a crew, and had been assigned the same quarters in barracks on shore. The Navy had its own way of doing things and were very particular as to traditions in some respects. They had this almost mystical love affair with the ocean that set them apart. I suppose really it was romanticism and the equivalent of the airman's love of the sky, and in my case at least when war came it all changed very much. There is no romance in killing at sea, believe me.

We did a lot more training as a crew, sometimes in small flotillas of U-boats, and then did war exercises which sometimes included our being hunted by destroyers and other warships who dropped small charges over us if they discovered our position. These were quite harmless and designed not only to show us we had been detected, but also to get us used to the sound of explosions underwater against the hull. Of course they were nothing compared to the real thing, as we found out later.

In my course some men failed at their jobs and were redesignated to warships or shore jobs or even the Marines and were not seen again. But most were competent, and in my own case I passed all the exercises and became a fully fledged helmsman. When I went home my family were proud of me, but I always had the feeling that my father felt I had betrayed him by not joining the Army.

By the spring of 1939 I had been assigned with my comrades to a regular U-boat and we had taken part in all the various single and flotilla exercises in the Baltic. We had been inspected many times by high officers including Dönitz who, as a fanatical believer in the U-boat arm, always had a great love for his men. I had become resigned to my fate; there was no sign of anyone being released owing to the international situation. When the day came when war was declared by England we were sitting about in our barracks and heard the news over the loudspeakers. Everyone went quiet. Someone began whistling an old sea song, others began discussing our chances of survival. Then we were all called outside to hear an address by the base commander in which he exhorted us to uphold the traditions of the German Navy in all ways and that God was with us in a just cause and that the Führer would lead us to victory, and all that kind of nonsense. We cheered and gave the usual 'Heils!' as directed and were then called to a lecture on British and French warships, merchant shipping and especially the latest known anti-U-boat measures.

For the first few weeks nothing much happened to us, though we heard that most of our operational U-boats had gone into the Atlantic; others were in training and this too we were obliged to continue. Then came news of Prien's victory at Scapa Flow and the whole Navy was in an uproar of celebration; we could only marvel at his very great audacity and bravery. True, we learned later that the *Royal Oak* was only an old battleship, but just the same the men did deserve their accolades and medals.

But news that a great liner had been sunk in the early days of the war was not good. The story of that sinking went through all the ranks of the Kriegsmarine and we knew that a big mistake had been made, even thought it was claimed that the ship had been an armed merchantman. The British claimed that women and children had gone down with the ship; this we learned because we had a barrack room radio and used to listen to the BBC sometimes, but in any case such stories always came around in time. We respected the BBC even though we thought at times it gave out Government propaganda; we were not so stupid as to swallow everything our own radio told us. We knew that civilians would die in the war at sea, it was inevitable, but for my part I hoped I would never be a party to the killing of women and children. The case of merchant ships was a different one: without them no government could fight a war – ours or theirs. But the British particularly needed a large merchant fleet to sustain their lives and especially in war, so they became a perfectly legitimate target insofar as war can dictate such things. It becomes a question of survival. After all, in the earlier war, as every adult German knew, the British Navy had so deprived us of vital goods and food that the population were starving. I'm not sure how many British knew that or looked on it as a war measure. But you see the truth was not always fed to the British in that war or the next.

It was early in 1940 when I first set off with my comrades on a war cruise. We were ordered to take up position west of Ireland to try and intercept shipping making for Liverpool and Scotland. We knew that the convoy system was in operation but that the escorts were a little thin on the ground at that time with no planes to patrol the Atlantic, and we also hoped to catch ships sailing alone. By then I had a close friend called Helmut and we worked together in the control room, I as helmsman and he as depth keeper on the valves operating the buoyancy tanks.

Once we were submerged the night-day sequence was upset; it became a life of on watch-off watch and without regard to night or day. I of course had my off-duty hours when my place at the helm was taken over by a relief, a good fellow a little older than myself called Willi from Hamburg, who had a family. We spent about four hours on watch then returned to our bunks or took meals. It was terribly cramped in the Type VII U-boat, but they were bigger of course than the smaller coastal type that we had trained on which were even more difficult to move around in. We had our meals in our own mess as there could be no question of half the crew sitting down together. Quite often we returned to eat our meals in our own bunk space, but when we ate together in our mess we had the radio blaring out dance music or sometimes someone had brought along a small gramophone and some records, and this helped to keep us happy. But mostly we listened to our own radio or the BBC or Radio Paris after the occupation if it played dance music mixed in with symphonies played by German orchestras, and of course war news and propaganda.

Our captain was a fine, humorous sort of man from the middle of Germany; he was not a sailor by tradition but had learnt his job and we had every confidence in him. We called him 'Ka-leun' (an abbreviation of 'Kapitanleutnant') at sea and he called us by our first names, so I was always known to him as Herbert. Later on we had a different commander who was much more formal and not so well liked.

The life of a submariner in any navy is far from easy, and any ideas of a romantic life on the ocean wave soon vanished. As a helmsman I did not take watchkeeping duties up top when we were on the surface, but I did my best to snatch some fresh air whenever possible. We always had to ask permission to go up top, and when we did it was often a spectacular experience as the sea was both magnificent and cruel, ferocious yet beautiful. I saw so many wonderful seascapes, sunsets and sunrises; the vast tracts of ocean were mostly bare, with not a ship to be seen. When we docked it was like returning to a strange and alien life, we had grown so used to being closed up in a tight-knit community, mostly under the sea with no company save ourselves and the fish outside the boat. Sometimes the porpoises would rush alongside and in front of us and this was always a sight to see. Our captain of those early days was always very good and allowed as many men as possible to come up into the fresh air.

We sailed to our allotted position on the war map and waited, partly on the surface with five men on watch and then beneath the sea for a spell. We cruised only very slowly this way and that on our patrol, waiting and watching for a target. Our orders as far as I know were to sink only merchant ships; the crew could be warned beforehand but sunk at once if carrying armament. I do not know of any contravention of these orders, but of course later on the war became much more bitter. I can only speak of my own experiences and the stories I heard.

I remember our first alarm. I was on watch and the First Officer sighted a small convoy steaming west; the captain hurried to the bridge. I had to maintain an even keel on the boat with the help of the others while the captain assessed the situation. Apparently there were six ships including one destroyer and we had no way of knowing if they were loaded or not as there was quite a sea running at the time. Our captain decided to draw closer if possible so course was altered to intercept the group for a better look. At the same time a message was sent by radio in code reporting our find and action to U-boat HQ.

It took us about two hours to reach a position from where we could ascertain the nature of the convoy, but we were disappointed when the captain decided not to attack as the ships were in ballast. It was a waste of torpedoes to sink empty ships he told us; later on it would be different as the aim became to destroy not only valuable cargoes but shipping space.

That first alarm was such a big disappointment for us as we had trained for so long for such a moment. But very soon afterwards we found an incoming convoy and this was a much better proposition: it was quite large, about twenty ships with two destroyers, and we were told by radio that two more of our boats were already in position.

We took our time in bringing our boat into a good firing position and at last all was ready. The convoy was passing before us slightly off the port bow at slow speed, heavily laden merchantmen, and one of these, our captain reported, appeared to have aircraft parked on its decks. He decided to aim for this one in particular and one of the two escorts which would be passing on the same general course.

At last we heard the command 'Los!' and the firing of the torpedoes began. I felt the slight jar and thump as the weapons left the tubes and the waiting began. It was three or four minutes later when we heard a loud crump and everyone began cheering. The boat rocked slightly and the captain, with his eye glued to the 'scope, told us that one ship had been hit and had broken in two. He allowed his officers to see the results and then called for a change of course which would take us round the rear of the convoy and hopefully into an attacking position on the other side. We were alert for the sound of pursuing destroyers or our own boats, which were somewhere in the vicinity.

The destroyers raced about and one came within a hundred yards of us but failed to detect us. By then we had passed round the rear of the convoy and saw that one of the ships had stopped to pick up survivors from the sunken vessel which had vanished. We felt sorry for the crew and those who had lost their lives. No true sailor ever rejoices at the destruction of a ship, no matter what type or nationality.

We passed close round the rear of the convoy and then heard another explosion quite close at hand; our captain reported that another ship had been torpedoed. This meant from his observations that another U-boat was on the same side of the convoy as ourselves so our watch was intensified. It is possible to hear sounds passing through the water from a great distance, but without better equipment than we had it is not easy to determine just how close another submarine could be, and we feared a collision which could be fatal for both.

Then the worst happened: a fog bank came down and hid the enemy ships from view. The captain ordered us to surface and report to base. We tried to follow the convoy but it was useless so our captain decided to conserve fuel and wait at a shallow depth, so down we went with all hands alert.

We heard diesels which soon faded and decided that it was one of our boats trying to follow the convoy on the surface. Some hours went by and that night we heard more explosions some distance to the east; then the fog cleared with a strong westerly breeze but we saw nothing. The captain ordered us to resume our patrol but we saw no more ships and were obliged to return to Kiel where we were given a grand welcome and a leave period of one week while the boat was serviced and reprovisioned.

I went home and received a royal welcome; my brothers were there as they were both stationed in Berlin, though the third was still a civilian and working as a car mechanic. I think my father, despite his reservations, was quite proud of me as I was now able to wear the U-boat war badge on my uniform. He was however anxious that I should try for promotion, but I tried to explain that this was not easy, it was a slow business. Little did I realise that as the war grew fiercer so would our losses rise until eventually they were so heavy that promotion came very fast to anyone competent if only to replace those lost, and most of those brave lads were.

I had a very good leave and also acquired a girlfriend for the first time. I also had to visit some relatives. As far as the girlfriend goes I think the uniform had a lot to do with it as I am not a particularly good looking fellow. Her name was Ilse and she was a brunette and not in the slightest an Aryan blonde. For that matter neither was I, so we made a pair. I had been out for a walk in the local park with my family, and when they wished to return home I decided to remain out for a while. I was always very conscious of trying to get as much fresh air as possible as I spent so much time at sea shut up below in a mass of machinery. My family quite understood this and left me alone sitting on a seat in the sunshine. I had been alone with my thoughts for a little while when a young lady came by with a little boy, then sat down on the seat beside me. The child was about ten I supposed and I assumed it was her son. He was very interested in my badges and naturally we got talking and I discovered that the boy belonged to a neighbour which made me quite happy as I found her rather attractive.

I had only two days' leave left so decided to take the plunge and ask her to go out with me for a meal and perhaps the cinema or even a walk round the park and woods. Somewhat to my surprise and delight she agreed, so we met twice before I returned to Kiel; we seemed to enjoy each other's company and decided to keep in touch by letter. Naturally, she knew I was in U-boats and realised I might not be able to send any mail for several weeks on end, but she did not seem to mind. She told me she had a sister at home but no parents and gave me a photograph which I kept carefully in my wallet. It was sad to part from her.

On our next cruise we passed round the northern tip of Scotland as the Channel had become too dangerous with some of our boats being lost, though we had our successes in that area too. We sailed at high speed on the surface into the north-west Atlantic in poor weather; it was April 1940, I believe, and still cold. We reached our patrol area and submerged. We had a new watchkeeping officer of the old school of rigid discipline and he got on our nerves. We called him the 'banana' because of his long curving nose; he was unpopular but very efficient.

When we reached our patrol area I was off duty and asleep in my bunk. In those days we did not have quite the variety of clothing that we had later, but it was usual to wear an old jersey or shirt beneath our U-boat leathers, and these protective outer garments were not worn all of the time anyway; it could become very hot and stinking in the confines of a submarine. This we had soon found out even in training and it was very much worse in the Atlantic, so that a short spell on the surface to let in some fresh air was a gift from God. I myself tried hard to keep clean, but it was difficult as fresh water was rationed and we had to use sea water for washing. Everyone grew beards though we were still young, and in some cases looked more like schoolboys, so their growths were very sparse.

In my bunk I was suddenly awaken by the alarm and everyone rushed to their stations, for even off duty it was necessary to get out of the bunk and take up a certain position, especially if emergency trim was called and the boat had to crash dive, and then we all had to rush forward in a mad scramble to make the nose of the boat heavier and increase the angle of dive. This was a fairly new thing in that period and we had practised it once or twice in our last bout of training, but it had been a shambles and rather unpopular. Of course everything flew all over the place on such occasions, all our belongings got mixed up with smashed plates etc, and even jugs of milk and lemonade flew over the deck and the resulting mess was awful – even worse was the cleaning up afterwards.

On this occasion everyone leapt from their bunks, myself included, as the alarm sounded. I had no idea what was happening but guessed some sort of enemy ships were close in sight. I stood near a hatchway and word soon came that a convoy with strong escort was heading straight for us, intended for England and therefore a rich target. I thought of Willi at the wheel as I stood there feeling the changing motion of the boat as the captain brought it round into a firing position. At this point I must mention that the manoeuvre took hours owing to the convoy's speed and the state of the ocean. We had to be extra careful when the escort was strong; to get into a favourable position to attack and then escape reprisal was the aim. The captain had to figure out his moves in advance and act accordingly.

We heard the noise of many ships passing not far away, a very strange and fascinating swishing, whining hum; and then I believe we had got out from the van of the convoy and turned about to try and get just ahead of the leading ships. I believe there were at least three or four warships around the convoy, continually changing position, so this made our task more difficult. It must have been at least three more hours before I realised our boat was stationary and I felt the torpedoes released. The boat shook as the first whirred away. Some minutes passed and we heard absolutely nothing. We were very disappointed after so much effort, and the captain decided to take a better look. The boat was taken up to periscope depth and we began manoeuvring all over again, not knowing why we had failed but intent on having another try.

Another hour went by and I sat on my bunk, and then the captain decided to call off the attack. Apparently the situation was unfavourable and it was impossible to reach a good attacking position, so we had failed and wasted four expensive weapons. But that was the way it sometimes went, and there was in those days the problem of defective torpedoes. This was because the new magnetic triggers were inefficient and the problem was not solved for a long time; a great deal of frustration and anger resulted. We were obliged to rely on the old contact heads and these never failed.

But on that day we had no success and were obliged to reverse our course and report accordingly. Fortunately, Dönitz had himself been a U-boat commander and knew about the problems. However, success was about to make up for our failure, for within twenty-four hours we had sighted a fat target some miles away and heading alone at high speed for England. The captain identified it as a large refrigerator ship, probably full of American beef which we could have done with ourselves, I thought later; if only we could have stopped the thing, taken off some sides of beef for ourselves and then sunk it. But I had no part in the decision making.

We made a parallel course, all the while coming closer; our captain did not want to miss this one. At last, after about an hour and a half, we were in a position and fired four torpedoes. Two at least struck the unfortunate vessel and it went up in flames, but took some time to sink which was just as well as it gave the crew plenty of time to escape. We hoped they would soon be rescued. The war at sea was always a cruel one and never more so than for those brave seamen.

We celebrated with cheers and schnapps and reported our success to base and then resumed our third week of patrol but had no more success and returned to

Kiel. I was very much looking forward to seeing Ilse again but only had a very short leave as we were due to sail again within a week, so I made the most of it and met my lady friend every day – or night. We went to the cinema and saw a fine musical film and then she took me to her flat where I met her sister who was also a charming girl, so much so that I asked her to write to my shipmate Willi and she agreed to do so as a friend and with no romantic attachment suggested. My parents and Ilse were sad to see me leave on the train but sent me off with many small gifts including sweets and cakes that I could share with my shipmates.

By that time the battle in France was underway and we were all overjoyed at our victories. We sailed again and made our way around Scotland which used up a lot of our fuel, but this could not be helped. When we reached the Atlantic we were sent to a point further south and were especially warned to watch out for neutral shipping as several had been sunk in error and this caused embarrassment to our Government. We listened to the war bulletins and cheered the enormous successes of the Army in France and began to believe it was all over and we could soon return to our homes in a Germany at peace. Then we found our first convoy and raced to take up an attacking position; I recall the details of these earlier cruises, whereas the later ones are more hazy: there were so many and some fierce battles and I never kept a diary I'm sorry to say. It would have made some amazing reading later on.

The convoy had two tankers in its centre and was watched over by three destroyers and a smaller warship. We did our best to penetrate this screen so that we could get at the tankers, but this proved difficult. But our captain fired four torpedoes which he hoped would strike one of the better targets at least. The moments ticked away in silent expectation; they were always very tense and bad on our nerves as we were stationary and waiting to be detected by the roving escorts. Then we heard one tremendous explosion which shook our boat and the captain shouted that one of the tankers had been hit and was erupting in flames. This was the first time that I had been able to look through the periscope during an attack; another man took the helm and many of us were able to see the results. It was a disturbing and terrible sight. A great column of black smoke was curling up into a grey overcast; the whole scene was very dramatic with the tanker still afloat and no sign of any crew. We did not know if they had perished or had already escaped. The destroyers were already racing towards our 'guesstimated' position and the captain had called 'scope down and a dive to three or four hundred metres or more, so we prepared to be attacked, and we were frightened I can tell you. We had not so far suffered attack and wondered how it would be. We knew the enemy had his detection apparatus and thought it might prove effective.

We went deep down and I did my best to maintain our course. It was a very tense few moments with total silence throughout the boat, only the captain and depthkeeping officer giving whispered commands. At last we heard the sound of the enemy detecting gear ping-pinging its way towards us and it really made us very frightened. Any second we expected to hear the plonk and crack of depth charges – and they came.

It was about three or four minutes later, with this awful knock-knocking about us in metallic fashion with the destroyers' screws threshing right overhead. It was quite terrifying: it felt like being trapped in a metal box with no escape. It was no place for anyone who suffered from claustrophobia, but then such people did not go down in submarines.

We did not hear any preliminaries, so were taken by surprise when the first charge went off. It was not too near but with our inexperience we thought it much nearer. The blast rocked the boat and sent our senses reeling; I was absolutely terrified, it was very frightening. The captain ordered us deeper and gave a course correction and we tried to creep away as two more charges struck not far away with the same devastating results. Some of the lights went out and I did not dare look round but guessed the other lads' hearts were pounding as hard as mine was. I had a sudden thought of my parents and Ilse, and wondered if this was to be my last on earth. I was sure it was the end. How little I knew. Later on, after suffering many such experiences, I realised that those early depth charge attacks were as nothing; the charges had in fact burst some way off. But the effect of even modest charges is amplified underwater because of the density, so if you are new to that kind of thing they can be both misleading and frightening to the point of panic. In fact panic rarely ensued in my experience even though in the circumstances it was understandable.

Several more charges came down and obviously further away, so our relief was very great. I glanced around and saw the captain grinning wryly.

'Well lads,' he said, 'we have come through our first enemy attack, so now it's back to business!'

With that he ordered another course change and a climb to periscope depth. When he was able to take a very brief and cautious look he reported that the enemy had almost vanished, but the tanker was still afloat – just – and blazing. One of the destroyers was not far off and had probably taken the survivors on board and may have been waiting to see if we surfaced. I wondered if our captain was going to attack the warship, but he let it go. Later on no such mercy would be given.

We returned to base with torpedoes unfired and although the base commander was never happy at such things we had scored a good success so he could not complain. But later on we were expected never to return with weapons unexpended, but it was unavoidable at times, so the wise U-boat commander made sure he fired all his torpedoes when targets were available. Once more I was able to go home and enjoy an even greater time for the campaign in France had ended in a great victory, so we watched the victory parades in Berlin where the crowds were enormous. I had taken Ilse and we also went to a theatre and a good meal afterwards. I now realised that I loved her and she seemed to recipro-cate these feelings. This time I felt even more stricken when leaving her, and once back at Kiel our base commander told us all that he expected some kind of accommodation with England to be made, but if they did not see sense then the war would go on until they did! What was more, we had captured valuable bases on the coast of France and big changes were afoot, and until England gave up plans were to go ahead with all personnel transferring to the new ports.

All this gave me mixed feelings. I was very anxious for the war to end so I could get home to Ilse, yet I was interested in visiting France. However, my fate was not in my hands, and within a few weeks we of the U-boat arm began trans-ferring to French bases. In fact, some boats were dispatched with skeleton crews while others travelled by train, stopping in Paris where a good time was had by all. I can say this with certainty as I was one of those on that journey: we were given royal accommodation in a hotel and allowed to roam at will around that fine city, and I managed to buy a few presents to send home. We then went on to St Nazaire and Lorient, split into different parties and I ended up with the same men in the former base where we were ordered to begin helping to prepare accommodation and general facilities of all kinds. A lot of workers and materi-als began arriving and even Frenchmen were called in to assist in some direc-tions, all under the direction of the Organisation Todt people and naval personnel, and obviously a very great effort was in hand to prepare U-boat bases for the continuing war in the Atlantic. This was very grim news as there was no sign of England's surrender, so the war had to go on until she gave in. At least, it did not seem possible for her to continue to fight alone. The island was under siege from sea and air; even our battleships had begun attacks on convoys in the Atlantic, and of course there was no sign of America entering the war to assist England.

I was billeted in a small hotel on the outskirts of Lorient and we got ourselves organised; we had a bar and canteen and good bath facilities. There was also a theatre nearby that had been taken over by the Wehrmacht. Special berths had to be built for submarines, though at first these were just wharves and jetties etc; in due course the huge and well-known concrete pens were built which remained impregnable for most of the war.* When a boat was being prepared for a cruise

*They were finally penetrated by the heaviest RAF bombs.

everyone had to assist in shifts to take aboard the necessary stores, including ammunition for the 88mm gun and a lot of food, even pineapples if available, oranges, lemons, fresh water, apples, pears, and bananas when we had them, lots of sausage, bread, potatoes, cabbage and other items, mostly in tins but otherwise in sacks and muslin bags. Naturally, on first leaving port the boat's interior was crammed with all those things which were even stowed through the accommodation and this made life even more difficult. But the longer the cruise lasted the less was the overcrowding as the supplies were consumed. But one thing dominated operations and this was the supply of fresh water which was severely rationed. There was a time when the so-called 'milch cow' U-boats were sent out to resupply, but these only met certain boats on special operations in the south Atlantic. Most U-boats had to remain completely self-sufficient for three weeks in the north Atlantic and in all weathers. It was never possible to loot ships sunk, though I believe on some rare occasions some cargo set adrift was picked up and made good use of. Mostly we ate and drank goods brought with us and this often included items from other countries including France, for there was plenty to be had in 1940 though things became much more difficult later on for the French.

The concrete pens were only just being built, so all my own war cruises in that year from France were commenced from wooden piers which were only really adequate for smaller submarines; when we needed more serious over-hauls we moved on elsewhere so that the boat could be taken out of the water for the engineers to get at it more easily.

I did several more cruises in 1940, all very similar and with no outstanding events, expect perhaps on one occasion when we sank a destroyer which went down very rapidly with all hands, a victory for us but very sad; so many thousands of lives were lost in that battle.

During my leave in October I became engaged to Ilse and we had a celebration party at her flat and also at my own home where she had already met my parents who approved of her. She had a job in a small factory making airplane parts and seemed quite happy in her work. Her sister married a young man in the Luftwaffe in this period so we had another party in her flat which was very enjoyable. I was quite anxious to marry Ilse but had a nagging fear that if I were lost at sea then she would be left alone and I did not want that. If the war was going on much longer then many thousands of men would die and it did not seem fair to inflict suffering on women in that way. I spoke quite forcibly to Ilse on this and she too said she wanted to marry but would defer to my wishes. Of course I had no idea then just how terrible our losses would become; if I had known then the thought of marriage would never have come up.

As it turned out fate took a very different course, for in 1941 my dear Ilse was killed in an air raid. It is very sad to recall that time. I was so shattered I considered taking my own life, I was so inconsolable. I tried to tell myself that as a soldier it was my duty to face such tragedies and carry on as do others.

It happened in the spring of 1941. I had been on leave, enjoying her company in outings and counting the days when I would see her again. We had a fairly quiet cruise in the Atlantic and sank only one small freighter. When we returned to base I asked for leave but was told it was not possible as we were sailing again in a few days; one needed two or three days for travelling time to and from Germany unless an air passage could be arranged, but these were only given in priority and I had none. The war had continued and since the collapse of France the air raids had begun on Germany and we wondered how safe our homes would be. But the raids were really quite small and we were not really worried; the Tommies had yet to get themselves really organised in that direction. It was far more dangerous at sea. But I thought of Ilse in the factory and how it would be a target, though I had no idea of the realities of that kind of thing and that bombs could fall all over the place. We had of course followed the news of our bombing of English cities and knew how much they must have suffered. But the RAF attacks on Germany were of little significance in those times and we never really worried about them. The chances of death or injury must have been extremely small.

Small chance it may have been, but it was enough to kill dear Ilse in her flat while alone. Some bombs fell in the general area and a few were killed and injured. I assume it was supposed to be an attack on Berlin's war factories, but it's a big city and things go wrong, I know. I was away at sea and heard that an 'insignificant' raid had been made on our capital but did not take too much notice. About a week later I returned to our base in France and was told to report to the orderly room, where I was handed a telegram by a female who looked very sad. I wondered what on earth it could be and thought for a moment my father had died from natural causes. He had not been in any action and was attached to the transport planning staff.

Of course when I read the message I could hardly believe my eyes: not my dear Ilse – how could it be? I could not believe it. I was taken into a small office, numb with shock, and handed a glass of schnapps, but I could not drink it. I was devastated that such a lovely girl who was part of my life could be so cruelly taken from me. The staff were very considerate and sent a message to my captain that I was sick with the bad news and he came to see me and was very kind. In the circumstances he said he would grant me leave at once and made all the arrangements. I reached home in a day or so to find my parents in a state of great sadness. I asked if I could have some of Ilse's things but they said they had been destroyed; in fact she had already been buried with only her sister and fiancé in attendance. It was all very devastating and sad as no one from my family had been to the funeral; I believe they had expected me to get home right up to the last minute so that we could all attend.

That was the end of my connection with Ilse's family, such as it was. Her sister got married soon afterwards and I never saw her again.

When I returned from leave I received more bad news; my boat had been lost with all hands. I was shattered all over again, yet marvelled at my good fortune in that all my comrades were probably dead, yet because of Ilse's own passing I had been spared. It was the most extraordinary turn of events. In fact I joined up with a few other crew members who had been off sick, and we were told to wait so that we could join another crew then being completed.

This was not a good time, for apart from my own sad news there was the task of starting all over again with a new set of shipmates. I got to know very few of them because unlike myself most were newcomers, and there was a new commander who was less experienced, and experience counted for a very great deal, but this we gained in plenty in 1941–42. After the war began in Russia the Americans grew bolder in escorting convoys into the Atlantic, and this was a new departure and introduced special difficulties, for although we were not at war with them their actions were a serious provocation. After all, the Allied ships were our targets though mostly in the eastern half of the Atlantic, but the Americans began escorting convoys into mid-ocean and there were some encounters at the end of which, if I recall correctly, an American destroyer was sunk and one of our boats damaged.

I did four or five cruises before the Americans came into the war, and during that time my new boat sank twelve ships including another destroyer. Whenever we reached port there was always a band and girls waiting for us. The ladies were mostly Navy types but sometimes civilian employees in the various facilities, and it must be said one or two collaborators from the French. We had strict orders not to go off around the town and to avoid making close contacts because of the nature of our jobs with security a high priority, but as everyone knew, liaisons with French girls of one kind or another did happen. When a lot of healthy young men reach port after a dangerous voyage their thoughts are very much on wine, women and song! I myself did not mix with the available women as I was too sad over my loss for a very long time, but there were brothels controlled by the Wehrmacht and private arrangements whereby bolder sailors slept away in private homes with lady friends, and these lads wore civilian clothes on such leaves, but everyone including the French knew who they were. Inevitably there were heartaches and disasters and even one or two desertions, but in the main the men kept their heads and morale even if they lost all their money.

I took my own leaves home in Potsdam, but they were rather dull, sad affairs, and despite the dangers we faced I was glad to get back to my comrades. I had missed my old friend Willi, but my new comrade at the helm was a stout-hearted fellow also from Hamburg called Peter. In fact we tried to get away together on one leave as he had invited me to his home knowing how sad I was and unhappy at the prospect of going home to no Ilse. So I agreed to go with him and it was in Hamburg that he effected a great change in me. I met his family who were very kind to me, and also his sister called Paula who I had to admit attracted me, though it was too early for anything more, though I agreed to write to her. She knew all about my loss and did her best to cheer me up, and in this she succeeded, so that after we returned to sea I again felt I had something special to go back to, though I could never forget dear Ilse.

That next cruise was a memorable one for us as we penetrated the US seaboard for the first time. You may have heard that the next few months were a period of great triumph for the German U-boats in that area before the Americans got organised into a proper convoy system. The American shipping was largely confined to their coastline, and now they had us to contend with off the Atlantic seaboard and we found plenty of good targets.

I will always remember the first sight we had of the American coastline. It was spring 1942 and we took turns to climb into the tower to look at the land, which was the coast of Maine some ten or twelve miles distant. It looked just like peacetime: the lights were stretched all along the coast and we even thought we could hear the traffic and music! It was an extraordinary sight and will always remain in my memory. But we were not there on a sightseeing tour and crept away on the surface, moving south, watching out for other U-boats that were also in that area. Dönitz had ordered several of our submarines to take advantage of American laxness, and he was right inasmuch as terrific slaughter took place. It became quite commonplace to see the night sky lit up by the flames from burning tankers which were en route to New York or returning to the Gulf to load up with more oil. We often saw the silhouettes of ships against the shore lights and thought that the Yankees were crazy to be so careless.

The first victim we found in those waters was a large freighter moving north and some twelve miles off the coast, with our boat a mile or so beyond it. We fired four torpedoes in a surface attack and the ship was blown open and sank quickly. We always listened on the radio to identify any vessels from their signals, but on this occasion heard none. So we watched events and it was an hour before a seaplane came on the scene by which time we had submerged and were safe from prying eyes.

Our next target was a small tanker which cost us one torpedo but did not sink at first though the crew abandoned ship and made for the shore. So we went in closer and our deck gun crew finished off the ship with about twenty rounds of high explosive, and it sank. We then moved south and found another tanker. Although that one was in ballast, we sank that too, or at least it grounded on a reef, the crew taking to the boats.

When we reached base again I disappointed my family by going home with Peter to Hamburg, but I had so looked forward to seeing Paula and enjoyed a really good leave. I did telephone home several times to let them know all was well and promised to see them on my next leave. Peter's family lived in a large apartment block which was not too convenient when the air raid sirens sounded, as they did twice during my leave; we had quite a long trek downstairs to the shelter as there was no lift. We would much have preferred to stay where we were, but the family felt very vulnerable as they were near the top floor.

Paula was a fair-haired girl and not very tall but always laughing and I found I was growing fond of her. She had written to me not knowing when I would return and I had found her letters awaiting me when I returned to base. This was always the way of things with sailors.

Unfortunately, the family were to undergo great tribulation later when the big raids devastated Hamburg. By then the war had taken a very serious turn for our losses had risen enormously. I myself had some narrow escapes but our losses in boats were never announced to us, but every time we entered port safely the word got around and we soon learnt who was overdue, and in most cases they were never seen again. Now and then we heard that some crewmen had survived and were prisoners of war in England, Canada or the USA, but in most cases when a submarine was blown open like a tin can there were no survivors.

Our war continued through 1942 in all weathers. Some of the Atlantic storms were terrifying and our boat rolled alarmingly and few were not sick, so the interior of the boat became a real stinkhouse, if you will forgive the expression. Our language was rather descriptive I'm afraid; our life became very crude in such circumstances. We lost two men overboard from a watch when I felt we should have been submerged. The storms could go on for days on end, and from ashore would be seen only as a rather windy day perhaps, but the same gale at sea played havoc with us. As you can imagine, a cigar-shaped submarine will roll over almost onto its beam ends, so you can guess what conditions were like inside for the men. On our way home it was not quite so bad as we were running short of supplies so there were fewer goods to go rolling about. This rolling motion went on for hours and brought misery as the men could do nothing but vomit and retch; eating was out of the question, as was any kind of action. We lay on our stomachs in or near our bunks in abject misery. Then the storms subsided at last and the boat became calm again which was the signal to start cleaning up and, if possible, the hatches were opened to let out the foul air and in with the new. A hose was used to blow seawater through the decks to clean them out. These were bad days that tended to make men out of boys, and some of those crews were indeed little more than boys, kids in some cases who had just come out of the Hitler Youth and Labour Corps knowing very little of life and with no service time at all. Nothing can compare on land to the terrors of a full-blown storm at sea when survival at times seems remote. But those U-boats were very strongly built: no matter how much they pitched and rolled I have never heard of one turning turtle.

We got through 1942 with many losses, but there were great victories. When we went to the bars and theatre back at base we always looked around for the old familiar faces and characters, but too often found them missing. We had no idea how much longer it could go on for, and we became rather worn out by those endless Atlantic cruises, but were glad not to be in the icecap patrol off north Russia where things were worse in some ways.

I saw a few men go under. Some simply cracked up, their eyes hollow sockets, their faces lined and they chattered continuously or just went into complete silence. They had become old before their time and had to be sent away to rest camps in Brittany or Germany. Sometimes these cases returned, sometimes not.

I resolved to stick it out to the end, whatever that might be. It was possible to harden oneself to the war, but some men could not do this and suffered accordingly. Some of our cruises brought distressing sights when whole packs of U-boats tore convoys to pieces; the sea became filled with burning and sinking ships all at the same time, with tankers blazing and the poor seamen struggling in a flaming sea. I saw one such sight and had a great urge to avert my eyes, but could not do so. We had gone on deck in turns for some air after an attack on a convoy; the escorts had vanished somewhere leaving two ships including a tanker to sink. The latter was a mass of fire and we assumed the crew had long got away. But suddenly we saw some men on the deck trying to launch a boat, but the flames had caught it and it was destroyed. They leapt into the sea in their lifejackets and I wondered if we could rescue them. But then the tanker broke in two and all the men were engulfed in flames. It was a sickening sight and I was glad to get below again.

We never wrote home of such things; our letters were censored anyway and we didn't want our people to hear such things. I was questioned at home by my parents and told them the war was horrible but gave no details, though I did describe some of our normal tribulations though not mentioning the horrors seen.

In 1943 the back of our U-boat arm was broken. Things became so bad that all boats were temporarily withdrawn. We lost a great number of boats every month, the worst losses occurring in the opening months and especially in the spring and summer of that year, and it was incredible to find so many faces missing when we returned to base. It was the biggest threat to our morale so far, and although we were very depressed we never cracked. We may not have believed in what our Government told us but we were fighting for our country and it was our duty to do so.

We stayed in port for several weeks but were not idle. The air raids had become serious, but although they destroyed everything around they failed to knock out the bomb-proof shelters. By far the greater menace was the Allied air power extending far out into the Atlantic and the Bay of Biscay. Then there were escort carriers with anti-sub planes, and we would have been very foolish to cross the Bay on the surface which was something we had always done in the past. The enemy carriers and their own submarines lay in wait for us which meant we were no longer secure from the moment we left our shelters.

We were obliged to help clear bomb damage and even on occasions supply the flak guns with ammunition, which was very hazardous during raids with bombs raining down and splinters flying. We lost several men that way. We set sail once more in subdued mood, our boat fitted now with an experimental schnorchel tube and a new commander and first officer. We had no orders to practise with the new tube but had been assured that it was fully tested and not found wanting. So we submerged and hoped we could reach our operational zone without being intercepted by the enemy; many boats had been lost en route with their crews missing.

On this occasion we travelled submerged for some days before coming up, which was very much easier with the schnorchel tube. Our hunting area was with at least twelve other U-boats, yet it took us nearly two weeks to get any-where near a convoy. First of all the weather thwarted us and then there were so many escorts, it was hard to get through this screen. Finally one commander more daring than the rest managed to evade the warships and began his attack, torpedoing two ships at once. This caused enough of a diversion for the other U-boats to close in, but the escorts were well trained and knew what to expect so we found ourselves hemmed in and exposed to real danger. We had no chance to fire any torpedoes at all; we were harried and chased and realised that the enemy had perfected his detection devices, and even our new homing torpedoes were of no use in such situations. Our new commander felt he had to do something so he let two torpedoes go in the general direction of a sloop which had been chasing us, if only to see what happened. There was a large explosion and the enemy ship vanished, but almost at once our listening watch discovered that the other torpedo was running in circles. So we submerged further and heard no more of the damned thing. We assumed it had finally sunk to the bottom.

When we tried again, the convoy had gone over the horizon and we could not catch up with it in a reasonable time. However, we soon received a call from a spotter U-boat of another convoy to the west of us so we began a chase to reach a suitable firing position. It took us two days to get there, and when we arrived we found the biggest convoy we had ever seen – some sixty ships in great columns and looking quite majestic. The escort was suitably powerful and included two carriers with planes taking off and landing. We knew other U-boats were joining us and wanted to make a concerted attack, but were rather in the dark as to their position, so our CO crossed the van of the convoy and came up on its port side, being careful not to show much periscope to the escorting planes and warships.

The weather was good, just right for an attack, and we moved in closer and closer until we had a clear view of some of the best targets and fired four torpedoes, submerged at once and went astern. We counted the seconds and at last there came a double detonation as ships were struck. Heavy breaking up noises were reported by the listening watch and our commander decided to take a quick look at the situation. When he did so he was surprised to see that one of the escorting destroyers as well as a merchantman had been hit. The warship went down quickly, but the other ship burned and stayed afloat.

We then went forward again, our intention to attack the leaders of the central column, but before we reached a new firing position we were intercepted by an escort and forced to dive deep. This evasive action went on for two hours, and by the time it was safe to take another look all chance of a good sighting was lost. We did our best to retrieve the situation, but the British were now employing 'killer groups' of escorts, and these roamed far and wide irrespective of the convoy itself and made life very unpleasant. Their tactics were very sound, and it seemed to spell the end of any more great success in this war.

We heard the news of the invasion of France over the BBC. In a way it came as a relief and most of us knew that the war was lost. I only hoped that having survived that far I would live to see my lady friend and parents again. In the attack just described, we lost five U-boats which is a measure of the desperate times that had come to us. I saw all the empty bunks when we returned to base, and although we had plenty of volunteers it could never be the same again. The new men had not been given enough training; if they had been, then with the radical new U-boat designs we might have stood a chance of prolonging the war, but to what purpose?

The U-boats failed to intervene in the Channel so our main source of action continued to be the Atlantic, but with only a minimum of success. By then we had been home and seen the effects of the bombing and were shattered by the devastation; Peter's parents lost their home but were spared, thank God, though many thousands were not. The ruination was unbelievable – I will not say unforgivable, because the Germans had caused far more in Hitler's war. But obviously, to see so many poor civilians slaughtered was very distressing and inevitably led to calls for reprisals from the most effective weapons. There would be little sympathy for the British after the bombing of Germany and, of course, I refer to the V1 and V2 weapons, terrible though they were.

Peter's parents were forced to move in with relatives outside Hamburg, and they suffered very hard times. When we returned to our base once more in Germany after the fall of France it was only with the greatest difficulty, and entailed sailing round Scotland again.

By early 1945 I was no longer a U-boat helmsman but had been promoted to senior NCO and sent to the U-boat training school where new crews learned something about the new-type submarines (prefabricated) including the electro-boats. This was all very interesting but much too late not only for the war but for me personally, for I had grown sick of it all and longed for an end to it. I never went to sea again after January 1945. Many naval men were now converted to infantrymen, which was a complete waste of time. I myself was on a commander's course in Bremen when the war ended, having escaped the Baltic training areas ahead of the advancing Red Army. Thank God we were all taken into the British sector.

My own family had not wished to leave their home but changed their minds when they began to hear tales of Russian atrocities; they escaped with as many valuables as they could carry in a car and joined me in Bremen where I had, despite great difficulty, been able to find them a room just outside the city which was itself in ruins. Even though it was a close thing as the Russians were still advancing and clearly intended to grab all they could; I'm glad it ended the way it did. I was waiting with my men for the British to come, having heard that surrender was imminent, and when the first reconnaissance units came into sight with some paratroops we paraded outside to await events. All went smoothly: we were told to remain in our barracks and certain officers were taken for questioning, and to ensure that no facilities were sabotaged.

I remained a sailor for six more months until I was released and rejoined my family. It was a hard time, but a year later I married Paula and we have two fine sons.**

CHAPTER 5

Anna Wendling

Jt has long been recognised that the profession of nursing is one of dedication which brings its own special kind of reward; it takes a very particular kind of person to devote themselves to tending the sick – remuneration in financial terms has never been the chief incentive.

Those who took up this vocation before or during the recent world wars were tested as nurses had never been before, but especially so in the second conflict when during the air raids they themselves came under fire. In Britain the threat and probable effects of air bombardment had not only been taken seriously before World War II but greatly exaggerated: one leading military expert pointed out that during the earlier 'Great War' only seventy-four tons of bombs had been dropped on England, killing 857 people, wounding 2,059 and causing material damage to the value of £1,400,000. On this basis the expert reckoned that almost a quarter of a million casualties and £100 million worth of damage might be expected in the first week of a new war. Indeed, such was the fear in Britain of Hitler's new Luftwaffe that the Ministry of Health gauged casualties at 600,000 in the first six months of the war, with a possible 200,000 wounded. All such estimates were based on a faulty calculation of German bomber strength and their bombing capacity which the officials estimated could produce fifty people killed and wounded for every ton of bombs dropped on a built-up area. British air raid precautions were based on such wildly inaccurate and gloomy predictions; in the event the total number of British civilians killed by air attack was around ten times less, or sixty thousand in the whole war, most of them occurring in the Blitz of 1940–41.

In Germany the story was the exact opposite, for although the Nazi Government laid down tentative air raid precautions in the mid-thirties and intensified them before the war by the forming of an air raid protection league – the Reichs Luftschutz Bund, or RLB – no great guesses as to possible casualties were made or any extensive building of shelters undertaken. Certainly there was no distribution of personal coverings as protection as in Britain which, under the then Home Secretary Lord Anderson, issued the back garden shelters ('Andersons') free to everyone earning under five pounds a week. The Germans did not see the RAF bomber force as strong, and therefore was no threat to the security of the Reich. In any case, Göring had assured everyone in an ill-chosen phrase that would be much thrown back at him later that no enemy bomber would be permitted to overfly the Reich. Despite this utterance the RLB made sure when war broke out that every household and commercial enterprise instituted small routine precautions, yet the great victories in Poland and the West bred a great feeling of complacency which was not quite eradicated when the RAF began bombing Germany after May 1940. Many German homes had cellars, but it was not until the raids became worse in 1942 that more serious attempts were made to build tough public shelters, and by then the die was cast: the German civil population was about to undergo a terrifying ordeal by air attack such as no non-combatant people had ever been called upon to endure before. But this was the total war which brought the front line to the population 'behind the lines', for it had been recognised that without sustenance in weapons and supplies from the home front no army at war could continue the battle. Both factories and morale were 'legitimate' targets, as those people attacked by the Luftwaffe already had discovered.

On the German civilians fell a whole new arsenal of weapons. Gone were the puny little bombs of the earlier years; now came four and twelve thousand-pound 'blockbusters', so called because of their great blast capacity to eradicate whole blocks of houses and other buildings. Added to the standard thermite incendiary bomb came the far more terrifying and deadly phosphorus canister which ignited into an almost unquenchable fire on contact with air, bringing casualties to the likes of Anna Wendling that could not be healed.

❝I was born in 1918 at a small town called Düren in West Germany. I had a sister called Greta who was two years older than myself. We lived in the middle of the town where my father was an official in the Post Office.

After the war life became much more difficult, but we managed to survive though often going hungry. After the Nazis came to power my father was angry, but he said at least we would not have one of those Bolshevik governments, or even a feeble democracy. As a young lady at school I was a bright pupil and was chosen to lead the sports day celebrations, and I also led the youth orchestra on violin, though I was not exceptionally talented. My young days were very much influenced by the Nazi organisations, for they controlled everything. So I was a member of the Bund Deutsche Mädel for a time, though I wanted to become a professional musician. I used to attend music school where we played classics and light music, and then I joined a Nazi orchestra which played concerts on public occasions.

But by the time of the great crisis of 1938–39 I had decided to go into nursing as I always wanted to help the sick and needy. My parents were rather surprised and my sister thought I was foolish, but I had made up my mind and went off to begin training at Duisburg where I hoped to become a fully fledged nurse and be sent to a big hospital. The training lasted six months before I was sent to a hospital as a probationary nurse in a general ward which I found quite pleasant, though the rules were very strict. The patients were mostly elderly and included some difficult ones, and I grew unhappy as it was not the kind of nursing I had expected. But I was only a probationer and it was my duty to stick it out or quit, and I did not want to do that.

When the war came nothing much happened except that we were lectured on air raid drill and on how to remove the patients in an emergency, how to cover the windows and deal with small fires. We carried on very much as usual until the next year when I was assessed as competent and transferred to a different ward where the patients were all pregnant women. This was a new kind of experience for me which I enjoyed very much. But as soon as I became used to this it all changed. The big offensive began on the Western Front and I was selected to go with other nurses to a hospital in Bonn to be ready to receive the wounded, and this I was very glad to do.

The military had a lot to do with this hospital and we came very much under their orders. The first wounded began to arrive, and I recall my very first patient: he was a young boy who had lost his right foot and I felt very sad for him. But he was quite cheerful and said, 'It could have been far worse.' I helped him to get comfortable and to write to his home. The next man I tended had his head bandaged and had been shot. He did not survive. I was very upset about this as he was my patient. I had been speaking to him and telling him he was in good hands. I went to ask the sister if I could feed him some liquids and she said she would see him first, but when we returned to him his eyes were closed and he had stopped breathing. We were very sad.

The ward soon filled up with young men, all of them badly injured in some way and some of them were moaning, others very cheerful. All had come back from the fighting in France where the advances were very great and, I suppose, the losses not too big. But to us it was distressing to see so much suffering. This work went on for some months, as although the campaign ended fairly soon the men needed time to heal and convalesce, and one or two did not survive. I remember a sergeant who had been hit in the eye by a bullet or splinter. He was very upset as he said he could not see well out of his remaining eye. I did all I could to cheer him up, but he seemed to wilt away with depression and died. I found that some people did not have the will to live once they were wounded, even though they might easily have recovered otherwise.

Eventually the hospital was cleared, the soldiers gone by one way or another, their wounds healed or else they were discharged from the Army if they had lost a limb. I was wondering where my career would take me next when I heard a rumour that we were to become a permanent military staff. I was not sure how I felt about this as I really wanted to vary my career and even advance up the ladder a little. So I applied to become a surgical nursing assistant and was told I must attend a course with others. When this happened I found the course took place in the same hospital complex where there was a training wing. We had to relearn all the parts of the male and female body from the surgical point of view, and all about anaesthetics and operating procedures. We were given tests in writing and talking and taken to witness operations being performed. Some of the girls did not like this; some fainted and a few asked to be withdrawn from the course and their wish was granted. I found it all very interesting, though not very pleasant at times, especially when the operations resulted in death, but this was something that we as nurses had to get used to. The power of life and death did not rest with the surgeons or ourselves, but with God; this I told myself sometimes as I watched them cutting into people to relieve them of this or that. If they were to survive they would; if not, then no. I found this attitude helped me no end, but later when I saw so many wounded and dying including the children I found it much harder to understand.

Those who completed the course were assessed as fit to serve in operating teams or otherwise; in the latter case they returned to general nursing. In my case I passed all the tests and was told that as soon as a vacancy occurred I would be sent to an operating team in a hospital, and this would not be where I was. So over the next few weeks I worked as a general nurse, helping civilian patients as, despite the earlier rumours and experiences, we were not militarised at that time after all. But I remember a few soldiers and airmen who came into the hospital, and among them was a Tommy who had been shot down over Germany and was about to be operated on for a stomach wound. I spoke to him once or twice and he seemed a very pleasant young man but in some pain. He went off to the theatre, survived and was taken off elsewhere. Later I saw many more Allied airmen.

Eventually I was told my appointment had come through: I was to travel to Berlin and take up a position in a big hospital in the Charlottenburg area. I packed at once, telephoned my parents and left the next day, and when I arrived found the nurses billeted next to the hospital in a barrack-type block, but it was all very comfortable and I shared a room with three more nurses who all came from the city itself and they made me very welcome.

I was put to work at once and attended my first operation as assistant to the surgeons; it was my job to lay out all the various instruments, and this I was well trained to do – there was nothing unfamiliar in the procedures. I recall the first patient, an elderly man with a hernia, which was soon put right. Next came an old lady with a displaced spine which was not curable, but she was helped in some measure I believe. Then there came a boy of about twelve who had fallen on to an iron spike or something and had badly lacerated his thigh, which required surgery. That completed a morning's work and it was fairly typical of the time.

After a hurried lunch in the canteen we began again. I believe the first was another hernia, the rest I forget. My days thereafter were much the same but were relieved in the evenings by outings about the city with my new friends. We used to go sailing on the lake and have a nice time, especially when the men called and whistled at us. Some of my new friends invited me to their homes as they lived with their parents, and this was nice as I was so far from home and would have been rather lonely in the barracks alone.

The routine did not vary very much until the summer of 1941 when there was a great influx of military wounded who had overflowed from the hospitals in the east. There were some very awful sights to see and I had to steel myself, as despite my experience these things were worse. Some of the cases were very pitiful, as although they had hope in their eyes they stood no chance at all. It was hard to have to bag up their few possessions to be sent to their families.

When contrary to expectations the war in Russia did not end, we were told that special teams would be formed to deal with the wounded on a mobile basis. Although our base would continue to be Berlin we had to be prepared to go anywhere at short notice, and this is what happened. We packed into a car or van with all our equipment and rushed off somewhere, to various districts but always outside the city and usually miles to the east, where we would set up ship in all kinds of temporary quarters to carry out operations. It was an ingenious way of dealing with the ever increasing numbers of wounded. Then we had problems as some of the patients were Russians, though I must say that I believe that many of these were left to die in the field, and this was part of higher Nazi policy. The combat units did their best but were overwhelmed and unable to cope. The organisation broke down and was insufficient to take such large numbers of casualties. Even so, we cannot excuse callous treatment, though I know from my own experience that all the Russian wounded passed to us received exactly the same care as our own men. What happened to them later I cannot comment on, but I suspect their treatment was abysmal.

After the first hard winter when we had so many frostbite cases, we set up specialist units and this worked well. Some of the most difficult cases were the burns patients, and very special treatment and new types of care had to be formulated. Most of these cases went off to special units and I only rarely saw any.

When the air raids grew more serious, the first civilians came into our care and some of these were very, very young or very old as most of the fighting men were of course away at the Fronts. I recall a little girl who had both legs blown off below the knee; she was quite cheerful but had suffered a great shock and did not survive. Another child had lost an arm and a leg and was in a very bad way. I remember him well as he clung to me so much after arriving and I had difficulty in putting him down. I believe his name was David, and although he was not Jewish he may have had foreign blood. We did our very best for him and he survived. Some of the older patients failed to survive as they did not have the resistance to shock and wounds and just gave up the ghost. I remember one old man who used a lot of very bad language not only against the enemy but Hitler, and a lot more before he died.

During 1942 I saw very many operations, not only the Russian Front cases but also some from Africa. These men were so sunburned and strong and looked like real heroes and were always in the very best of spirits. I recall one boy from Hamburg who had lost an arm and he used to ask me to write his letters which I was glad to do when able. Another was an officer who told me that though the battles were quite hard Rommel was a top General, and they would therefore win in the end and he was anxious to return to Africa.

In 1943 the air raids grew far worse and bombs fell all around us and on the hospital so that some of the staff were killed and injured. It was strange to be tending one's own people, but they were very good and gave the minimum of trouble. As the bombs came down everyone was very frightened and some wards had to be evacuated, but it was impossible to remove them all. We had large cellars and these soon filled up, but not with patients, so the police had to be called to remove people who had no right to be there.

I remember one night of hell when the RAF were dropping many very large bombs and it seemed that nothing could remain standing, and I wondered if I would see the night through. Then I saw a young man sitting up in bed looking at me, and he said, 'Don't worry my dear, it's only a passing storm.' He laughed at me. I could not understand how he could remain so calm; the noise was terrible and the whole city was lit up by big fires everywhere. Next day I had great difficulty in getting about because of the great damage not only in the area but to the hospital itself.

We had many air raid victims to attend to, including those burned by fire and phosphorus, and there was little to be done for them. It was heartbreaking to see so many young children and old ones carted away as dead. I felt I could not stand much more of it and wondered if I should resign. We received stern words of encouragement and a promise of wonder weapons that would not only exact revenge but bring a stop to it all, but we were very dubious by then of any such miracles.

I was not often able to get home, and when I did I found damage in our own town, though thankfully my family survived. They were very worried about me, especially as the Russians drew nearer. In fact our hospital was evacuated and we moved west quite suddenly and met the Americans. By then I had seen and nursed many an Allied airman who seemed glad to be out of the war, and I cannot say I blamed them. I remember one handsome American boy, a lieutenant, I believe, from a B-17; he had lost a foot and was in a bad state of morale but saw he was in good hands and would no longer have to face combat. Another I recall was a Tommy from a night bomber, and not too popular with the civilians in our hospital, but he received the best of treatment and was taken away as a PoW.

When the Americans came they inspected our work and complimented us and gave us bandages and drugs as by then we were terribly short of everything and unable to do the best for our patients.

Thank God it all ended and we could start to repair the ills of war.**"**

CHAPTER 6

Matthias Henken

he rapid rise of the new aviation technology was accelerated even more by the outbreak of war in August 1914. By then a number of nations including France, Germany and Britain had formed small military air units equipped with observation balloons and a few aeroplanes which were used initially for reconnaissance and artillery spotting. Inevitably, some planes were soon fitted to carry small bombs which were initially dropped over the side of the machines by observers.

By the war's end the combatants possessed large air fleets, the British Royal Flying Corps was about to be rechristened the Royal Air Force, while the Germany of 'Kaiser Bill' had its Imperial Aviation Service, which was allied to the Austrians. When peace came the RAF had about 20,000 aeroplanes on charge, and in a very few years this large number was rapidly whittled down to a few hundred. As for the Germans, their own air fleet was taken over and broken up and no more warplanes were permitted, much to the disgust and humiliation of men like Herman Göring and Ernst Udet, both air aces, the former having taken over command of the Richthofen Circus during the war following the death in action of the famous 'Red Baron'. Göring went to Sweden where he tried to earn a living selling parachutes and demonstrating civil aircraft all over Scandinavia.

But in the following years leading German aviators began building up their air force anew with the connivance of the Russians, who loaned them bases in their country. Men like Udet and others set about the forming of 'air sports' clubs throughout Germany, with a great emphasis on gliding. This went apace with the development of ostensibly civil aircraft types by German firms which in many cases were easily convertible to military use. In fact, a great hive of 'civil' enthusiasm for flying was really a cloak for the rebirth of a new powerful air force, and this was aided by the burgeoning Nazi Party which formed its own brownshirt aviation units, later to be reorganised as the National Socialist Air Corps.

By the time Göring announced the birth of the 'Luftwaffe' in 1935 it was too late to do anything about it, and from that time on the Allies and others were haunted by the spectre of a large and very powerful Nazi air arm capable of terrorising whole populations, above all by the use of poison gas bombs.

Ernst Udet had become a General in the new air force and was incidentally a talented artist who liked to portray new German aircraft as well as personalities in caricature; fairly recently a small collection of his plane sketches were offered in a London auction house. But it was Erhard Milch who proved to be the real wizard in creating the Luftwaffe's striking power, epitomised in the latest Heinkel, Dornier and Junkers bombers, especially the Ju 87 'Stuka' which was, however, pushed by Udet who was to fall out with Göring and commit suicide, as was also 'fat Herman's' chief-of-staff, General Jeschnonnek.

By pulling strings – merely by making one or two telephone calls – it was perfectly possible for a Nazi Party official to get himself transferred into one of the armed services, literally to step out of one kind of uniform into another. And this did happen. One such case involved a comparatively minor Nazi official who through boredom and an interest in aviation got himself transferred as an officer into a Dornier bomber group, learned to fly the plane and was eventually shot down in the Battle of Britain. In another case an official had been instrumental in helping to set up clandestine air units prior to 1935; he too moved from the ranks of the Nazi Party organisation into Luftwaffe blue.

Matthias Henken did no such string pulling, and some facets of his account are worthy of additional comment.

The bombing of Guernica by German Heinkels of the Condor Legion in the Spanish Civil War of 1936–39 proved a propaganda disaster for the Nazis, raising hostile headlines in the world's Press and becoming embedded in history as a prime example of Nazi German 'frightfulness' and terrorism, cited as an atrocity in every popular war history in books and on film ever since. There is some argument as to whether German military leaders ever intended to use the air weapon to cow civilian populations or not. It is probable that the Nazis did, for there were and are certain advantages to be gained: civilians fleeing in panic from bombing can clog up the military machine, for example. Frequent allegations of terroristic Stuka attacks on civilian refugees can be matched by similar cases when Allied fighter bombers strafed and bombed anything that moved on roads and railways in enemy occupied territory. From aloft in a fast moving plane it is often impossible to distinguish civilian from soldier, and in any case it is fruitless to open up arguments regarding atrocities from the air. After all, it was the British who as a matter of policy first used the air weapon to 'pacify' native villages and recalcitrant tribesmen in the far-flung Empire in the 1920s. The most blatant use of terror and inhuman tactics occurred when the Italian Regia Aeronautica used poison gas in Africa to suppress opposition in its battle to gain an empire in the 1930s.

And for all the decrying of German support for General Franco in Spain as a would-be fascist dictator, recent evidence suggests that he received some kind of clandestine support from Britain; despite being a Royalist nation, Britain had a far greater fear of the Reds, who were Franco's opponents.

According to German accounts the bombing of Guernica was one of those errors, a raid that began as a normal attack on a military objective but with bombs falling astray, owing perhaps to the target becoming obscured by smoke and dust. Grievous though all loss of life is in war, this attack was very small when compared to what was to come later, yet it stirred up a hornets' nest of anti-German propaganda – even Picasso executed a painting depicting the agony of Guernica, and ever since it has been linked with other German air assaults such as the bombing of Rotterdam and Warsaw.

Following the triumphant German success in the West in 1940, many Luftwaffe air crews enjoyed a haven of rest in the French and Belgian countryside while the Führer digested the spoils and bathed in his latest bout of glory. Their vacation was shortlived, for as soon as Hitler's vague peace overtures were rejected Göring was given a free hand to subdue Britain from the air. Those airmen not already engaged were moved forward to airfields closer to their targets, and 'Eagle Day' was scheduled for 12 August, going off at half-cock but being restarted the next day. Even if the losses suffered by the Luftwaffe were nowhere near as heavy as claimed by the British, they were serious enough – especially among officers – to bring an end to the daylight bombing campaign, one that the Luftwaffe had never been trained for in any case. As soon as the night flying over Britain took place on a larger scale losses began to creep up, not from British action but through accidents. Even so, from the military standpoint the losses of planes and crews per thousand sorties were very low over England, though every German airman now knew that their objective had not been attained and heavy losses had been sustained; not that they felt they had been defeated, certainly not the fighter pilots, though the bomber crews' morale was less high.

This period also saw the inception of pathfinder bombing techniques by the Luftwaffe's Group 100 which had trained in Germany in flying by radio beams. This proved generally to be very successful, despite British counter-measures. The British were, however, caught flat-footed by a lack of night fighters, and by the time some kind of force was becoming a viable proposition with the new airborne radar devices the Blitz was virtually over.

Matthias Henken survived by a miracle, for air crew downed in the Channel by night without a dinghy stood very little chance of being found before cold overcame them. There were no radio bleepers, but the Germans had rapidly installed an air-sea rescue system of small craft and seaplanes and were in advance of their opponents in this respect.

❝I was born in Cologne in 1918 into a middle-class family. I was an only child and my father worked as a bank teller, and we knew hard times, especially when our money became almost worthless. I know that in the 1920s my father shed tears of frustration and worry; he worked in a bank holding millions upon millions of marks, yet it was worth very little.

After I had left school I went to technical college to learn engineering, but soon changed over to aeronautical studies and became very interested in aviation. When I had finished my course I was able to find a place as an apprentice with a small aircraft firm, but after a while I became far more interested in flying. My interest was helped after the Nazis came to power and began to build up the secret Luftwaffe. I was able to join the Hitler Youth gliding lessons which I found very exciting, became proficient and passed all my tests so received more flying lessons in a real aircraft, an old Arado biplane.

Then I heard about the new air force and applied to join; being accepted, I was sent off for some recruit training. This was not too bad but I was only really interested in flying. I next went on to flying school and found it fairly easy as I had already gone through a fair amount of this tuition. We then received new uniforms, and Göring told the world about our new Luftwaffe and it was very exciting. I was now very interested in larger flying machines and, having passed all my tests, was told that I could go on to a bomber pilot school with other candidates.

When we arrived at the school (I believe it was near Dortmund), we were shown into barracks and saw some of the aircraft on the field, mostly Dorniers and Junkers 86s. Within a few days I had settled down into my new life with some good comrades. We began to receive lectures on multi-engined flying and were shown over the planes' controls and had the flight characteristics explained to us.

I think it was about a couple of weeks later that I received my first flight in one of these training bombers; it was a Junkers 86 with very noisy diesel engines with a gun turret hanging down beneath it. It was not very comfortable in those things, but we had to learn to fly twin-engined aircraft. Each plane had a pilot instructor plus three pupils who took turns at the controls. It was very different to the smaller aircraft we had flown and quite a handful. But we progressed, though not without mishaps and accidents. I saw one very nervous pupil pilot come in too fast and just miss the trees at the far end of the field; he then tried to go round again while banking but had lost power so he crashed and the plane burned, killing all aboard. On another occasion I nearly had a bad accident while turning to take-off; my Junkers' wing nearly severed the tail of another plane and we collided. I was severely told off and grounded for a few days to write down the basic rules of taxying.

But we gradually improved and began to master the beasts and were told that we would become one of the first bomber units of the new Luftwaffe to fly a new type of plane, which was the Heinkel 111. We were sent away to northern Germany, near the island of Wangerooge but on the mainland, and there we found a squadron of brand new Heinkels, the early type with the elliptical wings. We swarmed all over them and soon began to receive instruction and very soon became a Kampfgruppe (Bomber Group). We had to learn how to fly both singly and in formation over land and sea, being constantly warned against carelessness and crashes, for the new planes were in short supply. We were then inspected by high officers and I saw Göring in his fancy uniform and medals. We also had some Nazi Party bigwigs look us over, as well as, I might add, foreign dignitaries.

We flew almost every day, weather permitting, and by the time the Spanish Civil War came we were proficient. I had a very good young crew, though one man was a little older than myself, and we called him Papa. He was in fact the crew captain as observer and was responsible for our bombing results of which we had a fair amount of practice over the sea and on ranges inland. Then we heard that we were to be part of a special unit being formed to help General Franco. We had no objection and were under orders anyway. It was all supposed to be a big secret and we were given strange new brown uniforms with different insignia while our new delivery of Heinkels received the fascist insignia of Franco's forces.

Then came the day when we took off, led by a special navigation leader, and flew by a circuitous route to Spain. It was a very exciting experience for us all and we wondered how we would fare in combat for the first time. We had our own airfields and ground crews. I was now a sergeant pilot, our captain a lieutenant, plus two gunners, one of whom was the radio operator; we were ready for action. We were warned to watch out for Russian-type fighters as the Spanish Royalists had taken delivery of some which might even be flown by Soviet pilots. Not that we were worried as we had our own Messerschmitt fighters as escorts, though when these units first arrived they were equipped with older Heinkel 51 biplanes, while other squadrons had early Stukas (Ju 87a).

We began operations and all this was very experimental for us and our commanders. We were always briefed to bomb military targets, whatever was said about us later; on no occasion did we aim for civilian centres or anything like that. Of course there were times when bombs went astray as at Guernica, but that was in no way an international atrocity. It was one of the first bombing mishaps of the era, and there were plenty more to follow later by both sides. Our targets were troop concentrations, railway junctions, transport centres and bridges. We never bombed factories or that kind of installation. We also struck many airfields and saw defensive fighters including the Russian types we had been warned about – the Ratas. In all our service in Spain we lost only one bomber to fighter attack. Our own fighters were excellent in escort, but the enemy side had little in the way of really efficient planes and air crew.

The climate varied very considerably from very hot sun to a deluge of rain. All in all I cannot say we enjoyed our stay in Spain for we were at war and saw very little of the country. Two outstanding leaders emerged from our service in the fascist cause: one was von Richthofen who was, I believe, a cousin of the famous ace of the earlier war; the other was Werner Mölders who began his score of kills in that war and went on to improve upon it later. I did not see them at the time, but Richthofen was present when we paraded in Berlin later as 'heroes' of the so-called 'Legion Condor'. By then it was 1939 and the big war was about to begin. We had a short respite to rejoin our old bases, get back into our usual uniforms and assess our experience. A certain amount of reorganisation took place, and by the time the Polish campaign began we were flying slightly amended formations and also carried bombs of new weight and construction.

The international situation deteriorated rapidly and Hitler declared his war on Poland. We were taken by surprise as up till then everyone expected some compromise as with the Czech business. So we flew to Prussia and commenced operations at once, bombing all the troops we could find, transport centres etc. We also knocked out most of the Polish Air Force on the ground and the campaign was soon over; we felt we had done the job we trained for and retired back to Germany.

We were all given leave and my parents were especially glad to see me alive and in one piece; they were always very doting on their son and I loved them greatly. We were all treated like heroes, though I can't say I felt like one. I had a very good leave in Cologne and when I returned to my unit I felt refreshed though I was not expecting any great action. In fact the war on the Western Front stagnated into a sitting one and we were happy to leave it that way. Then we heard rumours of a coming German offensive in the winter, but nothing happened until May, when it all began. We were ordered to new forward bases for operations against enemy airfields in France, and in the early hours of 10 May we took off with loaded bomb racks.

Everything went like clockwork: we flew at ten thousand feet and found our target, which was an Allied airfield near Amiens, unloaded our bombs and turned for home. We had an escort of Me 110s to protect us and saw no enemy aircraft, only a few desultory flak bursts far away. We continued these flights daily, sometimes bombing rail junctions to clog up the enemy's transport system. Then we had our first loss when some French Dewoitine fighters attacked us and one of our Heinkels went down in flames. The Messerschmitts chased off the French and shot one down. One of my friends was in the lost bomber. This was my first close loss of the war, but would not be the last.

In our next sortie over an enemy airfield we were attacked by RAF Hurricanes and two of our machines were shot down. I don't know what happened next, but the enemy fighters were engaged by our Messerschmitts. When we flew home we were smarting from our losses and disappointed that our escort had let us down, but in reality it was not always possible to prevent surprise attack. Then we suffered more losses, but two of our crews survived to be rescued by our ground troops so we did not feel so bad.

Before long the French campaign was over. We settled into a base in the French countryside and enjoyed a nice time. It was a farm country and the farmers were agreeable to bartering eggs etc for beer and cigarettes. When we went into town the people did not seem unfriendly and we were always on our best behaviour.

But after a few weeks we were disappointed to find that our very pleasant life was to be interrupted because Mr Churchill had told Hitler where to go in so many words and England was in no mood to give up. This was a great shock as there had been high hopes that the war was ending; we could see no reason to go on with it now that the Allies were beaten. So we moved a little nearer the coast and prepared for operations against England. Our commanders told us that our first job was to eliminate the Channel shipping, then to smash the RAF fighters on the ground; after that we could perhaps land in England to finish the job. Well, it did not quite work out that way.

I can remember our first flight across the Channel and my first view of England; it all looked very green and tidy. I was sitting there in my seat and flying the bomber and wishing I could take a holiday there on the English coast and perhaps visit London. It was all so peaceful at that moment: the sun was shining and it was very warm in the plane and the war seemed far away. I think there were about fifty of us in that formation with some Dorniers further away. I did not see our fighters but knew they were there somewhere.

We crossed the Channel at about fifteen thousand feet and flew on over the Kent coast and then I heard someone shout 'Fighters!' – and the Hurricanes were among us. It all happened so quickly; I heard our machine-guns firing and the plane shook and rocked. We were supposed to bomb an RAF airfield in Kent or any other we could find, but the Hurricanes turned us away. Some planes were damaged in this assault and I saw one Heinkel turn away with smoke pouring from it. It was all over as soon as it started and then our formation leader told us of a change of target. But we did not get very far on this new course as more enemy fighters appeared, so we turned away and bombed shipping in Dover harbour instead. We then flew back to base without further incident. It had been exciting while it lasted and we could see the RAF meant business and that we would have a tough fight on our hands.

Next morning we were off again and I heard my captain singing to himself, and wondered if he would still be singing in an hour's time. In fact we took much the same route and as before were attacked by enemy fighters within sight of the same objective – the airfield. This time one of our Heinkels collided with another, one went down in pieces while the other tried to glide back to France. It was over very suddenly again and I myself saw no enemy fighters though I heard a lot of shouting. We encountered a lot of flak but dropped our bombs on or near the target and turned for home. And then we were attacked by fighters again, with planes zooming across our formation from all directions and our Messerschmitts trying to intercept them. I had my hands full flying the Heinkel and trying to stay in some sort of formation and did not see very much except for a few fleeting shapes.

We reached our base minus two more of our crews who had gone down in the Channel. That evening we held a 'council of war' in which closer escort was demanded from our fighters, but we knew they had their difficulties.

Next day the weather was dubious and we lay around near our machines for hours. But after lunch the clouds cleared and we took off, our objectives very similar: airfields and harbours in the south of England. This time we were also escorted by twin-engined Me 110s as well as the 109s, and this great formation made a very impressive sight as it was stepped up around and behind us in the deep blue sky. We flew from fifteen to twenty thousand feet, and again the sun was very warm in our glazed nose. We were still confident that we would win through in the end.

Once again we heard the shouts of 'Fighters! Fighters!'

We strained our necks to try and spot them; I believe the enemy were a little more wary of all our escorts. Then above the roar of our own engines we heard the lighter, rasping sound of fighters diving and the rattle of machine-guns firing and the 110s were twisting and turning under attack. We saw two of these twin-engined fighters going down in flames and a Hurricane smoking with the pilot baling out. Then the bombers too were under attack and all sorts of noises erupted: bullets zipped into our machine and I saw a Spitfire hurtle past, our gunners trying to hit it. The noise became continuous, and with all the evasive action being taken collision became a real risk.

Miraculously I did not see a single bomber go down, but then my view of the whole formation was restricted. When we crossed the English coast a lot of flak came up at us but it was not very accurate and did us no harm. But we had been disrupted by the combat and were no longer in impeccable formation. My captain pointed down at an airfield to our left which was already under attack and clearly visible. Our bombers turned in that direction, and at that very moment one of our engines stopped. I had no idea if we had been hit earlier, but the motor gave in and I had to switch off and feather the port propeller. This was serious and I had trouble in maintaining place in formation and we began to fall back. Other Heinkels had to avoid us and I wondered if we would now be singled out for attack by the Hurricanes and Spitfires. We ended up on the very tail end of our formation and dropped our bombs when they did, but without observed results as we were now rather unstable and bucking about in the slip-stream of all the other bombers.

We were very apprehensive and watchful as we turned for the coast, as well we needed to be in case enemy fighters appeared, but we remained unscathed, though we saw two more of our bombers dropping out ahead. That evening we congratulated ourselves on a lucky escape. We had landed on a fighter field and been toasted in their mess before returning to our own base by car while our plane was repaired.

The following weeks of that battle are a haze to me. We flew and flew and flew and wore ourselves out. I remember seeing bombers and fighters going down, flaming wrecks on the English countryside and parachutes descending. It was a very wearing time in which I guess we lost over half our boys while the rest, myself included, were exhausted by continuous flying.

When orders came to fly to London we were surprised and apprehensive; our leaders' claims to have smashed the RAF were not borne out by the facts.

On 7 September we flew up and near the Thames and achieved a break-through. I had expected annihilating attacks all the way and was not too hopeful of survival. In fact we bombed the London docks and turned for home before anything happened in the way of fighter attack, and when it did we came out unscathed. I saw some planes go down, including some RAF machines.

But that night it was a very different story: we felt disgusted that we had to bomb by night as well as by day. I did not see how the war could be won in that fashion. But we had our orders, and I believe it was soon after eight o'clock that we reached London and were one of the first over the target where great fires were burning from the attacks of the afternoon. I was amazed at this sight; we had never seen anything like it before. But we were obliged to continue the raids by day also and we became even more exhausted, and as we did so the accident rate shot up. I saw one of our best crews crash as they returned from a raid one morning. They were much too low and hit a fence; the bomber sprang up again into the air and then struck the ground and broke into pieces and burned, and not one man got out alive.

On another day a crew had taken up a Heinkel on a test flight and it flew too low and into the ground, as if the pilot had simply fallen asleep; there were no survivors. We grew used to all this and could not see how we could escape into a more sane life. In my case my great interest in aircraft and flying had been used up; I was now sick of it all and hoped for a ground job, or at least a long rest. There is no fun or enjoyment in that kind of incessant wartime flying; it just becomes a dirty, noisy, dangerous job that wears out your nerves. I have seen worn-out young men who aged before your eyes.

The schedule could not go on so the daylight attacks were stopped, partly because of the above but also of course as a result of our losses, which could not be borne indefinitely. The losses in officers had been particularly severe which led to an order forbidding more than one per crew in all operations. On every night crews were flying more than one mission to London or other British cities. I myself took off about four in the afternoon to reach London after dark, bombed the city, returned to base near Lille, had some supper and then took off again by about nine to ten o'clock. It was not a very long flight, but twice per night was too much and we were not trained for such night flying. We had heard about our 100 Group of pathfinders who used radio beams, but most crews were expected to find their own way to a target already lit up. We were directed to bomb other British cities for no good reason that I could see, such as Hull, Birmingham, Manchester and Liverpool, all of which I visited with the same crew but one, a gunner who was taken sick, and we lost him.

The worst raid I recall was one to London early in 1941 when the flak was bad and we were holed quite a lot but not severely damaged. I never saw a night fighter or any combat and of course the daylight operations had more or less fizzled out.

The flight of Hess in May 1941 came as a bombshell but was quickly superseded by other events, and when many crews were sent east we remained in the west, and although a change might have proved interesting at the time, in the long run we were best off where we were – at least we had decent billets. We then moved into Belgium and made a few raids on England from there. These were quite small affairs, yet it was on one of them that we were badly damaged and had to crash-land in the sea.

It was a fairly routine flight to the west coast of England to bomb the port of Bristol. This was in 1942, and when we arrived we saw flares and bombs striking the target. We went in and dropped our bombs, but as I turned the plane away there was a heavy explosion under our port wing which tipped the

Heinkel over and I had difficulty in regaining control. We lost a few thousand feet of altitude and tried to get back on course for our base, or at least reach France. But our port engine had been damaged and I had to switch off and feather the prop. We were losing height steadily and I had no idea if we could get back. For some reason we were also now short of fuel so our radioman sent out an emergency call and received a response from a ground station directing us to the coast of Brittany. We followed instructions and headed for the nearest airfield.

We flew lower and lower; it was a very dark night and we had only a vague idea of our location which was just off the north-west coast of France. I intended if I could to glide in and land the plane on its belly at the nearest air-field, but we were under orders from control and tried to follow them. But I was having increasing difficulty in controlling the Heinkel on one engine and flying into a headwind. Then our captain, who was crouched in the nose, said we were low over the sea, and I saw a shore light so guessed we were close to land. There was no time to change my plans; we were too low to gain height on one engine, so I told the crew to take up crash positions for a landing on the sea.

We hit the water with a terrific smack and I was thrown forward and hit my head on the control column. Everything happened at once: the nose glazing broke up on impact and pieces were flying all over the place, the sea rushed in and we were floundering. Then all went still and I struggled out with my face hurting badly; the top of the glazing had gone and I managed to pull out my radio operator and the others followed. The bomber was afloat but submerging, or so we thought, so we tried hard to get out and inflate our dinghy before the plane sank. This we managed to do fairly easily, and as soon as we stepped off the wing into the rubber boat we found that we were in fairly shallow water. One of the crew tried to use our only paddle and struck the seabed. Then we saw that we were only a few hundred metres off the shoreline, the water was less than a foot deep, so we decided to wade ashore as the sea seemed fairly calm. At that moment some soldiers came down from the cliff carrying torches, discovered we were German and helped us ashore. We found we were not too badly off: our radioman-gunner had a bruised arm, but apart from that and my face injury we were in good condition.

We were taken to the soldiers' camp and given treatment and a hot meal which did wonders for us, and next morning some transport was sent for us from our base. Our Heinkel was dismantled at low tide and taken ashore comparatively undamaged.

However, it was only a few flights later that something far worse happened to us.

By then the British night fighters were becoming more active and skilled and

I believe searched for us with radar by night. We had made a few more trips and I had just enjoyed a good leave at home. I remember the night very well.

We stood about our machine at sunset making small conversation. The storms of the Channel battle had passed, as had our schedule of 1941. We found life much easier and were content to remain in the west – anything rather than go east! Our target was the port and docks of Plymouth, and we took off in a Heinkel as usual, a good plane but by then rather obsolete. We climbed in a darkening sky to about twenty thousand feet on oxygen, and set course for Plymouth, making a small detour over the Atlantic to come in on our target from the west.

It must have been about one o'clock in the morning when we came in over Plymouth on our bomb run. We saw some small incendiary fires and larger flashes of heavier bombs bursting. There was quite a lot of flak coming up at us and I was weaving the plane slightly and varying our height to throw off the defences. Our captain released the bombs and the bomber jumped as usual and I turned for home. I had just completed this course change to the south when our top gunner cried out that he thought we were being followed. I at once began to lose height in a gentle dive, picking up speed and turning the machine this way and that. The gunner said he was sure he had seen a silhouette below us and the glow of an exhaust. I decided to try a gentle turn to port so that our gunners could try to spot the follower – it could have been one of our own planes.

At that very moment there was a tremendous flash and crash in our fuselage and our gunner called out 'Fighter! Fighter!'

I threw the plane into a violent manoeuvre in the opposite direction but it was very slow to respond, and even as I did so there was another great flash behind me and an explosion on the starboard wing, followed at once by a bright flame of fire which streaked back over the wing. I dived the Heinkel in an effort to escape; I was very frightened and hoped that we could put out the fire before our pursuer fired again.

I called up my gunner and the captain came up from the nose to see what was happening in the rear. The top gunner was dead so the lower gunner came up to try and take his place. All this took time and we were on fire with our attacker perhaps waiting to finish us off. I was terrified that we would blow up and I hoped that in diving the bomber the fire would be blown out. But as we roared down the fire grew worse and I felt we were doomed. But there were no more attacks so we hoped our pursuer had been forced to abandon the chase as we were well across the Channel and losing height too fast.

The captain suggested we send an SOS, and he did so while the remaining gunner tried to remove his dead comrade. At this point a piece of our burning wing fell off flaming and I thought we would blow up at any moment. But at about five thousand feet I managed to pull the Heinkel out of its dive and thought we might stand a chance of making a crash-landing on the French coast. I was not at all hopeful of bringing the plane down successfully on the sea again.

Then the worst happened: our whole wing was on fire and our captain yelled to me to bale out. 'Everyone out!' he shouted, 'Everyone out!'

Our surviving gunner was also wounded but managed to leap out of the lower hatch. The captain gave me a pat on the shoulder and said 'Come on!', and also baled out. I was terrified as I could not see how the plane could hold together any longer. If the blazing wing detached itself then the plane would just flip over and I would never get out. The machine was, however, on a more or less even keel, so I undid my straps and scrambled out of my seat. I thought of my dead comrade, the gunner, and saw him lying on the floor beyond the bomb bay. Then I dived out head-first without another thought.

The cold air hit me like a blow and the roar of the Heinkel seemed to fade away. I pulled the cord and the parachute opened at once, catching me unawares and giving me a terrific jolt. A few seconds later the Heinkel blew up into fragments with a great whoosh and a bang, and I saw flaming pieces falling towards the sea. Looking round I saw no sign of my comrades. The sky was black again and there was quite a strong wind blowing. I had thought we baled out fairly near the French coast and hoped that some rescue craft would be looking for us. I could not see much below but could vaguely hear the sea. There was no sign of coastline but I saw one or two small lights which I assumed must be on the French coast.

I hit the sea very suddenly and went right under in freezing water. It took me a few moments to struggle out of my harness and try to make out something in any direction. The 'chute floated away, but the sea was not very rough. Then I thought I heard the sound of engines but could see nothing, and in the darkness I began to lose all sense of direction. I was no longer certain which way the coast of France lay and wondered if I had in fact come down nearer England. I did not know which was the best way to start swimming, so I shouted in case my comrades were anywhere near. I called out 'Hallo! Hallo!' several times but heard nothing except the sound of the waves, and I realised that my calls would not carry far in those circumstances.

I don't know how long I floated. I was in my inflated lifejacket but my legs were becoming increasingly heavy and numb and I knew I could not survive long. My flying boots had to come off and I was becoming very drowsy. I turned over on to my back and tried to see the stars, but all I saw was blackness. I let my thoughts drift to parents and home and thought how nice it would be if I could somehow be transported to them as if by magic. I began to drift off into sleep or unconsciousness. At any rate I have no idea how long I drifted like that, but I suddenly awoke from this stupor as if someone had shaken me. I had almost no feelings at all in my body, and felt almost detached from it. I thought, well old fellow, you've had a reasonable life; if this is dying it isn't so bad!

But it was not my time to leave the earth. I found strong hands lifting me, but I was so far gone I hardly noticed. I was in a daze and almost oblivious of everything. I heard vague shouts and saw lights going on round me and knew no more.

When I awoke I was feeling delightfully warm and comfortable and under blankets. There was a dim light nearby and I heard a throbbing noise. I just shut my eyes and thanked God that all seemed well. But then I forced my eyelids open again. I felt so warm and happy to be alive – but where was I?

I now saw that I was in some sort of small cabin and in a bunk bed, and that it was German because there was a photograph of some sailors on the wall. So I closed my eyes and then a nice man entered the cabin and said, 'So you're back in the land of the living, eh?' I looked round. He wore a cap and a raincoat, and he was smiling and offering me a cigarette, helping me to sit up in the bunk. In a few moments I was drinking coffee laced with schnapps. When I could speak I asked him about my comrades and he said they were still searching.

They were never found.

I never went back to flying duties for I was too sick from my experience in the water, and after some months off duty I took over a desk job.**"**

CHAPTER 7

Wanda Holmeier

 anda Holmeier had the dubious honour of being born and growing up in the birthplace of Nazism, the city to which those who were to become leading figures in the brown party gravitated in the 1920s.

Josef Goebbels was a young man whose life had been blighted by a club foot, whose mother was determined to get him into university. In this she eventually succeeded, but by the time he found Hitler in Munich he had passed through half a dozen, and in one of these he found love and was prompted by the war to attribute his deformity to a wound gained at the Front.

Rudolf Hess, born in Egypt of good parents, a man of real but plodding intelligence who, when the Great War came, served in the same infantry regiment as Hitler, though with aspirations to become a pilot. This aim he achieved, but then the war was over and in Munich he embraced Nordic, anti-Jewish theories as a member of the crackpot Thule Society, but readily fell in with Hitler as a man he would follow forever. His flight to Britain in May 1941 caused one of the biggest sensations of the war, and saw the gradual waning of his questionable sanity.

Herman Göring, a man who gained notoriety as leader of the Richthofen Circus of fighter pilots, who lost his way after the defeat of 1918 but recognised in Hitler a saviour the very first time he heard him speak. His drug taking, extravagant tastes and boyishness hid a great and ruthless energy, yet he fell from grace as Nazi economic führer during World War II, but cheated the hangman at Nuremberg by suicide.

Ernst Röhm, ever the tough, professional Army NCO-cum-junior officer with a penchant for conspiracy and armed revolution, who was easily led into homosexuality. A violent man who sought to use Hitler but ended up a victim.

Heinrich Himmler, a physical coward who fainted on attending an execution after he had gained complete police powers in Nazi Germany. A rural type who nevertheless had organisational abilities coupled with racial theories which his awesome position enabled him to put into practice on a grand scale.

These and other leading Nazis took part in a yearly parade through the streets of Munich following Hitler's coming to power as they commemorated the abortive putsch of 9 November 1923, treading the same route clad in their brown shirts and swastika armbands that the original column of woolly-minded conspirators and would-be revolutionaries had followed in the bungled attempt to seize power in Bavaria. The exigencies of war put paid to the ritual, and in any case the RAF had soon demolished enough of the city to make the march impractical.

So bombastically confident were the Nazis in the early war years that they did not trouble to introduce conscription for women, though to some extent this reluctance was based on Hitler's conception and that of some others that the place of the German 'hausfrau' was on the home front raising children for the Wehrmacht. Only a trickle of females reached the German forces, while in Britain they were streaming into uniform in considerable numbers from the earliest days of the conflict. Indeed, in terms of manpower (and womanpower) no fighting nation was more mobilised than Britain in World War II.

"I was born in Munich in 1920, and by the time I was a teenager I had seen the rise to power of Adolf Hitler. Munich was the birthplace of Nazism, I'm sorry to say, although at the beginning it seemed that Germany did need a saviour of some kind. The Nazis were rough and ready in part due to the nature of the situation at the time; the Bolsheviks had a very strong hold on some parts of Germany, and although they promised bread and work for their followers their methods were very questionable, and in any case they threatened to overturn the whole system of life. We had no desire to become a colony of Moscow, or indeed any kind of 'collective'.

As a girl I often saw the brownshirts marching, the bands playing and the flags flying, and I suppose it was all rather exciting for the youngsters. I lived with my parents and older sister in the suburbs but spent much time at school in the city and loved to look at the shops. By the time Hitler came to power my father had himself joined the Nazi Party and thought it was a very good thing for the country. I was not really old enough to understand it all, and was in any case involved with my studies. But then many of my young friends joined or were almost compelled to join the various youth organisations, so I followed suit and became a member of the girls' league (BDM) and had a nice uniform. I took part in parades, went into the country on hikes, sang songs and attended all kinds of functions where we often received lectures on Greater Germany and on matters connected with the role of females in the new Reich. I was too young to take it too seriously and certainly never thought of it all leading us to war. Like all young girls I had my interests including books and films and, not unnaturally, young men; in fact there was one young fellow called Ernst who was always asking me to accompany him to the cinema and to cafés, but I liked to appear uninterested.

Eventually it became necessary for me to find a job, and in this we always received advice not only from our parents but also the heads of the youth organisation. My father had got himself a better job through his Party connections, while my sister Helga had got herself a job as a secretary in a large factory office. I was not in any great hurry to find work, but it was expected of me so at last I found work in the administration of the city college. It seemed a reasonable job but I was not all that interested in mere office work; perhaps I wanted something more adventurous. I had by then begun going out with Ernst, who was one of the older Hitler Youth members with a father of some standing in the local Party, which of course being in Munich was of importance.

When I told Ernst that I was not all that happy in my work he said, 'Leave it to me my girl, I'll get you a better job!'

I mentioned this to my parents and they were horrified because I had only been working at the college for a few weeks and they thought I was being stupid. But I was intrigued by Ernst's offer, and sure enough very soon afterwards when I met him he was looking very pleased with himself and told me that he had spoken to his father about me and that I was to present myself to him at his Party HQ as soon as possible for an interview. This surprised and excited me and I wondered what my parents would say. But as soon as my father heard it was at the Nazi Party HQ he too grew very excited and told me to go and make a good impression. My mother said nothing and did not seem too pleased; as for my sister Helga, she merely said 'It's your business!'

By the following week I had gone to see Ernst's father and was shown into his office. He asked me a few questions and seemed very polite and was pleased to learn that my father was a Party member. When he asked me what I could do I told him I was a kind of clerk and trainee typist at the college library, so after a moment he said, 'How would you like to work for me here?' I said that would be very nice, but what would I do? He said there was always plenty to do in his office, but that if I worked hard and proved useful then he might promote me to be his secretary. This sounded very promising, so I accepted and agreed to start the new job in a week or two. I had to arrange things at the college, and he assured me that there would be no problems at all, so I thanked him and left, running home to tell my parents the good news. That night I saw Ernst, who said, 'I told you so, didn't I? When I make a promise I keep it.' Ernst was tall and rather dark and I liked him a lot.

Not long after that we had a big parade in Munich in which both Ernst and I took part, and I saw his father watching from a platform, and I knew my parents were somewhere in the crowd.

Then I began work in my new job at the Nazi Party HQ and it was all very easy at first: all I had to do was maintain up-to-date card indexes of all the Party members in Bavaria. It was simple work and undemanding and I saw my new boss frequently; he always had a polite greeting for me. I also saw Ernst very often and he was becoming quite serious about us, but I told him we were too young and should wait awhile before rushing into anything. Which in the outcome was a very good thing.

It was during that job that I saw Hitler. He had by then become world famous as the new leader of Germany, and every so often he visited Munich and the old haunts of his early days of struggle (Kampfzeit), and of course came into the Party HQ. I was at my desk when my boss came in looking very flustered with some other officers all in their smart uniforms and told us all to stand to attention. There were a lot of shouts of 'Heil' outside and the sound of footsteps, and then Hitler came into the HQ with his large party. I only got a glimpse of him as he strode through on his way to one of the rooms for a conference. He was rather disappointing to look at, not at all impressive, but everyone seemed to treat him like a god. We went on with our work and later on there was a lot more hubbub when he left and I never saw him again in person. I believe Ernst and his father thought the world of him, and my own father had nothing but praise for Hitler also.

When all the fuss started later over Czechoslovakia and then Poland there was a lot more coming and going in Munich with many officials coming for urgent conferences and all that sort of thing, but by then a lot had happened to me personally.

After I had been in the job some time, I became very bored as there was not enough to keep me occupied, but then to my surprise Ernst's father was replaced. I don't know what happened to him, he may have gone to another job; all I know is that Ernst stopped seeing me as he was disappointed that I did not want to get married. We just drifted apart and that was that. I believe he went straight from the youth movement into the local SS and I never saw him again.

It reached the stage when I decided that if I could not improve myself at the HQ then I would look for another job. Obviously, the option of becoming the boss's secretary was no longer open to me and I did not care for the new man at HQ, so I decided to look elsewhere. There was little unemployment but good jobs were hard to find and I did not at first succeed. There was also the slight problem of leaving the Nazi HQ as they tended to look on you as one of their own, and wished to keep tabs on you. This was brought home to me when I finally did get another job. It was back at the college and, though on a lower pay scale, would be much more interesting work as it was concerned with research. When I told my immediate supervisor at HQ that I was leaving she was amazed and said that she would speak about me to the boss. I could not understand this, and when he sent for me he almost demanded to know why I wished to leave. Didn't I realise that it was a job for life and a career? I told him the work was dull and there was not much of it; I think he found me cheeky and dismissed me rudely.

But I managed to get away from the place to start my new job which did not please my father at all who, I must admit, was a rather keen Nazi supporter and did not understand my attitude. But he had to accept things as they were and I went back to the college and found it a big improvement. Then came the war which shocked everybody. It was a far more serious business than I then realised; I suppose I was not all that bright and did not look on life in that serious a fashion, at least not in worldly terms. I had escaped the first war and had no idea of its horrors. I thought we were quite happy and safe in Munich.

After the war ended in Poland I was startled to learn that my new boyfriend called Karl was also insisting on marriage. He was about to go into the Army and I was not at all keen on the idea. I think he was anxious as he was going away into the Wehrmacht, but I told him that if he loved me he would not mind waiting. To be truthful, I liked him a great deal but was not ready for marriage and children, despite what the Nazis preached. Karl grew quite angry with me, but I would not be swayed and in the end he went off into the Army and I never saw him again.

When the war erupted again in the West we were very excited and always listened to the news bulletins telling us of the great advances; even I began to take some interest, and in a few weeks it was all over. Great celebrations took place with parades in Munich and everywhere else in Germany. My father was especially joyful and told us that once again the Führer had been proved right. Our enemies in the East and the West had been floored, so the war was won.

By then I had a new boyfriend who was a sergeant pilot in the Luftwaffe, and he invited me to visit his base with him one Sunday. I thought this would be exciting and agreed, so in the afternoon he took me in his car and I saw all the Messerschmitt fighters and other planes. It was quite exciting to be shown over these machines, and my friend lifted me into the cockpit of his own fighter and explained the controls. Then we went into the canteen where I was introduced to some of his friends and had a drink with them. My new friend was called Frank and I was quite impressed with him; he was tall and handsome and wore the Iron Cross and looked very dashing in his uniform, and I was glad to take him home to meet my parents and also to meet his own, who lived outside Munich.

It was not long before I realized that I had fallen in love with Frank and we agreed to become engaged. We had a small celebration and then he left for the

Channel coast and I never saw him again. That was a bitter blow for me and I was very, very upset as I had loved him deeply. I received a letter from his comrades telling me that they had been involved in a heavy fight with the Tommies over England and the Channel and poor Frank had gone missing. I had his photograph on the wall of my room at home, and another small one on my desk at work. It was a tragedy of the war and I felt that I would never again become so involved with a serviceman.

I carried on working but it didn't seem the same without my Frank to look forward to. Then my sister Helga decided to get married herself; she had a good man with a steady job in the town, but he was due to be called up for the Wehrmacht later. I attended the wedding but it made me terribly sad.

I reached a stage where I was brooding too much, and I was not at all the lighthearted girl I had once been. Life had become much more of a burden, and by 1941 it became obvious that the war would claim many more lives. I felt so useless that I decided I must go away somewhere; my parents thought I was mad but they could not stop me. By then the war was becoming much more serious and it was spreading, and I knew I would have to think much more carefully about my future. I had one or two friends but did not know where I could go outside Bavaria. I had not travelled and lacked experience. So it seemed a very good idea to join the female branch of the Luftwaffe; this would enable me to get away to fresh places and situations. My parents did not object so I went to the local office straight away and signed up for training. I had no idea what I would be called upon to do, but I knew I had made the right decision.

My parents were sad but sympathetic to see me leave. I was sent to a training camp near the Baltic coast and issued with all the usual uniforms etc. I did not ask about duties at this time and was soon being taught the disciplines. There were five hundred girls of various ages and professions and we lived four to a room in brick barracks. It was quite comfortable and the life was not difficult. Our discipline training lasted about four weeks, and then we were lectured on the various duties undertaken by women in the Luftwaffe and what courses were open to us. In some cases special training was needed in the use of radio and other technical equipment, and of course there was the Air Reporting Service. I had not made up my mind what I preferred to do, but in any case the choices were not all open to us. We would have to wait and see.

When it came to my turn I was told that I could become a radio assistant on flak duties of some kind; I was not sure what this entailed but it had to do with gun control systems and communications. So I told them I was very interested and soon afterwards was sent away with other girls to a training school. This took place in Württemberg and lasted a few weeks and was very thorough. By early 1942 I was able to go home to my parents in Munich, and they were overjoyed to see me. The air raids had not yet become serious. When I returned to the school everyone was called on parade and names were called and I soon learned that I was to go with one other girl to a unit near Cologne. We set off and arrived at a rather lonely place later that same day; the personnel we found were almost all male and there were some flak guns. We were shown to our quarters which were in a hut with two other girls, one of them a sergeant who told us what to do. Our meals were eaten with the men in a barracks and we were introduced to the unit commander who was a Baron and a gentleman. Next day we began to learn our duties and were very soon in action as the Tommies were coming over almost every night.

My job was in a small hut with one other girl. We had to maintain contact with other flak batteries in the area by telephone and radio. This was interesting but made difficult at times because of the terrific noise of the guns, the like of which I had never heard before, but I soon grew used to it. Sometimes we were up all night and very tired the next day, but this was allowed for as we were on a rota system, and we could sleep in the day if necessary.

The air raids got worse and we were always in action and sometimes for quite long periods as the planes wandered all over the place, and if their target was Cologne then we had a very busy time. When we were off duty we used to go for walks in the countryside or sit in our canteen or billet reading or writing letters. We also had parties of a kind with the men when we sang songs, and these were quite jolly. I became friendly with a sergeant-major who was a decent sort of fellow, and he took me into Cologne; but there was so much damage it was not very enjoyable. I was, however, quite happy to go for walks with him and talk. My parents were quite worried about me but I told them, I was in no danger in my kind of job, apart from the shell splinters; the nearest bombs fell some way off.

One night some six months after I began these duties we heard a terrible noise. I managed to glance out of the window and saw a plane coming down like a flaming meteor. It was screeching and made a terrible bang as it hit the ground a few miles away. I believe our own gun battery helped to shoot it down.

I became worried as the air raids became more widespread and Munich was attacked and a lot of damage was done, but my parents remained safe. When I went home on leave I saw the ruins, but everyone remained cheerful. But by 1943 we could see that the war was lost. I used to hold long discussions about the situation with my girlfriends and the sergeant-major, and we were very pessimistic. But we carried on and things got much hotter as the American bombers began coming over too, and whenever we could we would watch outside if not on duty. It was quite a sight to see the hundreds of silver specks crossing the sky and the smoke trails and planes blowing up and coming down in flames with parachutes falling. One afternoon during such a raid I was standing outside our quarters when a B-17 came down very, very low trailing smoke, and we thought it would crash near us. All the men ran to the vehicles and I thought I would go too. But the plane vanished behind the trees and there was a big explosion so I stayed where I was. Some of the men went to see the remains and came back carrying pieces of metal with insignia, and one gunner brought back a human hand in a glove which was awful. I will never forget that day; it made a big impression.

Quite often our own planes crashed down on or near the many airfields and men were killed. It was a terrible war and I could see no good coming out of it all. When I went home I found fresh bomb damage and heard stories of people we had known who were no longer with us, and men lost at the Front, and it was all very depressing.

In 1944 we were moved to another site a few miles away and this was an improvement as the accommodation was better, the food good and two more girls were added to our staff. Some of the guns were now manned by older boys of the Hitler Youth with our own NCOs in charge, and they were very keen at their job.

We were soon in action again and it became worse and worse, and one or two of the boys on the gun crews broke down in exhaustion and had to be taken to hospital. I myself was becoming very tired because of the long hours of duty due to the increased raids, and we were not always able to get our full quota of sleep.

Then came the invasion, and we finally knew for certain that the war was lost. The Russians were coming in from the east and we grew very worried in case they should occupy Germany. When at last the Allies reached Germany we were very relieved, but we did not see them as we had been moved further inland. In fact, I was hoping that we would go south, nearer Munich, but this did not happen. By then my dear town was in ruins and our home severely damaged, but my parents and sister had got away into the country with relatives. Helga was now a secretary in an Army office job, so was quite safe.

At last it was all over: Germany had surrendered and we waited for the Americans to come. That was a day I will not forget. We were lined up with our CO awaiting the first American tanks. None of our men had run away and we were still complete as a unit when the enemy arrived. The Americans pointed their guns at us and searched us, although this was not really necessary as we had no weapons. They were polite but firm and made a few jokes about the women prisoners. We were then marched away in a column and locked up in a childrens' school under guard until being removed to a large PoW camp later. It was there that we were lectured by the Americans on the terrible concentration camps, and I can tell you that though we all knew they existed we had no idea of the awful crimes and conditions in them. We simply thought that they were a kind of open prison for Communists, Jews and all sorts of criminals. It was a terrible shock to hear and see the evidence, and I felt we had been betrayed by our Government. I was never a Nazi or political in any way, but I believed in my country; yet we were dragged through the mire of shame by what happened under the Nazis. The whole world seemed against us and it was the worst time in our history."

CHAPTER 8

Kurt Meissner

he rearming of Germany under the Nazis did not really get under way until 1935, by which time Hitler had been in power for two years and had been fully occupied securing his political and economic fronts. There were enemies to be eliminated both inside and outside his own ranks, and new allies to be coerced. The Communists had to be carted away into the special camps which the brownshirts had set up even before Hitler took power, though a few turned coat and joined the Nazis. The Nazis had promised revolution, but it turned out to be nothing of the kind, at least not in the sense anticipated by a fair number of diehard Nazis; Hitler had never had any intention of killing off or alienating the intelligentsia, the upper, middle or lower classes and least of all the wealthy industrial potentates and the Reichswehr. Rather he sought to weld them all together, patronising each and using them as he saw fit to construct a great mass of adherents entirely malleable to his will.

This special kind of Hitlerian 'democracy' was to be exemplified in the new 'Wehrmacht'. This was his brand of socialism of a nation bonded together in a common cause, which in practice meant the ideals of the Führer – ein volk, ein Reich, ein Führer! – a Fatherland destined to march on to its chosen destiny of a new and dynamic era of achievement that would stun the world. The Nazi slogan became 'Deutschland Erwache!' (Germany awake!). One song exhorted the nation to awake from its deep dream, to wake up and follow the new Pied Piper who would lead them to triumphs hitherto undreamed of – even under Bismarck.

In this new 'Third Reich' the German people would be regimented as never before; in fact, as one foreign observer put it later, the Nazi programme ensured that every male member of society would be in one uniform or another practically all of his life. This process began at an early age when he was permitted to join the Jungvolk, a kind of militarised boy scout movement, though later on the Nazis decided that the real and original boy scout movement, as instigated by the Briton Baden-Powell, was in fact not quite the innocent organisation it seemed, and by 1940 laid down that the British scout movement was subversive and would be proscribed once the country had been occupied.

The boy progressed into the Hitler Youth, thence to the Labour Corps and finally the Wehrmacht. But following that service he was then eligible for spare time duties (if fit) in the SA or other organisations such as those of the veterans.

Having secured his rear, so to speak, in 1935 Hitler began turning his attention to the armed forces as a necessary prelude to forcing through his global demands. Out went the old 'Reichswehr', in came the new 'Wehrmacht', and with it a plethora of new uniforms and equipment. A brand new kind of division was created called 'armoured'; for the first time tanks would operate in mass as laid down by certain German and British experts, the former thoroughly absorbing these new principles of armoured warfare, while the latter filed them away and stuck to the horse. Hitler chose an auspicious date to introduce conscription – 9 November, the anniversary of his abortive putsch in Munich in 1923. On that date the class of 1914 boys would be taken into the Wehrmacht. But before that Hitler installed a further plank in the militarisation of Germany: until 26 June 1935 the boyhood of the Reich had been invited to enrol in the Reichs Arbeits Dienst or Labour Corps on a voluntary basis. The force was completely militarised and any youth from the Hitler Youth could enrol for two years' service. It was, of course, a way of securing thousands of young men who had already been disciplined and toughened up ready for the Wehrmacht. But as from 26 June every fit youth was conscripted into the Labour Corps for a six-month stint from the age of twenty, and of course within a few months the call-up Act ensured that Wehrmacht service followed.

In November 596,000 young men were taken into the Wehrmacht, as compared with only 279,000 men of the same 1914 class in France. Thereafter, owing to the normal decline which occurred in the birthrate in World War I, the number of recruits declined, the minimum figure being 314,000 in Germany for the class of 1917 (171,000 in France). The French figures are quoted because that country still stood as Germany's principal opponent in the West, though with a far smaller population – under 42 million as against over 86 million for the Greater Reich and Britain's 46 million. These were the kind of figures that alarmed Winston Churchill, who was very well informed on German affairs and especially on rearmament.

In October 1935, again in defiance of the Treaty of Versailles, the Germans had blatantly reopened their Staff College in a formal ceremony attended by Hitler and his chiefs-of-staff. Yet by then the Germans had already formed ten army corps, which were expanded to thirteen by 1937. In 1936, 1,511,000 men were under military training in the Reich, and this figure did not include those of the Labour Corps or paramilitary organisations such as the SA brownshirts, who were a uniformed, disciplined body which even in 1934 had numbered about four million; many of these Germans had some experience of arms. By comparison the French Army in 1935 numbered only 623,000, of which only some 407,000 were actually in France owing to that country's colonial obligations.

The Nazi law of 16 March 1935 introduced a radical new departure, for thereafter every new recruit into the German armed forces would be required to swear an oath of allegiance to Adolf Hitler personally. This oath was to put many an officer in a dilemma later on when moral scruples were raised, while for the mass as a whole it implied that they had become 'national socialists'. They were no longer mere soldiers, but sworn by oath to uphold Hitler and his Nazi socialist state. Ten years earlier Hitler had written in *Mein Kampf* that the German Army must become 'a school for the mutual understanding and adjustment of all Germans'. He did what perhaps no other political leader had done before, with the possible exception of Josef Stalin: he introduced ideology into the military masses. Despite all this, Churchill, surprisingly in view of all he had learnt earlier, would refer later to the 'dull mass of the German infantry' as if they were a great herd of plodding, dim-witted yokels. He may well have been surprised had he known of the 'democratic' spirit that had been infused into the German forces despite all its hard training as compared to the oft-quoted, Prussian-style militarism; not democracy on the American model, for example, but at least with a far greater degree of informality than would have been imaginable in an earlier age, and with no connection to the class-ridden methods of the British Army.

Yet another 'Führer decree' became law in the summer of 1935, for it attempted to enfold the German Army even more firmly into the arms of the Nazi State, and of course Hitler. The second clause of the law read: 'The Wehrmacht is the armed force and military education of the German people.'

The German Army had long enjoyed a special place and esteem in the State in a way far beyond the armies of other nations. It tended under its stiff-necked Prussian leadership to see itself as leaders of the people, as haughtily superior to them, the flagbearer and almost the *raison d'être* of them. Hitler now went further, introducing new laws and 'honourable bindings', actually playing on the officers' code of honour so that once they had been sworn to him in fidelity they would remain forever his cohorts and follow him anywhere. There was more to this though for, as indicated, Hitler sought by all his measures to draw the people and the Wehrmacht even closer together with a view to gaining greater ascendancy over them. Despite their pride and self-esteem, the old guard of the German Army by and large was quite ready to fall in with his schemes, for in Hitler they saw a man who would, despite his lack of breeding and his coarseness, give them even greater power, and above all a brand new army of unparalleled might. Hitler wooed them and flattered them and, as seen by the events of June 1934, was quite ready to wipe out his own followers among the Nazi old guard in order to win them over. The Brown Army had contained actual revolutionaries who were little removed in style or ideas from the Reds, and who saw themselves as the new army of Germany and were thus in conflict with the old established military hierarchy.

So well informed was Churchill that he was able to confirm later his mid-1938 estimates that the German Army comprised about fifty-six infantry divisions plus four armoured, with a trained reserve of some thirty-six more of infantry, many of them motorised. These alarming reports Churchill was able to confirm from reliable French sources, for whatever these Allies lacked in stable government and political leadership, they were never short on the intelligence front.

Certain deficiencies that showed up in terms of mechanical reliability among the panzers during the German occupation of Austria in 1938 may have given some comfort to the Allies, but by 1 September next year no problems were encountered during the Blitz war on Poland. The following spring the long-planned German assault in the West took place, for Hitler had no intention of allowing his momentum to be stymied by a stagnating trench war as in 1914–18. The German armies proved themselves masters of swift, moving armoured warfare and drove deep wedges into the fixed positions of the Allies who had no answer to this kind of tactic, having based their training on earlier concepts; even the British, despite a considerable amount of motorisation, had few, if any, officers capable of modern thinking in war. This thinking, as exemplified by their enemy, embraced great use of combined arms – panzers, mobile artillery, infantry, and above all tactical air support by both Stukas and multi-engined bombers.

This great use of combined arms was further refined by the Germans in their later campaigns and was never quite learnt by their enemies, even when the Allies possessed a great and superior weight of air and artillery power. The German use of combined battle groups and above all, fast thinking and movement confounded their opponents time and time again. Even after the defeats in the West in 1940, the British soldier continued to train in outdated fixed bayonets and 'over the top' tactics, and was to a large extent a prisoner of national characteristics and certainly a curious blindness among their leadership corps.

The most powerful army the world had ever seen bled itself to death in the vastness of Russia, but it must be conceded few troops could have stood up to the winter of 1941–42 without general retreat. No matter how far their morale fell, the German troops in Russia never broke, and it is generally conceded that it was Hitler's order to stand fast that saved the Army from disintegration, despite its terrible losses. Those that remained were awarded the 'Ostmedaille' or East Front Medal, 1941–42. But Hitler and his generals had assumed that with an army of around three million soldiers the campaign would be over within a few weeks, and it would have been hard to find anyone in the West to disagree with him. Yet like Napoleon before him, Hitler was drawn irretrievably on into the wilderness of Russia, and the Army was simply worn down by the endless miles of steppe and the inexhaustible supply of Russian manpower. Even the superior direction and performance of his panzer corps meant nothing once the revitalised Russian Colossus began to bear down on him, Soviet armies much sustained by a stream of Allied aid, and in particular American rations and trucks.

It has often been stated that the Germans lost the war in Russia, that the affair in North Africa was a sideshow, and that whatever happened in Normandy or Italy the 'real' war was fought on the East front. This is true to an extent, but apart from figures it is also true that despite all their efforts, which were extraordinary, the German Wehrmacht could never have been defeated in Russia had it not been for these Allied 'sideshows', which cost the Germans an army in Africa (a quarter of a million Axis troops surrendered at Tunis in spring 1943), a very sizeable force in Italy, while in Normandy all the top SS armoured formations were confronted and decimated by the Allies (mostly by the British and Canadians), for even these crack troops were bogged down in positional warfare and fell victim to annihilating air and artillery bombardment.

However, it was that eminent military writer Max Hastings who concluded that in World War II the German soldier proved to be the best in the world, his observation being based on his findings that whenever the Germans met their enemies on an equal footing, they won.

Kurt Meissner's account of his experiences gives new insights into the harsh war in Russia which robbed Germany of so many of its sons.

"I was born in Hanover in 1922 in the time of the Weimar Republic, a rather confusing time for Germany. I did not know much of these events, but as I grew into a little boy there were many discussions and arguments in my family on our country's problems.

My parents were Lutherans and I had an older brother by one year called Lothar. My father had been a junior officer in the war and was very downhearted over our defeat. He remained in contact with old comrades and used to meet them from time to time to reminisce and discuss the current situation in Germany. Although my father was not a Nazi he was very pleased when Hitler came to power as he felt we needed a strong man at the helm to guide us out of our troubles, and this Adolf Hitler certainly proved to be.

When the Army was expanded again he went back into it and became an instructor. He was always a very proud, God-fearing man and I recall him telling us that God would protect Germany from all evils. These words always remained in my mind later on.

As things began to improve in Germany so my parents began to see that Hitler and his Nazi gang were not quite the kind of saviours we had hoped for. But at least the country was back on its feet again, and when I was called up into the Army I had already done my labour service. I did not mind this as I had no special aptitudes and my father always wanted me to go into the Army.

I was sent to an infantry depot to do training and was then asked if I would join my father's regiment which was a great surprise to me, but I understood that he had asked for me so that he could keep an eye on me. I agreed to go although I was not in his unit – he was a battalion commander and I was put into another and soon settled down to the life. The war had already started by then and we were sent in reserve into France after the battles. I was able to see my father quite often and later we visited Paris together. There was little or no hostility among the population and that was a relief, but we did behave very correctly and did nothing to give offence.

A few weeks later we were sent to the Channel coast and learned that the invasion of England was a real possibility. This was very exciting, though we never thought it would be easy. Next we received motorised barges and began to learn how to embark and land from them on to the beach, yet we never did it in rough weather. Our Luftwaffe was overhead every day, and we used to watch the big formations leaving over the water and saw many air combats and planes crashing.

We were often inspected by generals and I remember singing the songs of the period: 'We're Marching Against England' etc. But after a few weeks had passed we began to realise that the invasion crossing was a far more difficult enterprise than we had imagined, and my father told me that without a complete victory in the air it was impossible, and in any case he did not think our Navy was strong enough to defeat the Royal Navy and protect our barges etc. The battle in the skies did not quite go as planned, and the great fat Reichsmarschall Göring, who we saw at times, ordered the bombing of London. All our barges were dispersed and we knew that the invasion was cancelled, for the time being at least.

Late in 1940 I went home on leave with my father for a whole month and we enjoyed a good time. I had by then found a lady friend who was glad to see me; she always wrote to me when I was away and we remained in touch for a long time, though I had no thoughts of marriage. My father then tried to persuade me to become an officer, so I did my best and reached the rank of NCO – a top sergeant officer candidate – which meant going away on a long course of instruction. This lasted well into 1941, and then the war in the East began.

I had just completed my examinations and expected to pass out a lieutenant when I was called before the CO of the school with the other candidates and told of the big attack on Russia. It was an enormous surprise for all of us as we thought Stalin our ally. Our CO told us that the Russians had been playing a double game and really intended to attack us and had already taken over those small countries in the north; that they were trying to bite off slices of Hungary and Romania and were putting pressure on Turkey. They were up to all sorts of tricks, so the Führer had decided to smash them.

We new officers were to take part in this campaign and would be assigned to new units comprising replacements. This came as a big surprise to me as I had expected to rejoin my old unit with my father. In fact we were dispatched at once to Prussia outside Berlin and arrived at a training depot where we were introduced to our commands. As a new lieutenant I was put under a more experienced officer in an infantry anti-tank detail. It seemed we were to leave for the Eastern Front the very next day, so there was a great rush to get everything ready.

I knew very little about anti-tank guns as there were none actually in my unit back in France, though some were attached to all infantry regiments. We only had 37mm guns which were becoming obsolete, but were told that more powerful equipment was on the way.

The next day we boarded a train to begin the long journey across Poland and into the Soviet Union. We were very interested in all we saw and spent much time gaping out of the windows. We saw many destroyed homes and Russian prisoners in dirty brown uniforms. It took us two days to reach our destination and we finally climbed out at Lwow, in Poland. We began marching and marching and only stopped late that evening for a meal and sleep in a ruined village. I was quite exhausted but excited at the prospect of going into action for the first time. I had done my best to get to know the men under me and listened carefully to all the Lieutenant in charge told me. He was very experienced and knew what he was talking about.

Next morning we were relieved to find trucks awaiting us and we boarded these to start moving forward through dusty roads packed with all kinds of transport and a lot of Russian PoWs going back into Poland. Then at last we were told to disembark and again began marching along a terrible road which was little more than a broad track. We grew very tired and were thankful to stop for a meal and some sleep.

That night we heard the sound of the guns for the first time and were told by some returning troops that a huge battle of encirclement was in progress and that a whole Russian army was almost in the bag. Early next morning an officer came and told us that we were to help protect the flanks in case the Russians tried to break out, as they had many tanks with them. So we moved forward and saw huge columns of smoke and dust ahead as our artillery and Stukas did their work of containing this army in the cauldron. We were shown to positions, dug in our anti-tank guns and told to wait.

The heat was very great and we had nothing at all to eat for many hours, and I thought of my father safely back in France. Then we heard a most peculiar noise over the constant rumble of our artillery. I find it hard to describe as I had never heard anything like it before or since – not outside Russia that is.

We were on the alert and searching the horizon through our binoculars, but could only see a lot of dust clouds. The Russian steppe consists largely of arid land, otherwise of corn or sunflowers, and every movement seemed to raise this dust. The heat was very bad and we were very uncomfortable as we had used up our supplies of food and water. The noise we heard was rather like a subdued howling, but then it grew louder and louder and we began to see the great droves of Russians all in dusty, dirty brown uniforms and at first we thought it was a vast army of PoWs. But then we realised there were no German guards in sight. Then a squadron of Stukas came over us and waggled their wings; they had used up their bombs and were warning us that the Russians were coming.

This was our first glimpse of the enemy 'in action'. So far we had only seen dejected prisoners in huge columns, but this was a little different and I wondered if any other army in the world presented such an amazing spectacle in attack.

You see, there was very little cohesion among their units, a complete lack of direction we thought. They resembled a vast crowd who had just emerged from a stadium, all chattering excitedly at once, but looking like brown dummies. That is how they looked to us. You may have heard of the Russians' love of calling out as they charge the enemy – 'Hurraaa-Hurraaa-Hurraaa!' This is to try and keep up their spirits, but from a mass formation it can be a little startling.

This great mass of singing humanity had only been told to break out in our direction. We were actually facing west and thus barring their way back to their own areas. I suppose in a simple fashion those poor devils were just following orders without too much thought. We had to see them as the enemy, however, who had their orders to kill or be killed. They came on in a shambling, shuffling gait and all the way they were calling out in this low, moaning way, and every so often they would break into this great mass cry of 'Hurraaa! Hurraaa! Hurraaa'

We were quite scared as we had never seen anything like it before, and of course most of the men were new to action. I had a fleeting thought of the old cowboy and Indian films and gave a short laugh so that my Lieutenant wondered what was the matter with me. When I told him he also laughed, but remarked that this situation was a little different. These Russkis meant business and in a few moments we opened fire with all our weapons, including the 37mm anti-tank guns.

There was great carnage as our bullets and shells struck them; the dead piled up but when the rest saw our positions they turned towards us, forced on by the thousands pressing behind them. It became a wild charge by an army desperate to escape and I began to wonder how we could stop them as we were only comparatively few in number.

It was a vast plain. We had dug some weapon pits and depressions for the 37mm guns, but before us the terrain was flat over which this army of Russian infantry was passing and we saw not a tank or single vehicle among them. And as we fired and fired so the heaps of dead made a barricade for those Russkis behind, and they used this bloody concealment to start shooting at us, and then tried to leap the corpses to rush at us. I suppose we must have killed or wounded hundreds in our sector alone, but there were thousands more behind and in the end we were simply forced to retreat in a hurry and take up new positions as otherwise we would have been overrun by this brown tide.

I was in a sweat, very hot and frightened. It was an extraordinary introduction to battle and I remember thinking that I would have a fine tale to tell my children one day – if I survived!

At last this brown tide of the Russian Army turned away from us and tried to break out in another direction and we continued firing into their flanks, inflicting huge casualties. Then a strange thing happened, and this was even more extraordinary: the whole mass of surviving Russians – and there were still thousands of them – simply stopped dead about a kilometre from us as if on an order. We wondered what was happening and then saw through our glasses that they were discarding all their equipment. They then turned about to face us. All the enormous sacrifice they had made had been in vain. They simply sat down on the spot and we received orders to go in and round them up. So we moved forward out of our positions, warily, until we could see that they had indeed given up all thought of further combat. We moved over hundreds of dead, dying and wounded; they had no apparent organisation for dealing with the latter. We began calling them to face the other way and start marching; we would say 'Russki-komm! Russki-komm!', and they understood.

I was amazed at their broad faces and the spectrum of age groups, both young and middle-aged and dusty and dirty, each man retaining his rolled blanket if he had one. All their arms and packs they dumped on the ground, and grinning at us they started marching away in a very broad stream, raising great dust clouds as they shuffled away. I no longer looked on them as dangerous enemies but more as pitiable human beings and my first thought was – how on earth are we going to feed all these men? There were thousands and thousands of them, far more than we had at first realised; it was in fact a whole Russian army.

We waited and waited as the hours rolled by, and that evening had seen the great tide of Russian prisoners vanish westwards, and at last our ration trucks came and we could relax a little and discuss the amazing events of the day.

So this was the war in the East? Is this how it is to be, we wondered. We slept on the ground where we were, wrapped in our blankets, and next morning a Lieutenant came and gave us our orders: we were to move north and help to mop up the few remaining pockets of the enemy. We listened to the radio news from Berlin and felt that within a few days or a week or two the Soviet empire would collapse for lack of men.

How wrong we were!

We moved off on foot with two vehicles towing our guns and marched for hours across that endless plain of corn and dust and saw only a few stragglers who we simply pointed west and they cheerfully went their way. At last we had completed another exhausting day's trek and settled down for the night. Our bombers droned overhead and the weather continued to be fine. We were in good spirits, despite not having had enough to eat and drink, but this was normal in the field; the cooks could only send up minimum rations. We could only look forward to an occasional blowout when not on the march.

We heard many bombastic claims as to our successes and knew that propaganda played a part, but we had the evidence of our own eyes and had seen the vast areas of territory and thousands of men lost to the Soviets. So for once the Nazi claims were not really exaggerated.

Another night and we halted once more. It was now July and even hotter. We slept in our shirtsleeves and pressed on next day and at last began to see ruined villages, collections of hovels, shacks with nothing in the way of more substantial buildings. We knew there were towns and cities in the western Soviet Union, but we had yet to see any. My Lieutenant had a large map and tried to follow our progress, but it was difficult. It is an extraordinary thing in an army, you are reduced to only units. There were two or three million men on that front but all we saw of them most of the time was a few dozen of our own people. There were great gaps between regiments, and if the Russians had been properly organised they could have played merry hell with us despite our great victories.

We were now able to spend some nights in villages which were mainly mud and straw hovels with earthen floors. There was nothing to eat in these 'cottages' but a few small apples; the Russians had removed everything eatable and usable as they retreated. We saw our first civilians, and these were country peasants, very simple, backward folk of the crudest kind but friendly to us. In fact they used to say 'Stalin nix! Stalin nix!' and make a slashing sign across their throats. The girls were friendly too but very grubby and we stayed clear of them as most of these peasants had lice or other parasites. They had lived on so little for so long that their latest hardship was taken stoically. They were a hardy people, and this is why later on their soldiers were able to survive on so little and give us a hard time – once they were properly organised and led.

Weeks went by and in that summer I don't believed we suffered a single casualty through action, only one or two through sickness. As the landscape changed so did resistance stiffen, and it became obvious that the Russian Army had huge reserves. How else could we explain it? We had knocked off millions, yet there were more facing us, and more, and more. We reached the end of summer and encountered our first real combats and had to deploy for battles and I remember the first of them.

We had been following one of the usual dirt roads and round a bend saw a crude log jam ahead. It was flanked by woods and was obviously a perfect place for an ambush. We were the leading unit in that area so had none of our own people ahead or on the flanks. We became very cautious and deployed off the road to enfilade the woods and avoid the road barrier, but we were fired on from all these places and found that the enemy had at least two guns of anti-tank calibre lined up against us. Two of our men fell as we rushed forward past the road block and I saw several dead Russians. The bullets were flying and I was very frightened. There was a great deal of noise and suddenly I felt something hit me in the right leg. I fell down yelling into the long grass but then tried to shut up. There was a lot of shooting close by but I had no idea who they were. I heard my Lieutenant calling me but could not see where he was. I called that I was wounded and told him not to expose himself as I would attend to my wound. I took out a bandage and found a small hole above my boot; the bullet had passed through my leg and I could not stand on it. I did my best to bandage the wound while lying down as the bullets were still flying. Not long after it went very quiet, and someone shouted that the Russkis had gone. My Lieutenant soon found me and with his help I staggered back to one of our vehicles where I collapsed. I was given an injection by the medic and passed out as I had lost more blood than I realised.

When I came to it was evening and quiet. I could hear voices and found that I was lying in a tent with other wounded. My leg felt painful but was well bandaged. I heard more voices and then the doctor made his rounds and told me that I would be evacuated to a small hospital where they would decide whether I was a 'home case' or not. My first thought was one of disappointment that I had been separated from my comrades, but then I felt glad that my wound was not a worse one or that I had been killed. I managed to scribble a few lines home and settled down for the night. Next morning I was loaded on to an ambulance after a breakfast of bread and coffee.

The 'hospital' I was taken to was a makeshift affair set up in a Russian house, a wooden building that may have been a 'town hall' or something. The locality was a small town and actually contained some stone and brick buildings, but mostly it consisted of the usual mud and straw huts. A lot of these had tiny gardens with fences; the Russian peasants had their little plots of land in which to grow vegetables.

I was placed on a proper bed and examined at once by the doctor who told me that if all was well I could return to my unit in two or three weeks. I had mixed feelings about this as by then I had begun to dream of sick leave in Germany; but unless a wound was serious we had to convalesce in Russia. So I resigned myself to my situation and just hoped I would soon be fit again. I was reassured by a message my Lieutenant sent back to me via the ration truck – he said he would keep my job open for me!

In fact it was a month before I was pronounced fit for service, by which time I had become terribly bored with the place. We had a daily routine when the doctor made his inspection; no female nurses, only men. The meals were inadequate, there was so little to do, so little to read. One man had a chess set that we took turns with, another had a good radio, and these things alone kept me sane. There was nothing to see in the locality, or at least nothing worth walking around for. At that time the travelling theatre and music shows for the Wehrmacht had yet to be organised in Russia for no one had expected a long war, so boredom behind the Front was endemic.

I returned to my unit healed. It was late September and the heat had gone from the day. We had advanced much further but the enemy resistance was growing stronger and I found that half a dozen men had been lost. We had only three replacements, but my Lieutenant was very pleased to see me back again and told me that we would soon be in Moscow. I told him I doubted this, but he would not listen to my pessimistic talk and insisted that the war was as good as over.

I was given extra responsibility as a new unit had been formed and included more powerful 50mm guns, and these we had to master. We began to encounter Russian tanks and these were difficult to stop as they were fast and well armoured and their crews determined. We did not have suitable tanks to counter these in straight combat, so the panzer boys used to rely on us. I recall our first anti-tank action.

We had halted while our planes softened up a locality ahead, but as soon as we advanced again we saw three Russian tanks coming at us over the fields. We rushed forward with our three new 50mm guns and concealed them as best we could before the Russians saw us. We were of course hoping to catch them in the flanks, but they spotted us and drove us to ground with well aimed machine-gun fire so that we could not get in a shot at them before they raced passed us. This was not good as they were then in a position to hit our infantry. But our Lieutenant called some men together and they chased after the Russian tanks clutching a bundle of grenades, managing to catch up with them while we kept our eyes open for Soviet infantry. That was the way with the Russian Army, their co-ordination was very poor; they had no proper tank-infantry co-operation, so we were able to deal with the tanks. Our brave Lieutenant simply dropped grenades on to the tanks' engines and blew them up so that they caught fire or were destroyed. All the crews were killed as they baled out and no prisoners were taken. That was war. There were times when such things happened. If we felt we could not collect or care for prisoners then they were killed in action. But I do not mean that they were killed after being taken prisoner – never! I can only speak for our own men; what happened elsewhere I cannot say, and when Russians were exterminated behind the lines they were never killed in action by fighting troops – never.

When October came so did the rains, and we had a very miserable time; the roads turned to mud and all movement became difficult. The vehicles and guns bogged down and we squelched about in mud up to our knees. Those Russian roads were indescribable; it was a great rarity to see a proper paved highway. Then the rain turned to snow and this was actually an improvement as the mud-caked terrain froze over and we could move again. But of course the great drop in temperature affected men and vehicles; we had no warm clothing and suffered accordingly. In the north the situation turned to disaster as the Russians launched a great offensive, and in fact attacks started all along the line. We were forced to dig into the frozen ground in our first Russian winter. It was hell and beyond all our expectations and experience. No provision had been made for this and the sick rate leapt alarmingly. We were down to half strength. I myself was in a bad way from the cold and prayed that we would either be relieved or given proper warm clothing. Suddenly the food improved, but this was because we were in a static position and it was easier to reach us. But the Russkis kept sending in attack after attack, and because of our small numbers it was hard to drive them back. We began to think of Napoleon's Grande Armée in the previous century and wondered how they had fared. Here we were, the most mobile army in history, but reduced to static warfare in the worst of circumstances.

We began to receive extra clothing a few weeks after this terrible winter started, but by then thousands of German soldiers had been taken from the Front with frostbite and other complaints. Hitler ordered no retreat so we stayed put, freezing in our foxholes and dugouts.

We did not advance one metre after October 1941 and actually cringed in our holes for week after week. The best that happened was when we could slip away to a proper dugout about one hundred metres to our rear, and this was a great blessing, so long as the fire was maintained. We were wrapped up like mummies with scarves around our heads and faces with only our eyes showing. Outside we were covered in frost and ice and had to keep on the move to prevent freezing up. This was difficult in a foxhole with a better equipped enemy waiting for a chance to kill you; they were very good at sniping and it was fatal to show any part of oneself at all. They had sharpshooters who lay camouflaged and still for hours, just waiting for some incautious German to show himself and then – bang! One German less to kill. I saw several men lose their lives this way, which was very demoralising as we were in no position to exact retribution or escape.

One week followed another, and the only bright spot was the receipt of mail from home; but those letters showed how little they knew of what we were suffering. All the bombastic claims over our radio concerning the annihilation of the Soviet Army had now given way to a very different line – we were now holding back the Mongolian hordes!

When we tried to advance or straighten out a flank to improve our positions it was a failure; the enemy had had ample time in which to strengthen his line and we were stymied and reduced again to static warfare. The Russians in that winter held all the cards. So long as our panzers and other mobile units were prevented by the weather from operating in the way that they alone knew best, then we poor infantrymen were stuck in that frozen hell of a wasteland. It would not have been so bad if we had been able to move back into a town, but there were none near and in any case we were unable to disengage because of Russian pressure in constant small or larger attacks.

Christmas came and a little bit of good cheer for we received parcels, not only from our own folk but from strangers who donated something for the brave lads on the Eastern Front, and it made our lives a little easier. But it also made us rather homesick. The foolish exhortations by the propagandists we found absurd and disgusting: they sat at home in comfort while we froze in the wastes of Russia.

Eventually, the cursed dull days began to grow longer, but then came the snow blizzards and we were in an even worse state. It was hard to keep our weapons in action because of the abnormally low temperatures, and if the Russians had come over in strength in our sector we could never have stopped them. But their attacks never got them very far, so all in all we felt we had sur-

Above: German welfare workers depart on holiday.

Right: Marriage to an SS officer brought real benefits.

Below: Moment of parting – often the last.

Left: Labour Corps service was compulsory.

Below: Engineers of 76th Infantry Regiment construct a wooden bridge over the River Bug in Poland. *(IWM)*

German engineers use logs to construct a bridge between Naikov and Kahienka; Russia, Summer 1941 *(IWM)*.

The Hitler Youth Leadership schools were intended to provide future leaders of the Third Reich. The curriculum ranged from politics to cultural activities and sport.

Above: A Gestapo agent's identity disc (enlarged).

Below: A tutor explains Nazi geopolitics to a class in a Hitler Youth school.

Left: A U-boat skipper in the Atlantic.

Right: The business end of a U-boat: torpedo-tube doors record victories gained.

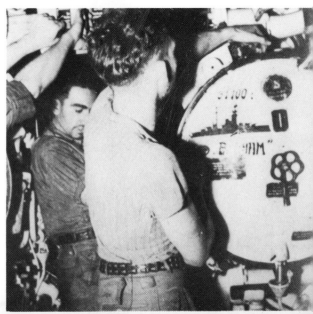

Above: A chance meeting with another U-boat in the vast expanse of the North Atlantic.

Below: An attempt to celebrate Christmas in the cramped confines of a submarine.

Right: Another hit, another Allied ship destroyed.

Below: Death of a tanker by night. The merchant seamen were the unsung heroes of the war and suffered great losses to German U-boats.

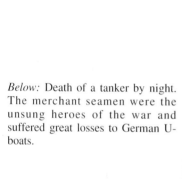

Above: Members of the Nazi League of Girls (BDM) are greeted by Hitler.

Below: Wounded German soldiers under nursing care in hospital.

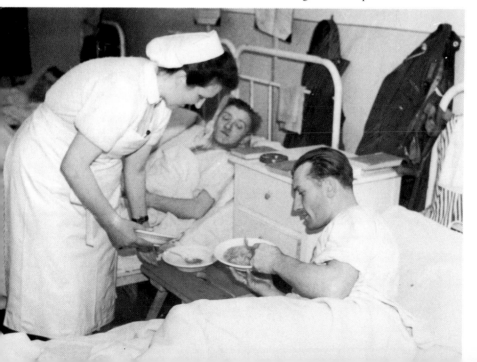

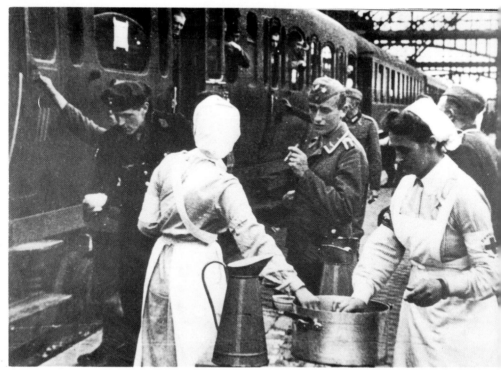

Red Cross nurses serving refreshments to servicemen on a railway station platform in wartime.

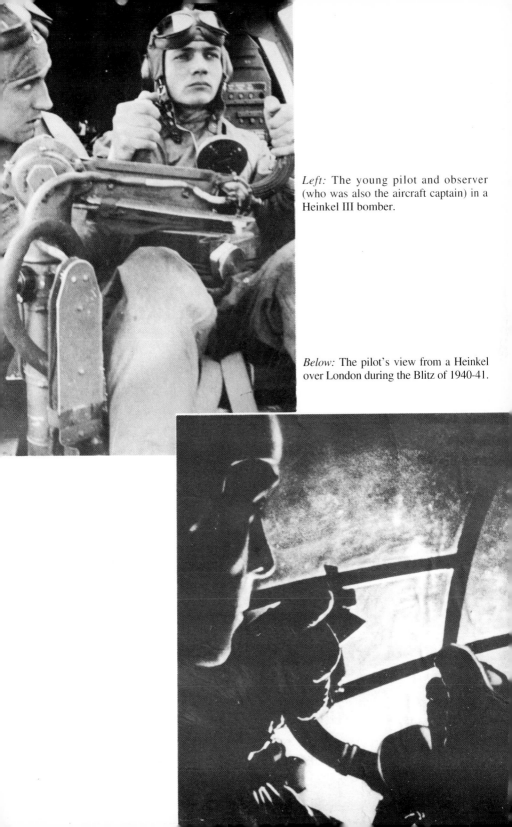

Left: The young pilot and observer (who was also the aircraft captain) in a Heinkel III bomber.

Below: The pilot's view from a Heinkel over London during the Blitz of 1940-41.

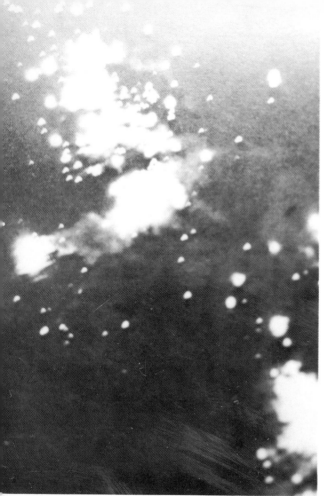

Left: Large fires and incendiary bursts in a British city.

Below: Luftwaffe aircrew prisoners at a London train terminus.

Above: Troops and airmen inspect a downed Heinkel, 1940. Most enemy planes were broken up for scrap.

Below: All that remained of a Dornier 217 and crew that crashed and blew up at Fairlight, near Hastings.

Hitler would not sanction the conscription of German women until 1943. Here, *Luftwaffe* auxiliaries serve on a flak site and reporting posts.

bove: A heavily laden young machine-gunner in Russia, ummer 1941.
ight: A German Lance-Corporal and his men inspect a oviet bunker.

Below: Summer 1941, the Russian steppe is awash with whole armies of Soviet prisoners.

Above: A German 'Ensa' troupe performs behind the frc Russia.

Left: A wounded Lieutenant remains in action.

Below: A few kind words from their General.

Left: Enthusiasm and ability assured good prospects for female Nazis – as for this BDM leader.

Right: Chic styling for two female SS auxiliaries.

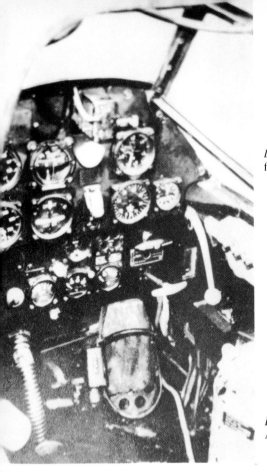

Left: The cockpit of a Messerschmitt 109E fighter was very cramped.

Below: An Me.109 lies in a field in Sussex – August 1940.

ove: A young fighter pilot just
arded the Knight's Cross is
noured by his comrades.

ght: The rudder of an Me.109
cords victories over Allied
ponents.

The ace Werner Moelders had a narrow escape in combat against the RAF in 1940 when a bullet passed through his canopy. Moelders died in an accident the following year.

Above: A female *Luftwaffe* auxiliary or *Hilferinne* in the volunteer days before conscription.

Below: Attractive German 'WAAFs' relax after duty.

Above: Thirsty work for ground crew servicing an Me.109F.

Below: The wing machine-gun pans of a Messerschmitt are replenished.

Left: Fraulein Betti Brockhaus, who strangely escaped the '1000-bomber' raid on Cologne 30/31 May 1942.

Below: RAF leaflets dropped over Germany spread the news and promised more to come in 'new style' air attacks.

DIE SCHWERSTEN ANGRIFFE DER LUFTWAFFE
VON DER R.A.F. WEIT ÜBERBOTEN

Mehr als
1000
Bomber
auf einmal eingesetzt

IN der Nacht vom 30. Mai griff die Royal Air Force Köln mit weit über 1000 Flugzeugen an. Der Angriff wurde auf anderthalb Stunden zusammengedrängt. Der deutsche Sicherheits- und Abwehrdienst war der Wucht des Angriffs nicht gewachsen.

Premierminister Churchill sagte in seiner Botschaft an den Oberbefehlshaber des britischen Bomberkommandos am 31. Mai:

„Dieser Beweis der wachsenden Stärke der britischen Luftmacht ist auch das Sturmzeichen für die Dinge, die von nun an eine deutsche Stadt nach der andern zu erwarten hat."

Zwei Nächte darauf griff die Royal Air Force das Ruhrgebiet mit über 1000 Maschinen an.

Die Offensive der Royal Air Force
in ihrer neuen Form hat begonnen

Above: Cologne's famous cathedral, almost one thousand years old, escaped the RAF bombing.

Right: The main gate at Wahn base with author carrying small pack en-route to Nr 202 Frankfurterstrasse.

vived the worst. It was a very long winter and by far the worst experience I had known, and of course that went for my comrades too, of whom I cannot speak too highly. By the time the thaw began we had lost two thirds of our original personnel and had new faces around us. In a sense it was like a new start, but we could not see how these new comrades could ever make up for our loss; neither could we see how momentum could ever be regained. However, as the better weather came so our spirits improved and we began to think of going over to the offensive, though I considered I would be very lucky to survive the war.

Our great offensive of 1942 did tear large gaps in the Soviet front and caused them huge losses; we captured vast numbers of prisoners and it was 1941 all over again. As the spring came a leave roster started, and I was at last able to get home to Germany. It was a very traumatic experience: I spent three days travelling just to reach Poland, but from then on it was easy and when I arrived home my parents were quite shocked to see me, for I was much thinner and my hair had started to turn grey. I had not really noticed this myself, what with all my other problems, and realised I must have given them a shock. It was hard to explain all that we had been through. My father had obtained special leave from his own unit in Belgium, and of course he was most anxious to learn my tale, On the one hand it was easier to talk to him about soldierly matters, but I did not want to upset my mother and give the impression of a son wasting away in Russia and facing certain death.

When I saw how easy things were in Germany I wondered why we were making all those terrible sacrifices in Russia. There were many Nazis strolling about in their fine uniforms who did not appear to have suffered in the slightest. I suppose my reactions were bitter, but I believe most men home from the Front felt the same. We could not see what it was all for, and certainly had little hope of final victory as the summer of 1942 wore on and we faced the probability of another hellish winter in Russia.

My lady friend was terribly sympathetic and knitted various comforts for me to take back. My brother meanwhile had entered the Navy and was on a destroyer in the Baltic facing the Soviet fleet, which was becoming more active. Then it was time for me to return, and although as an officer I was supposed to set an example and be made of sterner stuff my heart wilted, and I was reduced to some tears as they all saw me off at the station. I did indeed wonder if I would ever see them again.

Some four days later I had rejoined my unit and found that my good friend the Lieutenant had been killed leading an attack, his second-in-command wounded, so I was placed in charge and promoted to First Lieutenant. This was bad news.

There was a great deal of action over the following weeks: we were in the

Orel sector and facing us were a great number of Soviet mobile divisions and we were very short of anti-tank guns to combat their tanks. And very soon after my return to the unit I was wounded again during one of these tank attacks, this time more seriously.

It had been a night of artillery bombardment and we were cowering in our holes. At first light the Russian tanks thundered towards us with a lot of infantry behind them. We opened fire with all weapons and I was about to change my position when a great explosion from one of their tank shells buried me under a lot of debris. I was struck in the chest by something and passed out with a great weight of rubbish pressing down on me. I could not breathe and fainted, thinking it was the end. But then I saw the light again and it was much quieter; hands were pulling me free and I could breathe again. But I had a pain in my chest and when they removed my tunic they found I had a splinter lodged dangerously close to my heart. I was in a lot of pain so they put me out with morphia.

I came to in a dressing station on the operating table. The surgeon made some soothing remarks and I was put to sleep. I experienced all sorts of pleasant dreams of home, my family and lady friend. Then I woke up lying in bed with my head throbbing and wondered if I was all right. When I woke up again I felt very hungry and soon an orderly brought me some soup which I was able to eat sitting up with his help. He told me that all was well but that with my kind of wound I would be going back to Germany. I felt terribly relieved.

Within a week, I was transported by hospital train to Innsbruck in Austria and into hospital, which was heaven. The nurses were wonderful and the food good. I was able to sit up and eat and play chess and the doctor told me that I had had a lucky escape: a fraction to one side and I would have gone to heaven – or the other place!

I was able to write home and receive parcels, and I began to look forward to convalescence and some sick leave. This came a month later when I was ordered to report to the nearest Army medical centre.

A month later I was sent home on four weeks' leave with orders to report to the nearest Army medical centre at its conclusion. I enjoyed a blissful time which was only slightly marred by some air raids. My folks and lady friend were terribly relieved that I had survived again, but even more worried over my future in case I was sent back to the Eastern Front.

At the end of my leave I reported as ordered to the nearest district medical centre and was given a thorough check-up. To my great disappointment they pronounced me fit, but with a recommendation for service elsewhere. To my great relief and delight I was sent to France where I spent a very comfortable time until 1944 when the invasion came. I was once more placed in an infantry anti-tank unit, but did not see much action. Instead we retreated from our sector all the way back to the German border, where we became involved in more static warfare until the German offensive in the Ardennes, which did not involve me. I was in a reserve unit, and though supposed to move up into the Ardennes, we never did.

From then on we were only engaged in one or two street battles against the Americans, and while we came under great threat from the air all of the time it was nothing compared to the Eastern Front.

When the surrender came I was in southern Germany and went into a PoW cage for about three weeks before we were released back to our homes where we were able to try and get back into some sort of civilian life again.

CHAPTER 9

Gerda Klinger

or those Germans who enthusiastically jumped on the Nazi bandwagon life could be sweet, for anyone with ability and ambitions could succeed in the heady atmosphere of the mid-thirties when the National Socialists were enjoying their first taste of power. To show loyalty, espouse the Nazi cause and generally put oneself forward could bring big rewards, for those in command were not slow to make use of the zealous.

After 1933 a very great emphasis was placed on a Nazified youth culture. Hitler paid special attention to the young and appointed a Reich Youth Leader – Baldur von Schirach – to carry through a programme that would ensure Germany's boys and girls became sufficiently motivated and inspired for a future of service with the Third Reich.

'The generation which is ready for the final and greatest decision on this globe.' That was how Adolf Hitler viewed German youth. But that youth was already organised to some extent before Hitler came to power through a great variety of youth groups already in existence, many of them run by political parties such as the Social Democrats and of course the Communists and churches. The Nazis began their own youth league at an early stage. Their organisation had formerly been called the League of German Labour Youth, and was taken over by the Nazis as early as 1922 to become more permanently established as the Hitler Youth in 1925. This was right after Hitler's abortive putsch in Munich and a spell in jail. The next year the SA brownshirts took over the School Pupils League, while von Schirach, who had been leader of the Students League, was appointed in October 1931 as Reich Youth Führer. In those days a large proportion of members came from the ranks of the unemployed; sixty-nine per cent of the remainder were young labourers or apprentices, ten per cent in commercial enterprises, and twelve per cent high school students. Membership numbered 20,000 and was limited to those paying initiation and membership fees, yet 100,000 boys and girls marched past Hitler at the Reich Youth Congress at Potsdam in 1932.

Soon after Hitler came to power the Nazis pulled off a coup. Most youth groups were affiliated to the Reich Committee of German Youth Associations, and as such were taken over by Baldur von Schirach with the help of the SA. What few groups remained were gradually forced to amalgamate with the Hitler Youth, but this took a few years to achieve, for some groups, such as those run by the churches, resisted to the end. This came in 1936 when the Nazis promulgated their Reich Youth Law, which also put an end to any doctrines previously laid down by the civil service or educational establishments, for all German youth were to come firmly under Nazi control, and to this end deserving Party members were given the task of running the State youth organisation. Their job was to collect membership dues which commenced with thirty-five pfennigs for every 'pimpfe', or youngest member, the total yearly income being at least thirty-five million Reichsmarks.

But the chief task of the leaders was to educate their charges physically, mentally and normally in the spirit of National Socialism. As mentioned elsewhere, pressure existed to ensure the enrolment of every German boy and girl into the State youth movement, yet actual legal compulsion did not come until April 1939, when membership was made obligatory between the ages of ten and eighteen years. The general 'Hitler Youth' admitted even those with non-Aryan grandmothers, whereas the 'Stamm HJ' was a more exclusive élite to which only the most deserving were admitted. The moulding and regimentation of youth continued with the setting up of special schools intended to provide future leaders of the Reich, but apart from these the Reich Minister for Education Dr Rust decreed that every Saturday be set aside for indoctrination, while Sunday must be 'family day'.

By 1937 there were two classes of leader under preparation in sixty-five Nazi Führerschulen: these were the professional and the non-professional. The aim was to select those of higher calibre who had already proved their worth at high school, or by passing a handicraft or professional graduation. Those accepted would need to complete both labour and Wehrmacht service before becoming Führerantwarter (leader aspirants), and undergo four months at the Hitler Youth Leaders staff offices, eight weeks in the Reich Leaders School, a one-year academy course, three weeks in industry, and finally up to six months in a foreign country. If the candidate passed all these hurdles he or she would then become eligible for twelve years' service as a Reich Youth Leader.

It was estimated that some 30,000 had become youth leaders by the outbreak of war, but it is improbable that all the above course curriculum was fulfilled in each case. By 1939 several hundred thousand minor leaders existed; in fact by 1938 a total of 562,000 male and female leaders were in place, a very great number which indicates the scale of effort undertaken to organise completely

German youth. But only two rank tiers had actually completed a spell in the military, which was in some cases as little as two months. The insistence by the Nazis that only youth could lead youth was never really adhered to since a number of leaders were up to thirty years in age.

The Nazis made a 'career' in the youth service sound so attractive that this led to a serious shortage of teachers in state schools. The Party met this crisis by simply lowering education standards, which led to protests by the Wehrmacht of lowering standards among recruits.

In 1938 a new organisation was added to that of the BDM or League of German Girls; this was the BDM Werkglaube und Schönheit (Belief and Beauty), with the membership voluntary, the basic aim being to instil a belief in Nazi motherhood and the production of perfect Nordic specimens ready to serve the new Reich at home and abroad, preferably blond hero types with an unlimited faith in Hitler and new horizons.

Ability and suitability of the Deutsche Jungvolk to go forward into the Hitler Youth, or BDM, was matched later at eighteen when young people were again assessed for suitability for the higher accolade of being admitted to the Nazi Party, and such a 'glorious' event could only be gained after a solid period of Hitler Youth activity. Physical handicaps were a bar to membership of the HY, but special groups existed for the blind and hard of hearing. At the beginning of 1939 the total membership of the Hitler Youth stood at 7,287,470. This included 502,571 BDM, but not those of the Belief and Beauty organisation which was intended for older girls and numbered 440,789.

The Nazis forbade any scholastic approach to HY training, and from the age of ten the whole emphasis lay on the hardening of young bodies in military training, mostly by marching about the countryside carrying equipment, flags and singing songs. The rules included the girls of the BDM, but this brought dispute so they were allowed only to 'ramble' while singing their songs. The military became involved in this programme, disputing the best way that para-military training should be undertaken, for there were those in the Wehrmacht of the old school who preferred a measure of scholarship which was anathema to the Nazis and also to some in the military. Yet even conservatives agreed to new methods and so the political officers arrived to prepare publications and lectures of indoctrination which included an amount of starry-eyed claptrap on mystical lines and the inevitable near-divine being of the Führer.

The greatest accent on German youth training lay in the physical: 'The German youth of the future must be as hard as Krupp steel,' Hitler said in 1935. The young bodies were indeed hardened, for the boys were fitted out with packs and given compasses and sent off across the countryside, not on paper-chases or picnics and to play boyish games, but to indulge in Kriegspiel, or war games, which mostly consisted of what would today be called 'orienteering' or map manoeuvres. Mass physical jerks went hand in hand with school lessons, and as soon as he was big enough the boy was shown how to hold and use a rifle, for at the butts he could begin training for his Leistungsabzeichen, the honour badges which unlike boy scouting merit marks and badges included awards for shooting. They were in fact the precursors for later military sports training in the SA and SS or Wehrmacht itself. All the tests of stamina could gain him his Fahrtenmesse, or HY knife, by which time he had learned to sing the Nazi anthem – the Horst Wessel song.

The toughening hikes were strictly controlled as to distance and weight carried: ten- and eleven-year-olds were limited to ten kilometres a day; up to the age of fourteen this was raised to fifteen kilometres. By 1939 the Army had agreed to lend a hand in the process of militarising German youth: in future the 30,000 youth leaders would receive supervision from the Wehrmacht. As a result, and the appointment of military liaison officers to every 'bann' or unit of 453 youths, the HY lads were able to loose off no less than sixty million rifle shots in 1938, the rate for the following year being seven million per month.

It would be wrong, however, to suggest that German boys in the 'thirties spent all their non-school hours hiking with backpacks and shooting rifles. The Nazis set up special Hitler Youth homes, and a new Reich Law of January 1939 decreed that every township over a certain size must itself provide such a home where the local HY unit could meet for studying. The list of subjects to be followed was laid down in monthly guidance folders which reached a circulation of 620,000 copies. These topics included: the healthy family, the healthy nation, a hereditarily diseased nation, 5,000 years of Germania, how to overcome Versailles (the Treaty), from the Old to the New Army, the theatre, puppetry and music. Music was also emphasised, with bands and orchestras being encouraged and organised; the curriculum in this direction would include the classics, light music, folk songs and Nazi anthems, but of course no jazz or music that was Afro-American or Jewish in origin. Discussions were also encouraged, but as usual these centred around the new saviour, the Reich and the decadence of the democracies.

In the BDM the girls were extolled as to the virtues of Nazi German womanhood, with duties to their menfolk and the bearing of children, the proper female activities on the social scale. As the boys grew they were able to receive specialised instruction in aviation, marine and military matters, vehicle maintenance and driving. Tutors from the Wehrmacht and Party organisations such as the NSKK motor corps attended to all vehicle instruction. This programme of mobilising the youth as part of the process of preparation for mobile warfare produced 102,000 members of the Motor-Hitlerjugend by 1938 who were organised in seventy Stamme, or 'tribes'. Yet the driving test for these boys was so severe that only ten per cent passed it.

Reichsführer Himmler's love of the peasant life led to one-year courses for Hitler Youth in land service, hopefully leading after military service to the applicant being classified as a 'New Peasant' and entitled to a hereditary farm of between 120 and 400 acres. During the war a further chance for boys to 'return to the land' came with the introduction of Country Service, and of those entering the scheme it was claimed that almost one third elected to remain on the land, and as many as eighty per cent in the former service. As indicated, the driving force behind this pet scheme was Himmler, who was nursing dreams of settling SS families on the land to be conquered in the East.

When the war came the Hitler Youth organisation was well prepared: as early as 1938 some had already been trained with fire brigades, and when in 1942 the air raids grew worse, more and more were taken to serve in flak units and on air raid defence as rescue, fire and messenger boys. By January 1943 it was decreed that boys as young as fifteen could be used to fight raid fires; by that time an incredible 250,000 youths had already enrolled in fire fighting units. In the previous October thirty boys aged fourteen to seventeen had been presented in Berlin as winners of the War Merit Cross, while two more received the Iron Cross for allegedly shooting down British night bombers.

From April 1942 the Nazi labour boss Saukel decreed that boys of fifteen and girls of seventeen could be compelled to work on the land and directed to any province. The older ones would be accompanied by HY leaders who would attempt to continue their education. The Nazis directed the expansion of Hitler Youth activities throughout Europe following Hitler's conquests, encouraging the recruitment of foreign boys and girls into similar organisations.

As the war progressed the further corruption of youth was pressed by the setting up of camps for pre-military training at which well-decorated 'front heroes', who had formerly been members of the HY, gave lectures on the glories of combat and the triumph of German arms on all fronts. The fate of one such camp member is typified by a death notice inserted in Goebbels' own paper, the well known *Völkischer Beobachter*, on 30 October 1942. The advertisers were the youth's bereaved parents who lamented the loss of their son Wolfgang, who had been a gunner with the Waffen-SS in Russia, a holder of the Iron Cross 2nd Class, Wounds Badge, and the Hitler Youth Honour Badge in silver:

'Died on the Terek River, aged 17, bravely staking his all for the Führer and the Reich. Ever since he joined the Hitler Youth at the age of eight, he had lived as he has now died, for Germany's future.'

By 1942 it was stated that ninety-five per cent of the pre-war HY had gone into the Wehrmacht, many of the leaders joining the crack Grossdeutschland regiment, including Baldur von Schirach himself. In that year it was also claimed that ninety-eight per cent of all German youth belonged to the Hitlerjugend, which then had a membership of ten million. Yet, in the years of Nazi supervision, as one researcher pointed out, German youth showed a surprising rise in delinquency in the 1930s, though such figures when compared to those of Western youth today must seem minor. In 1931 the number of court appearances resulting in punishment was 2.9 per cent; by 1936 it had risen to 8.6 per cent; while the rise in homosexual offences were shown as jumping from 121 cases in 1934 to 481 in 1936. But in view of the fact that it is impossible to say how many of such boys were members of the HY, the figures cannot lead to any great and damning conclusions.

The tale of Gerda Klinger is an unusual one. Obviously a young woman firmly reared in Hitler's New Germany, she was energetic and ambitious enough to rise through the ranks of the German girls' league to what must have been a position of local eminence. So much so that both she and her youth leader husband, to whom she was well suited, were both plucked out and dispatched to the 'holy of holies', the Reichsjugend HQ in Berlin. This must have been a very great honour and an enormous leap up the. ladder, for Berlin was where it was all happening in the later 'thirties, where the élite from Germany and foreign parts congregated.

The restless ambition to fulfil herself in the Nazi hierarchy prompted Gerda to get herself moved out of a plum job into that of a mere filing clerk for the SS bureaucracy, an extraordinary step down that must have pained her considerably. Yet she refused to take this as a lasting setback and persisted with her claim to something better. Her story might easily have ended there in the labyrinthine file rooms of the SS, a leader of German youth brought low in a sense and doomed to spend the rest of her young days in obscurity. But her renewed quest bore fruit in a way she could hardly have expected, and this is where her tale takes such an unusual twist.

'I was a Nazi, and I will tell you how this came about.

I was born in Paderborn in Westphalia, and was an only child. The year was 1920 and the war was over. I knew nothing of our great troubles and only began to learn something about it when I had reached the age of ten in 1930 at school. Although I began to learn something of the world in general I knew little or nothing of the great struggles for power that had been going on in our country itself, but by the time Hitler took over I had grown used to upheaval and turmoil so it was all very normal for me. Even so, I was an ordinary child with the usual desires of a carefree life. My parents adored me and gave me everything I wanted, so perhaps I was a little spoilt.

We lived in a very nice home which had once belonged to an aunt who had far more money than we ever did. So we were comfortable. My father had been in the war but had escaped injury, though he suffered in the great period of unemployment when things were bad for everyone. We could not get enough to eat, especially as my father had no work, so we were in great difficulties. But somehow we came through that period and it all faded into my childish past and I cannot recall much about it.

When I went on to high school the Nazis had taken over and changed the whole curriculum. This meant that we were taught by Nazi teachers who told us of the terrible injustices of the Versailles Treaty and the loss of our colonies, taken over by the Allies who, we learned, were led by Jewish businessmen, corrupt lords in England and all sorts of profiteers who had no interest in anything except wealth. All this was churned into us over and over again, not only in school but in the youth movement, which I joined as did almost every other child, first in the Jungvolk and then in the BDM where I learned a good deal about the 'new Germany' and our great leader, who would take the country into its right place in the world – so watch out everybody!

For Germany was on the march. We wanted justice, that was all. We did not want war, all we needed was greater living space; after all, we had far less than the other Western nations with smaller populations. Some of this I later realised was untrue, but parts of the Nazi philosophy seemed reasonable and as youngsters we had to believe it; we did not have the reasoning powers of an adult.

In due course I was made a leader in the BDM, and as such it was my job to look after all kinds of matters including discipline, hygiene, the role of women in the new Germany, the need to produce fine children and to support our menfolk in all things. My parents were very pleased with my progress, though a little dubious about some of the beliefs taught in the Nazi books that I showed them.

Apart from my duties in the BDM I worked as a full-time staff member of the local Nazi Party. I was always diligent in my duties in the youth movement and the Nazis were always watching out for new material to turn into leaders and specialists. One day I was asked to attend an interview at the Party HQ, and there the woman overseer asked me to take on a full-time job at that place. In fact I was about to start a new job in civilian life, but I leapt at this opportunity to advance myself in the Nazi hierarchy. I have to admit that. It seemed a very good idea at the time, and they had some good points, especially on the social side, for they always did their utmost to attend to the needs of the people, however much they failed in other ways.

It would be a paid job and would include the organising of all kinds of events for the local BDM, attending meetings and discussion groups concerned with the advancement of our cause and the Party on all levels. This sounded a very challenging and worthwhile job and I was glad to accept; I could begin at once and I knew my parents would not object, so I agreed.

I was provided with full uniform and an expense allowance; I had my own office and shared a secretary, so it all seemed perfect for one so young and inexperienced of life in general. Some of my friends were very envious and desired to know how they too could advance. So I told them to work hard for the Führer! That was exactly what I said, and I believed it.

I began my duties and seemed to prosper well enough. There was so much going on and so much to do in those days. The Nazis were always holding meetings and parades of some sort, promoting themselves all over the place and especially with important people in industry. They liked to show off their skills with youth, and this is where I came in as I was called upon to parade my BDM. These events included sports and formations with the Hitler Youth boys, who provided the music.

Through the late thirties I worked on and received promotion to a higher staff job, and then met the man who was to become my husband. Herman was himself working in a similar capacity to myself in the Party staff, and we became great friends and it was not long before we decided to get married. This was quite a big affair with all of our work colleagues and parents in attendance at the church and the reception in his home, which was quite a large villa. We had lots to eat and drink and a very happy time was enjoyed by all.

For our honeymoon my husband had arranged something special: we took a train to Berlin for a week and then flew by Ju 52 airliner for a further week in Paris, where we had a very fine time and I was much impressed by the beautiful city. It was hard to return to our duties afterwards, but we had to, and then came a great change.

I was asked to transfer to Berlin where they had need of my organising ability. I was very honoured but not too happy about leaving my parents, but they assured me that if need be a home could be found for them also in the big city! This surprised me greatly, but I learned later that once you were a member of the Nazi hierarchy, even in a comparatively minor role, you could get almost anything.

My husband had also been promoted so we decided to accept our new jobs which meant having an apartment in Berlin, so the arrangement seemed ideal. I said goodbye to my parents and left with Hermann in his car, arriving in Berlin after dark the same day to see all the wonderful lights of the city about us. We had never been city folk, you see, and to us it was all very grand, and when we reached our offices the next day we were further impressed: they were quite sumptuous with all the furnishings you could ask for. I had my own secretary and my husband was on the floor below.

So you can understand that to be comparatively young and in such an exalted position in one of the great cities of the world at that time was quite an experience for a small-town girl. In fact, I was very surprised that I had got that far, as although I thought I was competent I did not think I had any great assets. But at the time the Party was still enlarging and building up its empire and anything seemed possible. So we settled down into our new life and very grand it seemed too. We had much to learn concerning the actual organisation and the plans made for overseas, or should I say the organising of German youth outside Germany. We had to attend many conferences and meetings, but in our spare time tried to enjoy ourselves on the wonderful lakes and in the parks, the zoo, circus, theatres, and in fact everywhere in Berlin. It was something of an idyllic existence and my duties were not too hard, mostly concerned with the reception and advice of delegations of all kinds and the drawing up of tables and schedules etc. I was not overtaxed at all, but after a while it all began to pall and I needed new horizons. My husband was appalled, but I was not to be put off; I really did need a change and knew that from our vantage point something could be found.

I spoke to the woman above me and she told me to wait a while and she would see what could be done, and I could see that she was disappointed in me. But I was not exactly in the armed forces and under orders, even though to be a Party member in uniform was almost an exact parallel.

But several weeks went by and I heard nothing from my superior, so I went to her again and asked her if she had found me anything. So she picked up the telephone and spoke to a man and sent me along the corridor to see him. I was surprised to find that he was in SS uniform, but realised I had seen him about the building so assumed he was some kind of liaison officer with the Party. He was polite to me and asked about my work and background and husband, and said he thought he could help me but that I must be a little more patient. When I told my husband that night he shrugged his shoulders and remarked that as long as we could remain together in Berlin he had no objection.

A day or two later I was told to report to the same SS officer, who welcomed me again and said that he had a post for me in his own organisation, but that I would have to move to another address though it would still be in Berlin. I said that I did not mind this at all, so he told me to report to a certain room number at the address and gave me a letter of introduction which was already sealed and no doubt about my career to date. He said I should go along there at once, so I did so.

The building was the main SS HQ in Berlin and I felt a little nervous as, although I was a Nazi myself, the SS had a certain reputation as the Party police and were always on the watch for infringements in any direction. I showed my letter to a clerk and he asked me to wait, and soon afterwards I was shown into the office of a high-ranking SS officer who asked me to sit down while he read my letter. He then said he knew about me, and how did I feel about working there in the HQ? The work was confidential and I would have my duties explained to me. He said that otherwise it was routine, with good prospects for promotion. So I accepted and asked when I could begin. I was taken into an adjoining room where another SS officer took charge of me, showing me along a corridor and up to the next floor. The place was a hive of activity, and when we reached the office that was to be my new workplace I found two females. One of these was in charge and she took over to explain the work.

This room was wholly concerned with racial Germans; that is to say those who were not actually born in Germany but were German by marriage or some other way, both at home and abroad. The work was mere indexing, and in fact I quickly realized that I had walked into a far worse situation than the one I had left. But now there was no turning back. I said yes to everything and was told to return to my old office at Party HQ, wind up my affairs and report back to this SS building a week later.

When I told my husband he was actually interested, but when he saw my own lack of interest he grew irritated and told me I was feckless but that it was my affair and that he only wanted me to be interested in my work.

I began work at SS HQ and first had to take an oath of allegiance not only to that organisation but to Hitler and Himmler as well, signing a document pledging loyalty and confidentiality about my work. All this I did. I was then shown a desk and told that all of the cabinets containing card indexes were to be my responsibility. It was my job to keep them up to date using letters and other documents received from my superior. So I settled down to get into the routine, examining the contents of the indexes, and soon found it was all very simple. In short, I had reduced myself from a national youth organiser to that of petty clerk in the SS! It dawned on me that I had made a terrible blunder, but I tried to console myself with the idea of promotion. In fact, when I had the opportunity of being alone with the other girl clerk I raised this question and she told me not to worry as I would be watched and if thought worthy would automatically receive a promotion.

Before I began work I had been taken to a tailoring department for the fitting out of a uniform; if I had been an SS officer I would likely have been asked to buy my own. I had been an officer in the Party, but this fact did not help me in the SS. I was fitted with a grey suit without any rank insignia. I felt quite demeaned and very dejected, and when my husband saw me he said what a fool I had been. This was no help. Furthermore, I had realised that joining the SS was rather like becoming a member of some secret order, at least in terms of 'belonging to', an order which looked on you as a privileged member of society who should be grateful and honoured for ever having been allowed into their ranks at all. Many had been rejected, so I was one of the lucky ones. Not that I felt like that at all, and I could see no way of getting out of the situation. I sat each day at my desk with these stupid cards and recalled how much promise there had been in the old days at Paderborn. I did not see how a woman could ever reach a higher position in such an organisation, though later on I came to realise how little I knew about the SS with all its branches.

However, I decided to stick it out and the months passed, and we were then into the various crises of 1938–39 and war seemed a possibility. The SS people were very busy in various ways, and I learned that there were other formations just like the Army and I wondered if I could somehow transfer to them in some capacity. It was a futile option as no jobs existed. Then came what I thought was as small ray of hope – the supervisor over us was moved to another place and I took over the office, but by then there seemed even less to do than before, so I did my best to occupy my time by marching around the various corridors, finding out what was going on. This was not really a good idea, but I could think of no other way to stave off utter boredom. I then found there was a department concerned with signals and intelligence of some kind, so I decided to try and get a transfer.

This is what happened. I went and saw the same officer and explained that I had hoped for a more interesting post concerned with organisation. He listened to me, picked up the telephone and made two calls, and that was that. I was told to report to the signals department where a controller would instruct me in a job there. I was delighted as I had noticed the department was much larger with more personnel and activity. In fact I was shown to a small room alongside the main office where there were files and cabinets full of signals and all kinds of correspondence of a secret nature. I had already taken an oath, but was reminded that everything I saw must be kept in my head.

When my husband heard about my new job he was amazed and could not understand how I had had the nerve, but congratulated me just the same. But when we next went home to Paderborn my parents were anxious as they did not think it a good thing to work for the SS, but once they heard that it was just an office job they were reassured.

Then came the war, and with it a great increase in activity in our department though my own work was routine as the messages were mostly concerned with the reports of various SS posts around the country, and not every exciting. All kinds of matters cropped up such as uniforms, pay, status, etc, though occasionally something more unusual turned up concerning suspects and arrests and that kind of thing. There were files and indexes on subversives, all kinds of criminals and political detainees, and all these had to be kept in meticulous order by me with the help of a young assistant.

During these months I learned a good deal about the SS organisation which was huge and growing. I also, I might add, received a few 'offers' from various members of the male staff, all of which I refused as politely and firmly as I could. In fact I decided it would be a good idea to keep a photograph of my husband in uniform on my desk, but as soon as my boss saw this she told me to remove it.

The outbreak of war could, I thought, bring various changes, though I felt secure. But there seemed no immediate prospect of promotion and I felt I had ended up in a dead-end job. But I carried on, and in the end my patience paid off. The same high officer was touring the departments one day and asked me how I was enjoying the work, so I at once told him that I felt my career had come to a full stop again. He laughed at this and said that he would bear me in mind if a further opportunity came up.

My supervisor heard this exchange and was furious with me, but I was not worried by her. Some weeks went by, however, and she then came into my room one day and told me to pack my things. I was amazed but she said nothing except that I must report to the personnel department and receive further instructions. I went to that department and found a Luftwaffe officer awaiting me which surprised me greatly. He looked me up and down and asked my name and if I was willing to take on a job he had for me. I was amazed as I had no idea how I in the SS could be of use to him, but he said that he often worked with them and was in fact a member of that organisation, which again amazed me.

I wondered what he was doing in Luftwaffe uniform, but he told me he would discuss everything at his own office, which was not far away. So I left the building with him and got into his car, which had a driver, and we were soon entering his own block which was smaller than the SS offices. I thought this might be part of the Luftministerium, but I only saw a few uniformed women about.

When we reached his office he asked me about myself and he told me that he would require another oath of confidentiality. This surprised me but it seemed reasonable enough, and after that was done I asked him what my work would be. First of all, he said, I would need to change into Luftwaffe uniform, but this would not affect my SS status, and in fact I would continue to be paid by them through him. He went on to say that the job would entail acting as his secretary and liaising with the SS in security matters, which was why it was all so secret. I was quite surprised and interested as it sounded like something special. He told me that some travel beyond Berlin would be involved, and he hoped my husband would understand.

This was all very surprising and intriguing to me and I wondered what we would be involved in. He told me not to worry as it would all become clear and that I could begin working in that office at once but be prepared to go away with him at short notice on various jobs. I agreed to this, but told him that I ought to discuss it with my husband. He knew about my husband, he said, who had been cleared by security so all would be well, but the work would be confidential and should not be discussed with anyone – not even my man.

Once again I told my husband about my latest move and he was amazed, especially when I told him it would be secret work and I was not allowed to discuss it even with him. He seemed rather upset and mystified but tried to accept it, I believe.

This must seem like a strange story, but it is true. I must have been one of the few females engaged in espionage on the German side in the war, although when I accepted the job I had no idea that anything of the kind would be involved.

During my first few days at the office my boss showed me various files on foreign dignitaries, especially air attachés and the like. These reports concerned anything that had been said at receptions and meetings on aviation, plus anything at all in the way of gossip and pieces of news. I now wondered if my 'Luftwaffe' boss was in fact in the pay of the Gestapo, but said nothing. I had never had any experience of them, and in any case the SS were rather different in some ways.

I had to do a certain amount of work collating the files and reports while my boss was away seeing various people both in that building and elsewhere. He was a middle-aged, not bad looking man called Horst, and I believe he spoke at least three languages. He was well travelled about Europe and appeared to know various politicians, including foreign ones and, of course, air attachés. I believe he was usually involved in receiving them at receptions and even showing them over our bases. Apart from this I knew little or nothing about him, and thought it prudent not to ask.

Then after a couple of weeks he told me that we were off to Bucharest in Romania; I was astounded and could hardly believe it. He told me to pack some things for a three-day stay and be at the office early next morning. I was very excited when I got home and told my husband, and he likewise was in a state of amazement and wondered what I had got myself into.

I was very nervous as I knew that we would fly in a Junkers of the Luftwaffe, but everything went well. We took off from Berlin Tempelhof and had a nice if noisy flight with a meal en route. My boss carried a satchel with him, and when we arrived in Bucharest a car was waiting for us. At the hotel another German was waiting, but I did not hear the ensuing conversation. My boss then showed me to a room and said he expected me to join him for a meal shortly. Although we were considered allies in Romania I had, as instructed, brought along a civilian suit, so I changed into this and later went downstairs to find my employer, also attired in civilian clothes and deep in conversation with several people. When he saw me my boss introduced me to them, and two were a Romanian couple who spoke to Horst in French but greeted me in German. Another man present was German but he soon left and we were shown to a table where a meal was served. It was all so unusual and amazing for me that I was rather tongue-tied, while my boss conversed with the two others in French, throwing in a little German now and again. I enjoyed the food and drink, and as there was a small orchestra we had a dance or two. I thought of my poor husband back in Berlin at his boring office job and wished he could be with me.

We left in a car with driver lent by the German Embassy, and Horst asked that we be driven around the city so that I could see some of the sights. Of course, everything was lit up and looked wonderful and I enjoyed it immensely. My boss returned me to my room at the hotel and asked me to join him at breakfast next morning when he would have a surprise for me. I could not think what he meant by this, and could not imagine how I had come into such an agreeable situation.

I enjoyed a good night and next morning went downstairs to find my boss already seated at a table and in conversation with a gentleman in a dress suit. When he saw me Horst stood up and introduced me to this man in English, to my very great astonishment, so that I stammered and could only say 'Hallo'. I believe Horst called the man 'Mr Cartwright', though I cannot be sure as I was so dumbfounded that we were with an Englishman that I just sat down in a whirl. On seeing my expression my boss said, in German, 'Oh, don't worry, he is an old friend of mine. We often meet here for a drink and a chat about old times.' I was suitably amazed, and wondered in view of all the supposed secrecy what he was really up to.

We ate breakfast and then this 'Mr Cartwright', or whatever his name was, stood up and shook Horst heartily by the hand then my own, thanking me politely in German for my company and left. Then we sat down again and my boss saw the look on my face and laughed.

'You see,' he said, and I remember this perfectly, 'war is not all unpleasant.'

Next we made several trips around the city by car, but I had no idea what Horst was up to as he left me waiting outside during his calls. I did not mind this in the least; in fact I got out of the car to stretch my legs and even looked in a few shops. I wondered if I could take back one or two presents for my family, but had no chance to buy anything.

We spent three days in Bucharest as expected, and I enjoyed it all, but we never saw that Englishman again. Horst did tell me that the British were up to their usual tricks in the city, trying to influence the country and royal family to go over to their side, or at least remain neutral, as well as trying to infiltrate secret agents into the country for various purposes, but we had the situation well in hand. I asked him about the Englishman and he told me that he was probably mixed up in it somewhere but it didn't matter as they would always remain friends. All this was very amazing and a revelation to me.

Back in Berlin I found myself in difficulties as I wanted to tell my husband about my adventures, but in fact there was little to tell so I just said I had acted as a secretary making notes and that I had not actually been present at my boss's 'mission' meetings, which was perfectly true.

From then on our trips out of the country were fairly frequent, and I realised of course that Horst was involved in some kind of spy work, though I had no idea exactly. I also wondered why he took me with him; it must have been as a front, as I did nothing. Our very next trip was to Paris, which had just been occupied, and this was a very big revelation to me as I was able to walk around some of the shops and look at the clothes, also buying one or two presents to take home with French money Horst gave me. We also drove around some of the countryside before flying back to Berlin where, to my surprise, my boss gave me a small present. It was a gift compact he had bought in Paris. I was very pleased and flattered, but decided I could not show it to my husband who would certainly begin to get ideas.

Our next flight took us to The Hague, Rotterdam and Hilversum. I have no idea what business Horst transacted there, but at one of the hotels we visited that had been taken over by our people I was introduced to a Dutch collaborator who was most charming and invited us to his villa for the evening, but Horst told him we had to return to Germany; this was not quite so, though we did fly back the next day. The evening before we had dinner in a small hotel reserved for Luftwaffe officers, and at this place I was introduced to some other men as Horst's wife. I said nothing, but realised later on that my boss was 'trying it on for size', as they say, with a view to using this as a cover. We were with other officers and the conversation was general and in no way connected with secrets or even official business.

When we returned to Berlin I tried to get on with the office work, but found that a new assistant had arrived, though Horst seemed to know all about him. He was in civilian clothes and I never discovered if he was in the SS or Luftwaffe and he told me nothing. He was about thirty and, judging by his accent, a Berliner, and seemed to know what he was doing. I wondered if I was being ousted, but it seemed Horst had other plans for me. He told me to leave all the paper work to the new man who was called Hans, so that he– as he put it – could 'make better use of me'. So I wondered what was coming next. I soon found out.

Almost at once we began circulating among the foreign diplomatic set. This was of course a new experience for me, and as this was before the air raids became serious there were many receptions and parties in the many foreign embassies and legations which German officials attended, taking along their wives or girlfriends, for it was important to get these people to relax, and I soon found that this is what Horst had in mind for me. When we attended such affairs it was customary to stand about making small talk, and when these foreign dignitaries were introduced to a lady they certainly began pouring on the charm, shall we say. For this purpose I had been fitted out with a special outfit, a gown which I was allowed to choose for myself in one of the best salons, and it fitted me perfectly. My husband was rather envious of the new life I was leading, but in view of the fact that I was home every night he had nothing to be alarmed about.

My routine would begin with Horst meeting me, rigged out in his best uniform, or even in tails occasionally, with me in my 'party dress'; we would travel to the appropriate embassy or legation or wherever the function was being held, and this was sometimes in the German Foreign Ministry where the ridiculous Herr Ribbentrop was in charge. We were expected to circulate among these ladies and gentlemen, sipping our drinks, apparently enjoying ourselves, but in reality listening to all the tittle-tattle and gossip and intrigue, and, in fact, everything. Before this new round of experience began my new employer told me quite frankly: 'I trust by now you can see that we are involved in a little fun and games including some mild cloak and dagger work. All you have to do is be charming to these gentlemen and engage them in conversation. Don't worry if I introduce you as my wife because then they will assume we are in confidence and talk more freely. And if I have to go off elsewhere just keep the ball rolling until I return. Above all, you must use your head and your wits and remember everything you hear. Do you understand Gerda?'

This is how I went into espionage. Of course it wasn't that really; it was just a little bit of eavesdropping, and I didn't ever hear anything really sensitive. I was a little bit surprised that Horst didn't ask me to go out with these men, but I believe he had respect for my marital status, so all I ever did was talk – but mostly I listened. Of course there were occasions when some gentleman would slyly wink at me and make suggestions as to a tête-à-tête, but it never came off, though I don't know what would have happened if they had insisted.

I grew rather used to this life, and saw a number of the top Nazi men, including Goebbels and Ribbentrop, whom I have mentioned, and there were others. I did see Hess before he flew to England, and that affair set the whole of Germany aghast and agog with speculation; certainly in the diplomatic receptions it was all the talk, and we were a little embarrassed as we ourselves did not really know what to think. We were obliged to take the Führer's view that the flight was unauthorised and Hess must be insane. We had our own views, but kept them to ourselves.

When my husband heard that the war had begun in Russia, he announced dreadful news; he felt it his duty to volunteer for the Wehrmacht, and I could not dissuade him. He joined the German Army and went off to begin training. I believe he could have pulled strings and become an officer, but he insisted on going through the mill as a recruit. It was a very bitter time for me as I was left alone in our flat which was, I suppose, why I allowed my boss to take me to a few theatre shows as his duties allowed. There was nothing improper in our relationship as I loved my husband. After a few months Hermann was promoted to NCO and then officer candidate in an infantry unit, and by 1942 he had gone to the Eastern Front. A few months later he was killed in action and I was distraught. I could not face my work and was given leave of absence.

I was away several weeks and I believe by then Horst had made 'other arrangements', as I received a call from him to that effect. He told me that as soon as I felt able he would arrange a suitable desk job for me, and I should let him know. I was now no longer the girl anxious to promote her career; I had only one thought and that was to return to Paderborn and my parents, and this I did.

However, it was impossible to stay inactive in a war of that kind, and I knew that the SS had kept trace of me, as after I arrived home I received a letter telling me to report to their local office. When I went to see them they told me that as an experienced Party member it was my duty to return to work of some kind, and that if I agreed they would arrange something locally. It was either that or the Wehrmacht, as women were now being conscripted. I decided that I had had enough of Party offices and, after discussing it with my parents, I opted to join the Navy. This meant leaving my home town, but by that time the Navy was in decline and I was not accepted. So I tried the Luftwaffe and was accepted at once, on receipt of my details. They told me that with my record I could become an officer at once, and if I wished could be posted to a unit to take charge of Luftwaffe girls, probably in one of the air reporting centres. I decided to accept a course of training at a school for officers. This course took me six months to complete, by which time I had passed my tests and was considered fit to command in one of the control centres connected with air raid defence.

The rest of my career was very humdrum. I seemed to lose all ambition, and longed for the war to end so that I could return to my home. The war went so badly and so much of our country was ruined, yet our town managed to escape most of the damage, I'm glad to say.

By May 1945 I was a prisoner of the British, but only for a short time, and then I returned home to my parents.**"**

CHAPTER 10

Norbert Limmiker

he notion of the superiority of German fighter pilots is a contentious one. The most famous fighter ace of all time was the legendary Baron von Richthofen of World War I, whose score of victories in air combat stood at around eighty when he was killed. This pales when compared to that of Major Erich Hartmann of the Luftwaffe in the next great war, which reached 352, of which 348 were gained on the Eastern Front. A number of other German aces of the Second World War also chalked up very large scores, and while sceptics have cast doubt on their claims, there is evidence to support them. The number of Allied (including Soviet) planes destroyed by the top Luftwaffe 'experten' seems fantastic by the norms of air combat, yet when the reasons behind such claims are looked at the figures are not so extraordinary.

By the outbreak of war in September 1939 one German fighter pilot had already opened his tally book by scoring fourteen 'kills' in the Spanish Civil War. Werner Mölders achieved this despite a great lack of enemy opposition: what fighters were put up by the Royalist side were inferior in all respects to the Messerschmitt 109. But the campaigns in Poland and in the West afforded little chance for Mölders or his contemporaries greatly to increase their number of victories; the chance came in the Battle of Britain, when for the first time the Luftwaffe's Jagdflieger came up against tough opponents in a well organised defence system. Mölders was able to increase his tally of Western victories to sixty-eight, and he went down in the record books with a final score of 115 before being killed in an accident late in 1941. His passing left Adolf Galland as the leading German ace, who went on to gain a total of 103 kills.

It has been suggested that on the Eastern Front at least the German fighter pilots found kills easy to come by, and certainly they never expressed much admiration for the Russian flyers. Yet the top Luftwaffe aces also ran up high scores in the West and over the deserts of Egypt and Libya. The German people came to venerate Hans Marseille, the so-called 'Star of Africa', who became a one-man threat to the Allied air forces in the Middle East, his score reaching 158 before his death, presumably by accident. Here we find controversy, for despite all that has been written about this Luftwaffe maverick in his capacity as an extraordinary flyer, some sources on researching his claims find that they are not borne out by the records of Allied losses.

Whereas the top Allied fighter pilots ran up scores of thirty to forty, and in some cases survived the war, the equivalent Luftwaffe pilots could see their names among the Knights Cross holders complete with Swords and Oakleaves for having downed between one hundred and over two hundred Allied planes. The RAF ace Johnny Johnson began his career at the tail end of the Battle of Britain and flew almost continuously until the end of the war, yet his score by 1945 still remained at thirty-eight. This kind of comparison makes closer examination necessary.

As every student of this subject knows, the German air crew were not rested or sent away to soft spots; there was no set 'tour' of operations; they fought on – with the usual leave periods – switched from one Front to another if needed, until they were killed or incapacitated. And there is no doubt that high scores were more obtainable because of two factors in their situation: first was the lesser skill of their Russian opponents in the East; and secondly, the great number of targets that presented themselves once the American daylight offensive got under way. Yet in time these two factors were to an increasing extent nullified by better Soviet abilities in air combat and the arrival of American long-range escorts in the daylight sorties over Germany.

By the usual rate of attrition the number of Luftwaffe experts declined, so that the average fighter pilot was much undertrained and had little hope of achieving high scores or indeed surviving at all. The German fighter force had once been formidable; it was worn down, stretched beyond breaking point by losses and lack of fuel. To sum up, the average German fighter pilot by all accounts was no better than his Allied counterpart, but the Luftwaffe's experts were superlative.

❝I began life in Gelsenkirchen in West Germany, an only child and son of a coal miner who always had high hopes for me. After attending ordinary schools I went on to grammar school where I learned French and English, though showing no brilliance in either.

When I left school I had a great interest in technical drawing, especially that connected with aviation. I learned quite a lot about aeronautics at college and wanted to join the air force. This desire was fulfilled after the Nazis came to power, when I was accepted into the new Luftwaffe as a recruit. My chief interest had been in the design and construction of aircraft but I allowed my name to be put forward for pilot training. This began after I had completed my recruit training in gliders, which I found very thrilling.

I then went on to a Luftwaffe flying school where we were taught to fly single-engined planes, mostly biplanes, and I enjoyed this very much. I saw a few accidents which was sad but inevitable. We were young and not too demoralised. After about three months I had managed to obtain my pilot's badge and volunteered for fighters. This seemed a very exciting prospect and I was very keen, as were all those who volunteered. We were sent to Berlin-Gatow where there was a training school with some new biplane fighters, the Heinkel 51, and these we were very thrilled with. At first we underwent quite a lot of ground instruction before being shown over the planes and allowed to sit in them. Next we were allowed to taxi them around the field, and then came the great moment when we could actually take off. It was a very thrilling moment and hugely exciting and I tried to remember all I had been taught by the instructor.

The plane was very fast and I took off and circled the airfield three times before trying a landing which was not difficult. All the pupils were very busy from then on learning how to handle the new machines, and although we had a few mishaps no one was killed. For the next two months we practised every day that the weather allowed both in single flight and by formation. We had flown high and low in mock combat and aerobatics until we felt confident in any situation.

Then came the day when we left the training school and I found myself en route by train with three other pilots to Dortmund, and then on to an airfield where we were received by the Sergeant-Major. I will always remember this man as he was such a stickler for discipline and told us at once to smarten ourselves up. 'You are absolute beginners,' he told us, 'and I will not have such untidy people on my field!' This seemed a bad start, but when we met our squadron commander he seemed much friendlier and soon introduced us to the other men, and later on after we had settled into our barracks we saw these other pilots again in their 'kasino' and had a drink with them.

We met our machines the next day and found that they were the same type of Heinkel 51s but with different unit insignia. We learned that we would soon take part in realistic exercises with the Army. This came about one week later, and after a careful briefing we took off in threes and then joined up into two squadrons over the field. We flew some miles on a course to meet some Junkers bombers, our job to escort them on a mock raid on the Army. This exercise took place over a large training area with lots of smoke billowing up from the mock fighting on the ground. The Junkers dropped practice bombs which emitted smoke to simulate hits. Then we all flew back to base where our commander told us he was satisfied with our performance.

Next day the CO took us up himself to test our skills in mock combat and I was amazed at his own skill in that type of flying. He tried to teach us all he knew and I learnt a lot and hoped I could remember it all if a real war came.

When I had leave at home my parents seemed very proud of me, especially, I believe, as I was their only son. Soon after that I became engaged to a young lady I knew, but her parents were not all that happy with this arrangement as they thought I was a young daredevil. I was always a careful pilot but nothing I could do would alter their minds; they felt their daughter would be better off engaged to someone in a safer job and above all with a lucrative future. So it seemed we were to languish, but we did not give up hope.

Around 1937 our Heinkels were taken away from us and we received new Messerschmitt 109 monoplanes. We climbed all over them in great interest and wonder as we had heard a lot about them and how fast they were. In fact we looked on them as world beaters. We were soon given the chance to fly them, though at first there were not enough of them to go round. I found the plane very fast but a little tricky in some situations, especially in take-offs and landings, and one had to be careful to remember to let the wheels down. They were the first planes we had flown with retracting undercarriages and some pilots forgot this and landed on their bellies and so received stern reprimands. If a pilot made too many errors of this kind then he was sent back to training school, which was something of a disgrace.

I myself did not do too badly. The problem with the planes in those days was that on the ground you could not see where you were going because of the nose-up attitude, so you had to jockey the tail this way and that. It was the only way of progressing, but at take-off it was easier as the tail soon came up off the ground enabling you to get a clear view ahead.

We then went into exercises and some aces from the first war came to inspect us and tell of their experiences. I remember Werner Mölders too as he had come back from the war in Spain; we found him a very good man, easy to talk to and anxious to assist in every way. When we went on air exercises we practised attacks on our Dorniers, Junkers and Heinkels, and always felt that we had come out on top. Those bombers were not well armed and we felt very sorry for the crews who seemed so vulnerable.

When the war started in Poland on 1 September 1939 we were moved to Prussia. We were told that the Poles had committed atrocities against Germans living in the border areas of Poland, and had then attacked a German radio station which was the last straw, as they say. We formed up on an airfield near the border and then took off to escort our bombers and intercept any Polish fighters attempting to interfere. It was always a thrilling sight to see so many planes in the sky at once in great formations. Our bombers attacked military objectives, but we saw no enemy aircraft in the air at all though many destroyed on the ground. We heard however that some Poles had been encountered and shot down. Their air force was very weak and mostly knocked out on its airfields. In fact we saw no combats at all in the air and only did a small amount of ground attack on enemy troops before the fighting was over. In a very short time we moved forward onto a Polish airfield which was partly cleared of wreckage to make it operational. The Russians had entered Poland from the east, but no one I knew thought this a wise arrangement – it only allowed them to get nearer to Germany. But after a month or so we were relieved by another unit and returned to our homeland.

Everyone went on leave and in the celebratory atmosphere we thought that surely now Britain and France would give up fighting and come to some agreement. But this never happened and when I returned from my leave I heard a rumour that we were going to attack in the West. We found this news both alarming and exciting, and knew that any battles would be more difficult and costly, though we believed in the superiority of our arms.

But no offensive came about and a terrible winter took over so that on many days we could not fly at all. The airfields were covered in ice and snow for a very long time and everyone had to lend a hand to help clear a path for the occasional flight of planes to get off the ground. Naturally, the Allies were in the same predicament so we had no fear of attack.

Then the thaw came in the spring of 1940 and everything returned to normal, and now we learned that the big offensive was imminent and very secret. We also heard a rumour that our plans had become known to the Allies and would be changed. But we knew no details of the overall plan, only what we had to do, which was exactly the same as in Poland: we would act as escorts to our bombers and shoot down any enemy interceptors we saw.

On the great day we rose very early to take off at dawn and meet with a formation of Heinkels. We then flew on over French territory where the bombers hit an Allied airfield. On the return flight we saw some enemy planes far below but had not the fuel to chase them.

This became our routine every day for the next week or so, and during this time we only saw half a dozen Allied fighters, some of them RAF machines which we engaged in one combat with indecisive results. These events proved a very disappointing time for our unit; although air battles did take place, these were on a comparatively small scale. Very many Allied planes were caught on the ground, I believe. We learnt a few lessons, but overall the campaign was one long run of success for our Wehrmacht, and especially for the Army which rolled across France so that we were continually required to pack up and move to new bases, and these were always captured French airfields where we occasionally found a few wrecked RAF planes such as Hurricanes, Battles and Blenheims.

Eventually there was nothing else for us to do: the opposition had collapsed and the French surrendered; only in small pockets along the Channel coast was there any fighting. The British Army along with some French troops had escaped at Dunkirk where we captured much booty so our victory seemed complete. I had a short leave and with some comrades made a short tour of some battlefields and then flew up to look over the beaches at Dunkirk and elsewhere. The Germans were extremely jubilant and a great victory parade was held in Berlin which I listened to on the radio. It was all very impressive. Some of our Luftwaffe leaders were decorated, though no one I knew received a medal.

In the next few weeks we enjoyed a very nice time in the French countryside near Arras and other bases. We were always very mobile and our duties few. We flew some patrols along the Channel coast but saw no enemy aircraft. Then we realised that England had refused to give in or parley so the war had to go on. We received this news with very mixed feelings. We wished to return to Germany and see more of our homes; on the other hand we wanted to fly over England to see something of the country! But we would fight if need be, though we never thought it would be easy against the RAF.

Then came our first combat across the Channel. We were escort to some Stukas who were to bomb a convoy, and I thought how peaceful it looked. From our height of about 16,000 feet we could see the ships like little toys far below with our dive bombers some one thousand feed below us. Then the Stukas went into their dives and released their bombs which mostly missed, sending up great water spouts around the ships. But at least two hits were obtained and two ships caught fire, so we flew back to our base, having seen nothing of the RAF.

That afternoon we flew off again to escort Stukas, and this time they did not have it so easy as we saw our first opponents. We climbed to nearly 20,000 feet and saw a convoy some way ahead and far below us. The whole Channel and a great piece of England was laid out to gaze upon, and down went the Stukas, and at that moment someone shouted 'Fighters!' We saw a lone Hurricane going down after the dive bombers. We at once turned over and dived after it, but as we did so more Hurricanes arrived and many combats broke out.

It is a strange thing; you see so many aircraft in the sky, but as soon as combat begins it all changes into a rapid whirl, a dizzy spin of action in which it is hard to find a target to fire on; it all happens so quickly. I saw a Tommy ahead of me and tried to get on his tail but he side-slipped and I shot past him. The Stukas had dropped their bombs; they were all over the place and getting in the way. Suddenly, when I looked around I could see practically no aircraft at all which I could not understand; where had they all got to?

I gained height again and then saw a few planes in the distance, and when I managed to draw nearer found they were Messerschmitts, so all was well. We flew back over France and soon landed at our base. Two enemy planes were claimed destroyed, but I had not fired my guns which was very disappointing. We were just learning that lightning-fast reactions were needed in such combats if victory was to be obtained, or if escape was to be made.

At this time we had little experience of fighting the RAF but believed Hurricanes slower and more clumsy. Later we found this to be true, but they were capable of taking much more punishment than the Spitfire.

That evening we had a lot of talk in our mess about this new battle and how best to help the Stukas, which were terribly vulnerable at all times but especially when starting their bombing dives. There was little we could do as we always had to try and maintain a height advantage and if possible attack out of the sun.

Next morning we were off again but this time escorting Heinkels and Dorniers in one great formation across the Channel and heading for Kent. I believe the bombers' targets were RAF airfields, but we saw little of that as we soon became involved in a fight over Dover with both Hurricanes and Spitfires, but once again with inconclusive results which was disappointing. The Tommies were brave flyers, but if you could catch them in a dive or by surprise then there was a real advantage. Our lads were now very keen to get on with it, but already felt that they were tied to the bombers and not allowed to use our advantage of speed and surprise. We had always believed in getting high and diving fast, but did not wish to leave the bombers unprotected.

The difficulty in such battles was that once combat was joined, everyone became lost in his own little affair and it was impossible to see if any more enemy planes came sneaking up to catch the bombers unprotected. I saw my first bomber blow up in this flight, and it was an ugly spectacle as none of the crew escaped. I also saw two RAF fighters go down with one pilot escaping by parachute.

The battle now entered its daily grinding routine and, like our opponents, we were only just getting the feel of it, so to speak. We had already found that the RAF fighters had excellent ground control, for whenever we appeared over their coast they always seemed to be there waiting to pounce. So we knew what to expect and tried to adjust our tactics accordingly. We flew very loose formations, unlike the RAF boys, which was an advantage in itself, for it is impossible to execute any rapid manoeuvre if you are stuck in a wingtip to wingtip formation as on a peacetime parade. We flew in fours or in a line echelon and always had a very rapid response to the 'enemy sighted' call. When we saw them we tried to dive down if at sufficient height, out of strong light in one very fast pass over or through them and continuing down until we thought we were safe enough to climb back up again. Of course it did not always happen that way, and we were caught ourselves as Spitfire formations pounced on us while Hurricanes attacked the bombers, so we would become so hotly engaged that we could do nothing. When we saw bombers falling it was very disturbing, especially when they had achieved nothing. It takes a great deal of courage to keep flying towards a target when you are under attack and seeing comrades to right and left falling in flames. I had the greatest respect for the American crews when they came over later on; they suffered severely but never gave up.

Not long after the opening days of the Channel battle the Stukas had been so severely mauled that they were withdrawn. Then our Messerschmitt 110s with their twin engines proved too slow and cumbersome and these too had to be taken out of the battle. We were not too sorry as they had become a liability.

Then we received new orders: we had to fly much closer to the bombers and do more to protect them. This was ridiculous as we could no longer manoeuvre and in this bad period we soon lost three comrades and very many bombers which vanished in flames or simply disappeared. We were gaining victories but not enough to keep the enemy at bay, and certainly the RAF was far from destroyed, as our leaders seemed to imagine.

I had achieved two victories in quick succession by September and before the first big attack on London. I had flown over the Channel as usual with many bombers below us; we were trying to follow our orders yet retain some sense of manoeuvre. We saw a lot of Hurricanes and Spitfires some way off in the clear blue sky. We had other formations on our far flank and as we drew nearer they suddenly broke away to attack the enemy. We were in a dilemma as the RAF group comprised a larger formation than usual, but we held our station as long as we could. Then those enemy fighters which managed to escape the scrap with our other comrades tore down after the bombers, so we at once made to intercept them, but not before two of the Heinkels went down from head-on attacks. I turned on a Hurricane as it dived away after attacking a bomber and saw the pilot looking round at me; he had his oxygen mask on and made a rude sign at me – at least I believe it was that. I went down after him, very determined, and fired a long burst from my guns. Pieces flew off his tail and his fuselage caught fire. The Hurricane fell over on its back, the hood fell off and the pilot dropped out. I saw his' chute open, I'm glad to say, as the plane became a ball of fire and vanished below.

I banked around in great excitement and climbed upwards again, hoping I still had enough fuel for another combat. Fuel was always our problem; once we had crossed the Channel we could only stay in combat for a short time. I was still over Kent and down to about five thousand feet, so still felt rather vulnerable. I decided discretion was called for as it would take too long to gain sufficient height again for safe combat, so I set course for home and arrived back safely, elated over my first victory.

A couple of days later we were over the same area and alert for the RAF interceptors which we knew would appear – and they did. A host of enemy planes came straight down out of the sun; some went straight for the bombers, more came on at us, and it was every man for himself. There were Spitfires and Messerschmitts and Hurricanes swooping down and around in all directions, and I felt I would be lucky to escape with my life. There were smoke and flames but from whom I did not know. I craned my neck and found two Spits on my tail and dived vertically to escape them. But they came on after me and then I saw two or three Messerschmitts below so tried a diving turn to try and lure the enemy fighters into a wrong move. And as they tried to cut the curve so one Spit was hit and went down. The other one tried to escape in a tight turn and succeeded in throwing off my comrades. But now I was myself on his tail, firing whenever I could get him in my sights. At last black smoke poured from his engine and the pilot baled out. I climbed away, jubilant, and set course for home, making sure I was not followed.

Then the Luftwaffe made its first big attack on London and we took part. It was a fantastic sight to see all those planes in the sky over England, and I will never forget it. Then we were over the Thames and a lot of flak came up and I saw the balloons; the bombers flew on, amazingly unscathed, and we wondered what had happened to the RAF.

Then as we turned away a lot of fighters pounced on us and once again it was a maze of combats with planes falling and trying to escape. I was forced to dive hard to the south to avoid being sandwiched between two Spitfires who were firing at me in turn. But I managed to shake them off at low level and made for home.

The following days were very hard as we were becoming very tired and had lost good friends, with few replacements who knew nothing and could not last long if the battle continued at the same pace. We were still confident but could see no great victory in sight. We felt we had drawn about even in the fighter versus fighter combats, but of course many of the Englishmen would fight again after parachuting down, whereas our people were being killed or captured. As for the bombers, their losses were much more serious and could not go on, so they curtailed the attacks on London and continued only by night which meant the virtual end of the air war over England. We flew a few more missions, and in some of these were equipped with bombs, but it seemed a useless gesture.

We were then taken out of the line and sent into Belgium for a good rest, thank God, and it was from there that we went on leave. Naturally, my parents were very relieved to see me safe again, but were very worried as to my continued survival. We heard the news bulletins about the constant night raids on London and marvelled that they could stand up to it. Of course, later on our own people would be called upon to undergo a weight of bombing previously undreamed of.

But for me the war was almost over, though I did not realise it in those happy days when I was on leave in November 1940. I had been able to meet my lady friend who agreed to go on writing to me but thought it best to postpone any more serious plans until the war was over. I could hardly blame her for this and returned to my unit to resume duties, which were thankfully much less hectic and consisted only of routine patrols along the coast.

I had just completed such a patrol one afternoon without incident and came in to land in my Messerschmitt as usual. Everything was normal until I suddenly realised my flaps were not working properly, and my speed as a result was much too high. I had to take quick action, otherwise I would have crashed over the airfield boundary. I had to raise my wheels and land on my belly – but it was too late. I struck something and all at once found myself turning over and over. The plane landed upside down and as it stopped with a jerk I felt a terrible pain in my head and back and knew no more.

The next thing I was conscious of was being carried away. I smelt the fresh air and thought how sweet it was to be alive. Thank God I was not trapped in a fire! I passed out again and next awoke in a hospital bed in bandages. I had a broken collar bone and other injuries and never flew again.

My grand passion for planes and flying had now been fulfilled and I felt thankful to have survived in more or less one piece. I was very slow to recover owing to my multiple injuries, and after a long convalescence was offered retirement or a desk job. I did not feel I could sit about at home doing nothing, so I accepted the pen-pushing job which helped me to see the war through in safety."

CHAPTER 11

Elizabeth Techen

bviously, Elizabeth Techen was no ordinary shop assistant, even though this was the occupation she had followed over many years. It needs intelligence and a quick brain to do the type of job that this girl took on in the Luftwaffe.

Her story is especially fascinating, as perhaps for the first time we hear at first hand how the other side spied on Allied warplane transmissions, but in particular those of RAF Bomber Command. This kind of war work has already been described by at least one ex-member of the Women's Auxiliary Air Force (as it then was) who worked in the 'Y' service stations beamed to pick up Luftwaffe air crew transmissions. This was all part of the intelligence set-up, and the Germans with their 'B' service proved very adept at turning every scrap of conversation they picked up to good use. The three branches of the Wehrmacht all maintained their own B Dienst and each had its successes, the German DAK, or Afrikakorps, in the desert war and the Kriegsmarine at home in following the Royal Navy's transmissions. Yet the Germans were unaware that their own use of the Enigma coding machines was betraying their own secrets as well as routine traffic; the Luftwaffe were especially unguarded in this direction.

The radio counter-measures game was played out to a great degree between the RAF and the Luftwaffe, though Elizabeth Techen was not involved in this. Her efforts lay in simply following the emissions of the RAF bombers as they went about their daily and nightly business. The RAF air crews did not realise the extent to which their activities were monitored every twenty-four hours of the day and night, and this included not only the listening in to simple messages broadcast by 'wireless ops' but the gauging of H2S radar transmissions. These sets, when switched on over England, were at once detectable by the enemy who had ample warning of a build-up of bomber activity by this and other means.

It is perfectly true as this tale relates that as the day wore on so did the RAF seem to 'wake up', with planes being air tested for the night's work and u/t crews making 'cross-countries'. It is rather poignant that the German 'Waafs' should have heard the innocent banter and scraps of popular songs from such lads who were in some cases making their last flights. Many a young air crewman unwittingly broadcast a final message to earth over the Luftwaffe's listening-in network, though it has to be pointed out that such scraps only sped out over the airwaves when a radio transmitter was inadvertently left switched on by a pilot or radio operator; normal intercommunication between the crew did not progress further than that.

"I was born in Berlin in 1913, went to kindergarten and junior school but left at fourteen to work in my father's shop which sold groceries, though when things became hard in our country we could not get enough supplies, and when inflation came we had great difficulty in paying. But things improved later and during the 1920s we probably lived better than most people in Germany.

In our area we had many Bolsheviks, as we called them, and they often came into our shop to try and persuade father not to sell goods to the brownshirts or Nazis who beat them up, and there were street fights. In the big parades the Reds sang songs of proletarian victory while the brownshirts had their own music and the best bands. They used to send men alongside on the pavements with collecting boxes shouting slogans. I did not take much notice of all this but I recall it as a very noisy period.

Life went on fairly normally for us, but after the Nazis gained power they got everything more organised and cleared every street of all known Reds who were taken away in lorries and not seen again, though some escaped into hiding. These things were not known to me at the time, but my parents told me things later so I had a much better idea of what had happened.

I had a little brother called Ernst who went on to high school after I had begun work in our shop. My father always tried to tread the middle road in politics; he did not want to become involved in either the Red or Nazi movement, though after the latter took power they soon took care to find out where your sympathies lay. There were informers about, and when children got together to play in the street or gather elsewhere they tended to quote the opinions of their parents, and that way little things reached the wrong ears, so before you knew it a man in a brimmed hat is calling to question you. This did not happen to us as my parents were very careful not to get involved in political discussion in the shop. They had opinions but only I heard them in the privacy of our home, which was a large flat over the shop. But I know it did happen; the Gestapo and others infiltrated everywhere as we discovered later, so we had to keep silent or only say the right things.

A little later in the 1930s I was told by one of the Nazi officials whose wife came into the shop that I should be in the BDM or Nazi girls' league. I didn't mind joining as it was nice to get away from the shop for a change. We had all sorts of outings, not only into the countryside but to museums of art and culture, even hospitals. We received lectures on German womanhood and the new Germany that was arising from the ashes of war. We had to write essays on all this, and naturally they had to reflect Nazi thinking. We were told that the democracies were decadent and corrupted by Jewish money and that we had a right to our just demands, especially in the question of 'Lebensraum' (living space). Hitler, we were told, was the greatest saviour ever known and would bring about all the changes necessary to raise our nation to its rightful place in the world.

All this was very interesting, but I went on working in the shop and by about 1939, just before the war when I had grown up, my parents began to think I might want to leave the shop and get married. This came about not only because of my age but because I had a young man friend I had known for years; he lived in our street and we had played together as small children. His name was Heinz and I grew very fond of him, though later I realised that we were no more than very good friends as we had known each other so long. But I began to go about with him after he had left the Hitlerjugend and entered the Labour Corps. He then had to enter the Army, which I thought bad as war was threatening. But it was 1939 and Hitler had saved the situation the year before, so we expected he would pull something out of the hat again. Everyone was very pleased when the British and French tried to make an accommodation with the Führer, but this time it all went wrong and we were terribly shocked when we heard Hitler announce that war with Poland had begun. That morning I was in the shop with my parents and I saw the look on their faces when they heard Hitler speak. My father looked at my mother and said, 'Oh, my God, the fellow is mad!'

I went out for a short walk and later on Heinz telephoned me. He did not have much to say except that he expected to be sent to Poland any day; he was in an artillery unit already on alert and ready to leave. I felt very sad but somehow fatalistic about it all.

Our neighbourhood was almost entirely working class, and they were always for whoever could give them the best deal in bread, as you might call it. By that of course I mean if a politician produced improved conditions, then they were all for him; most people are the same. In the case of Hitler he had not actually done much to improve their lot, but he had put paid to the Red menace which most felt was a very good thing as we did not wish to be another Soviet republic.

A week or two later I received a letter from Heinz. He said he had been sent to the war but hoped to be home again soon. Everything seemed to be going very well and in a month it was all over. I then received another letter from him saying all was well and he would soon be home. We were very pleased that the war in Poland had ended so quickly, and many thought that this was proof of Hitler's genius. My father said very little; I believed he hoped that France and England might now call it a day and come to an agreement with Hitler, but this did not happen.

Heinz came home on leave and we enjoyed some nice outings, though he now said he was being sent to the Western Front. I found that he had changed: he now believed in Hitler who he said had been proved right on every count so far, and he could no longer criticise him. He had, he said, 'seen the light', and I had to admit he had some powerful arguments in his favour, even though basically I did not agree with him. So I remained silent and just felt glad that he had come back in one piece. Heinz said that if all went well we could be married in a few weeks, early in 1940 or even in the spring. I did not show any enthusiasm, and when he saw this he could not understand. I told him that though I liked him a great deal we had to be very, very sure. With all the uncertainty of the war it would be unwise and unfair to start a family. I was not especially religious; my parents were not either, and had never forced me to go to church or anything like that, but I did have certain firm beliefs and one of these was the sanctity of the family and the need for a firm base in starting one. I could see that Heinz was disappointed and I believe he thought that he might not return from the Front.

Heinz went away to the Western Front and amazingly did not write to me for some time. I was sad about this as I had written to him, and because of the terrible winter I had sent him some woollen comforts, warm socks and a scarf. I believe he had been hurt by my remarks and saw that I was not in love with him. It was three or four months before he wrote to me, and then he thanked me profusely for the gifts but said that after much thought he had come to agree with me, that it was better to wait and see how things went before rushing into marriage, that he wanted me to remain his true friend and meet him when he had some leave. When I replied I told him it was fine with me and I would continue to write to him and send books and magazines etc.

I was then undergoing a change myself as I felt it was high time for me to find some other kind of job. I had been in my father's shop for so many years, but now I was a woman and could see how small it was and longed for a change. But I had no ideas as to what I could do as I had no skills and could not claim to be clever. My parents were very helpful and made various suggestions, but I decided one day to go into the city to see what I could find. I did this and spent a whole day looking around the big streets, walking in the park and taking a small lunch. In fact I quite enjoyed myself, and it was while taking lunch in a small café that a man began speaking to me and we had a nice conversation. He told me that he was a salesman for a ladies' clothing firm and did a lot of travelling about and enjoyed it as he could not stand being shut up in an office, though he did not know how things would go in the future because of the war. He used to carry samples of foreign clothes, but these had become scarce so he now had to rely on German manufacturers. He suggested that I might be interested in trying for a job with his firm making clothes; it was a small concern and most of his goods sold came from elsewhere. He said they had some big Army contracts for clothing, so this helped them along in business. But I was not interested in making clothes and knew nothing about such things, so when we left the café he gave me his card and said goodbye. I put it in my bag and forgot about it, but I still did not know what to do and started off for home. But as I made my way into the U-bahn station I saw some women in uniform and realised they were of the Luftwaffe; I had never seen any before and thought they looked very attractive. They marched past me so on impulse I plucked up my courage and ran after them; they were very surprised when I stopped them to ask how I could join their service. They told me it was not so easy as few women were taken, but gave me an address in Berlin which dealt with such matters. They wished me luck and I left them.

Having found the address, a quite large building, I went inside, intending to find out all I could and go home to think it over and discuss the matter with my parents. It seemed quite a good idea, though I had not fully made up my mind.

I saw a woman in uniform and she showed me into an office and asked me to fill in a form. She said my application would be considered, but that as I had no special qualifications I must not expect too much. But she could see that I was keen so said she would do her best and I would hear from her in due course. So I left the building well satisfied to make my way home and tell my parents the news. They seemed doubtful, but they were only really interested in my welfare and happiness. I saw my brother and he was amazed, but said nothing. I went to my room and wrote to tell Heinz the news; I think I hoped for his approval. By then my mind was fully made up and I really hoped for some good news regarding my application.

About two weeks later I received a short letter telling me to report back to the same building and that was all. So I did this and at the address a different woman showed me into the same office where I was interviewed. I learned that my application had been approved subject to a strict physical examination, and due to my lack of qualifications I would be trained in general discipline and then directed into a suitable job, or given the chance of a special trade, if I wished, on probation. All I had to do was take the medical examination immediately as they had some other girls about to do so. If I proved fit I could then take an oath of allegiance, go home and await a summons to the recruit camp. I was quite happy with this so was shown into a larger room where four other girls were just getting undressed with a woman doctor, and a Luftwaffe aide in attendance.

We had to undergo various tests with the results entered on forms and cards which we were given; we were then allowed to dress again and we waited in another room. We were soon called back one by one and I found my results showed I had passed fit for service in the Luftwaffe. So I went home feeling very pleased with myself to tell my parents the good news.

A month passed before I received a summons from Luftwaffe HQ telling me to report to the Anhalt station in Berlin where others would be waiting. We would receive orders on the spot and should take nothing but a case containing a few personal items. I had a week to prepare myself so I wrote to tell Heinz the news, and that I would write again with news of my new address. I had not received any word from him which surprised me, but I was not perturbed by this as we were not all that close, certainly not in love.

I said goodbye to my parents on the morning of my departure and they were almost in tears, though my father had already made his farewells the night before as he left rather early each morning. In fact he gave me a small diary and suggested I record my everyday life.

When I arrived at the station there were the usual crowds and I eventually found the girls waiting with a Luftwaffe woman and a male sergeant, so I hurried to them and gave my name. We had to wait for two more girls before we were given our orders. The Luftwaffe woman was in charge and told us that she would take us by train to the recruit training centre which was in the country to the north of Berlin. We would not be allowed home for at least a month but could send postcards; all other matters would be dealt with on the camp. So we boarded the train to start our adventure, all talking to each other in quite friendly fashion. I sat with a girl who had been a hairdresser's assistant and found that she was also bored and looking for adventure. Only one or two of the girls had been married and one was divorced; all were in their twenties and most not bad looking. I think they had a love of uniforms as this seemed to be uppermost in their minds as they chatted. Some had been typists or secretaries, others like myself had worked in shops, one was a factory hand. The Luftwaffe woman was an NCO and had left her male comrade at the station. She stood outside apart from us for the short journey. We looked out of the windows for some sign of the camp but saw only forest, fields and houses. At last we arrived at a country station and got out and found a truck awaiting us so we climbed in the back while our guide joined the driver in front.

It was a ten-minute drive to the camp, and when we arrived I saw huts, other buildings and a sentry on the gate. We entered a brick building and lined up while our guide checked our names again. She then left us for a short time and on returning asked us to follow her with our bags into a quite large dining room.

We put down our bags and were served a meal over a counter. The tables were quite long and had water and glasses. It was past midday and I felt hungry and was glad to get a meal which consisted of meat, potatoes and cabbage. Our NCO guide told us she would return for us in about an hour. We sat down and someone brought us knives and forks and we ate hungrily; the food was quite good and I enjoyed it.

After the meal was over we found the NCO waiting for us outside so we followed her with our bags into another building and were left to wait again. Then a male officer appeared carrying some papers and told us that we would be sworn in and given our uniforms and shown to our billets. We had to swear allegiance to our Führer and Fatherland while placing our fingertips on the German war flag.

The officer then thanked us for entering the service and said he was sure we would prove worthy. The air force, he said, was a comparatively new arm of the forces but had set up glorious traditions in the first war and would continue to show an even greater one in the West. We then rejoined our guide outside who took us to an equipment store where two female Luftwaffe assistants were waiting to help us find the right size of clothing. We removed our outer garments so that we could try on jackets and skirts until they thought we were well fitted. This did not take long. We were then handed side caps, though later on in the war these were replaced by the ski-type headgear.

Once the NCO assistants were satisfied that we had the correct size in jackets and skirts they gave us a spare set, plus all the rest of our equipment which we put into grey bags they provided. We also received hangers for our uniforms and were told that our civilian clothes must be taken home on our first leave.

We were then marched away along a little path lined with small trees until we reached some long huts and our guide halted us while she went inside one of them. When she appeared again she was with another NCO who told us to go into the hut and find places for ourselves. Inside we found two rows of cots piled with neatly folded bedding and had soon secured one each and put down all our new gear. There were large wooden cupboards around the beds but with sufficient space to move freely. I think there were about twenty beds to the hut; the windows had blue-grey curtains and the floor was a highly polished brown lino. The guide who had brought us vanished and we were now in the charge of the new one who told us to be alert and to listen carefully at all times, that we would be watched for our discipline and smartness and any girl who did not measure up to their standards would be dismissed, that we must salute officers at all times and do as we were told whether on duty or not. We had thirty minutes to settle down and then she would come back for us.

So we began changing into our uniforms and placing all the rest of our equipment into the wardrobes, which proved adequate. It was the summer of 1940 and the war appeared to be almost over, yet I don't believe that any of us in that billet were thinking about the war at all; all we had in mind was our new jobs and the adventures ahead. The change had been drastic so we were all excited and wondering what was coming next.

We looked each other up and down and made jokes, and then the NCO returned to call us all outside where we were lined up and given a lecture on how to comport ourselves properly when in uniform, to stop plastering our faces with make-up, the essentials of hygiene and to keep in touch with our families. I'm not sure why we were told this last part. We would be shown the various parts of the camp and then receive some drill and be taught how to march properly.

First there were the latrines with toilets, hand basins and a shower at one end, the location of the mess hall, and then we saw another group of female recruits marching past and were very impressed; we hoped to emulate them or do better. Then came a visit to the recreation hall where we could do all kinds of indoor sports including netball and climbing. Then we were taken to an open area of asphalt and began learning how to march in various formations and all the rest of it. We were then stood at attention while the NCO inspected us and made various rude remarks as to our deportment. She then demonstrated how to walk and march properly in uniform. So for the next half hour we were marched all over the place, backwards and forwards and practising saluting and all kinds of drill until we grew very weary. After that we were marched off to a hut where another NCO gave us a lecture on Luftwaffe rules and regulations, and we were shown a large chart of all the different ranks of the Wehrmacht. We were told that these had to be learnt to a degree, but that the only really important aspects were the rules and ranks of the Luftwaffe. We were then marched back to our own hut for a short respite before the evening meal.

During this interval the NCO returned to tell us that there was a canteen we could use behind the mess hall, and that after our evening meal she would return to inspect the billet and show us how to maintain the accommodation, and by this she meant keeping it neat and tidy at all times as there would be very strict inspections.

After our meal and some tea I went with two other girls to inspect the canteen where we found that it sold cigarettes, chocolates, writing materials and stamps. We later received special ration cards, but although we were allowed so many cigarettes on this we could also buy some, though I never smoked myself.

When we returned to our billet we found the NCO there waiting for us and she was not at all pleased to be kept standing about and told us not to go off without permission. She then showed us a little cupboard at the end of the hut containing cleaning materials including brooms and instructed us to maintain the billet in a high state of smartness as she would be making an inspection daily while an officer would come round weekly. She then inspected our wardrobes and made various suggestions, adding that on no account did she want to find any oddments lying about on the beds or floor during her daily inspection tour. We would be roused at 4.30 next morning, and this sounded fantastic to us and brought groans of amazement and disgust from the girls, but the NCO told us to be quiet and listen. She told us that there was a great deal to do on our first full day, but that as soon as certain things had been got out of the way we would find it easier as the normal reveille was at six o'clock, breakfast at seven, followed by the start of the day's duties at eight o'clock, so it did not seem so bad. She also said that after we had completed our preliminary training we would go before the assessment officer to see what use we could be to them. We would not be thrown out as the Reich taxpayers should not be expected to waste money on training even recruits to have them dismissed for one reason or another. And as a final fling she said that men were few on the camp but that no liaisons whatever were permitted and they must be avoided, but that whatever went on later was a different matter. 'Here,' she said, 'everyone works, there is no time for play, so forget men entirely as if they did not exist!'

She was a red-faced martinet and we felt she had never been with a man in her whole life. Even so, we had no wish to get into trouble so resolved to behave ourselves.

We were all very tired so I got out the pyjamas I had brought but found that most of the other girls had not brought any night attire and slept in their under-wear. The Luftwaffe never provided such items and we were always told never to leave any items of civilian attire in sight, but they tended to turn a blind eye if it was hidden away. I had no intention of sending my pyjamas home except for a change.

We had much to talk over and think about but we slept well, and were woken up next morning at 4.30 by martial music blaring out of a loudspeaker that I don't think we had even noticed. The music was very loud so it was impossible to sleep on. In a very few moments the NCO entered the hut to roust out any still in bed, and some were. I looked at my watch: it was only 4.40 and the sky was just grey. It was chilly and we traipsed out to the latrines in our greatcoats. Half an hour later we marched to the mess hall for breakfast to find we were the only girls there – the rest of the camp was still asleep. The meal consisted of porridge, a piece of sausage, bread and coffee. After that we marched back to the billet to put away all our equipment and make up our beds with blankets folded.

Outside again in the morning light we were marched across the camp to the medical centre where we received inoculations against various ailments, were collected together again and did fifteen minutes' drill outside (to warm us up a little, as the NCO told us). Then we marched back to our billet where we found that someone had deposited little notebooks and pencils on each bed; these, the NCO told us, were to be used for notetaking during lectures and for anything else we needed to remember, and trouble would follow if any were lost.

After a short break we were again assembled outside where a female officer told us in haughty tones what was expected of us and that Germany's future lay in the hands of young people like us, etc. She then inspected us critically before we were marched away to another hut to receive a lecture by a male NCO who told us to note down on our pads all the ranks we could in ten minutes from a large wall chart and that he would be testing us later. After that he unrolled more charts showing figures in combat gear of the various services followed by another one showing flags and uniformed figures of the Allied and Soviet forces, but we had no need to learn these. The NCO then left, his place being taken by a much older officer who gave us a lecture on air force history commencing with the first air formations prior to World War I and how they had fought in that conflict. He then explained how the Treaty of Versailles had forced Germany to get rid of all its warplanes, but that by being clever certain officers had been able to train and build up a small air force in secret which had led to the present Luftwaffe under General Göring who, he said, was of course an ace of the first war.

This officer then pointed out that as women in modern Germany we had responsibilities to assist our menfolk at all times in various ways, and that because we were no longer civilians this duty had not ceased. We would always be honoured to assist Germany's airmen of any standing or branch of the service and he knew we would do our duty, etc.

He was then replaced by the NCO who proceeded to question us on the ranks he hoped we had by then learned, or at least those of the Luftwaffe from the lowest private to chief of the air force. Then our own NCO returned and took us out into a field where we saw some Luftwaffe airmen erecting a signalling apparatus. It all looked very strange to us.

We marched away across the camp to a building containing a radio school full of students including a few females. Then it was more marching before a visit to the hairdresser where those recruits with long hair lost it while those like myself, whose hair was not in full control, were shown how to put things right. I believe a few female vanities were shaken that afternoon. We then went outside to undergo some physical exercises before entering the recreation hall where we found other female recruit squads in action, and they were quite impressive. Our NCO consulted with her opposite number before returning to tell us that if we changed into PT kit and returned within ten minutes we could enter into a netball contest with the other squad. So we raced back to our billet, changed hurriedly and returned to the hall where our NCO was waiting for us in great impatience and chided us for our tardiness.

The game was organised and in no time we were losing heavily because the opposing team seemed so much fitter and more agile. By the time an hour had passed we were worn out and the NCO was laughing at us and our feeble condition. We were then allowed to go for a shower, get dressed and break for lunch.

For the rest of the day we received lectures on hygiene, warfare and some technical trades of the Luftwaffe. By evening meal time we were very tired. I wrote home to my parents to tell them of my progress.

From then on the days passed quickly, being filled with marching, lectures and physical training which we sometimes took with other squads. We received copies of the 'Soldaten Liederbuch' (Soldiers' Songbook) and were expected to learn the songs and sing them on occasion. We found there was a concert hall which was later used as a cinema; amateur talent was allowed at weekend concerts and we saw some of these. One girl was a very good classical pianist while another sang 'lieder'. One man had a very good voice and could join in with two more to make a vocal trio. There was also a small dance band but they played mostly military tunes as they were trained musicians of the Luftwaffe, and when they played the soldiers' songs the vocal group sang the words. They were quite jolly evenings and I enjoyed them. At the canteen you could buy beer though I didn't care for it, though some girls did.

At the end of one month we were delighted to be given passes for home, and when I arrived my parents were amazed at how much I had changed. They said it was a 'transformation' and when I looked in the mirror in my room I saw a new woman. I wrote to Heinz, who by then had returned to Germany, and was stationed at Wiesbaden. He had been very slow to write, but my days had been so filled that I had not minded. I enjoyed a very good weekend in Berlin with my parents and some friends and relatives who had come over to see me, so when I returned to the camp I was in good heart.

We were then paraded and told that they were generally satisfied with our performance, though one or two girls needed smartening up otherwise they would be relegated to cleaning duties. We were to carry on for another two weeks recruit training at which point individual assessments would be made with a view to aptitude tests for trade training.

So we went on with our training, which had now become very routine and no longer a bother to us: we knew how to keep ourselves smart and presentable and maintain standards of hygiene and how to keep the NCO happy with a neat billet, and especially to sing well as we marched which pleased her no end.

At last came the day when we were taken for testing and given cards and examination forms to fill in. The results would give the male officer in charge some idea as to our abilities and what could be offered us if anything. The examination lasted several hours and at the end of it our NCO seemed glad to give us a thorough inspection and march before lunchtime. We were full of chit-chat about the exams and how we had fared with all the questions, which ranged from general knowledge and Luftwaffe history to ranks and also questions on Nazi history and Germany's place in the world and that of other countries. We were in a way being assessed politically, so had to be careful what we wrote.

Some days later our NCO told us that our work had been assessed and that we would now be assigned to various courses, though some girls who had not done so well would be given general duties on the camp or elsewhere. We were very excited as we marched back to the same classroom where the officer began calling out our names and numbers, and as he did so he stated which trade they had been recommended for although he warned us that this did not necessarily mean that we would enter them; much depended on our willingness and the availability of places in the course rosters at the technical training schools. At that time there were few women in the services and they could afford to be choosy.

When he came to my name he said he wanted to have a further talk with me. I was amazed and could not understand what he meant; I wondered if there was something in my exam paper that had offended him or if I had failed in some other way. None of the other girls were held back and they all left, leaving me alone with the officer who called me to him, and this is what he said:

'I have examined your papers very carefully and I believe you have a special qualification. Have you ever studied languages?'

I told him I had not, but that I had learnt some English at school and liked it; I had also learnt some French, but not so much, and preferred English. I had enjoyed reading about Shakespeare and certain parts of English history and traditions but I was no linguist. He told me that even so I did have a certain talent for languages and some knowledge of English and how to speak it, so his recommendation was that I be sent to language school to be given proper instruction with a view to special duties. I was amazed as I had never thought I had a talent or stated a preference at all. But I assumed the officer knew best, so I thanked him, saluted and left the room. Back at the billet all the girls wanted to know what sort of trouble I had got myself into, but were astounded when I explained what had happened.

I wrote home in excitement to my parents, having no idea what would happen next, and our training went on as before with plenty of PT and marching and only a very few lectures. We attended another concert and then the officer told us we would be sent away for specialised training. This was exciting news and six girls including myself were told to pack up and be ready to leave the camp next morning. I believe my friends were mostly going into the radio branch to work in the air raid protection service or controlling aircraft, but one or two were going to flak gun sites and had to learn how to use various instruments at technical school first. I alone was being sent back to Berlin of all places to attend language classes, and I was overjoyed. I had never imagined this possible and assumed I would be able to see my parents often. When I reached Berlin I found my billet was to be a barracks partly occupied by men but with some women too. It was not near my home but I would be allowed to go there at weekends for as long as the course lasted, which was splendid news.

On the evening of my arrival at the barracks I found I was to share a room with one other girl who was out at lectures, but she soon returned and took me to the mess hall with her. She was a clever girl and learning French and expected to be sent to France soon as an interpreter. I had no idea as to my own fate but received my orders on reporting to an office next morning: I would attend classes in English with other personnel, both men and women, and be assessed; the course had just begun and I had not really missed anything. The classroom was near the barracks and very convenient in all ways. Our tutor was an older captain and very personable, and he soon made me feel at home when he interviewed me and tested me on my English. But I was so rusty I was not in the least bit impressive. He knew of my background and lack of schooling and he told me he could not understand why anyone so bright had left school so early. I told him our home circumstances and he said that I should have gone to high school to learn languages. He set me some composition and gave me a short verbal test and seemed satisfied but told me that I would have to work hard.

I joined the class of about twelve and found it harder than expected, but after a few days it began to get easier because I studied in my room after school hours and my friend helped me, and at home on weekends my mother also helped me. My brother was very surprised at all this home studying and was expecting himself to go into the Wehrmacht at any time and become a driver of armoured vehicles, as his firm made tank parts.

After a month we were assessed and I was amazed to come top of the class.

We pressed on, learning all the different pronunciations and syntax and how to speak and write it and tested each other. We also listened to gramophone records of, I believe, BBC announcers broadcasting from London. It was all very interesting but we were far from perfection. We spent about three months on this course which was crammed as we were worked so hard. Then came a new kind of test. There was a radio in the classroom and the instructor switched it on and we heard an announcer reading the news in German followed by a commentator giving an exhaustive analysis of the events. We were told to take down what he was saying in English, but this was hard as he spoke too fast for us. Then came some music and the tutor switched off the radio and told us to pass around what we had written to assess each other's work. This was interesting and amusing as some strange errors occurred. After half an hour of this the tutor again switched on the radio and tuned in to the BBC for the news and anything else that was 'voice' only. This was especially interesting and we had to take it all down to be checked by him later, and when he did he said we had made good progress but had a little way to go yet. As you can imagine it is difficult to take down another language if it is not at dictation speed. But some interesting sidelights were to come.

The next morning a new tutor arrived in civilian clothes who I thought spoke perfect English and I wondered in fact if he was from England; if so, what was he, a traitor to his own country, or what? But I never learned anything about him and he went on to give us a two-hour lecture on English history right up to the war, which meant that the more recent events were 'Nazified'. We were supposed to be taking notes but I became so fascinated by what he was saying that I forgot much of the time. At the end of this lecture the tutor left and our usual man returned, to tell us that we had to write up a lengthy survey on all we had just heard. I was shocked as I had written down so little, but I did my best and I think passed this test as I have a very good memory. The rest of the course was mostly revision and every day we listened to the English radio and made a legible record of everything we heard in some fashion. If we used our own brand of shorthand that was all right, so long as we wrote it all out properly for the instructor to read afterwards.

Then we were told that everyone must take a typing course and this was a bombshell as I had never even seen such a machine and feared the worst. I doubt if my class mates had any knowledge either, and next day we went to a different room where every desk had a typewriter on it and a fresh tutor showed us a huge wall diagram of a typewriter keyboard and which fingers must be used for each letters etc. He then gave us a demonstration of how to begin, raising the right fingers from the start. We had plenty of paper and were shown how to load and make the machine ready. He next wrote a simple phrase on a blackboard and told us to copy it twelve times, which we did, with very slow and hesitant results as we had no co-ordination and could not make the keys work properly. Then he added another phrase and so on and we were hard at it all day while he walked among us criticising us and showing us what we were doing wrong. At the end of that day I felt utterly depressed, especially as things had been going so well in the language course.

But as the days went by we began to make progress and then a civilian woman arrived who went around each student showing him or her how to do better. This individual tuition was very valuable so that when we next had to type out lines we typed in unison with every student hitting the keys at the same moment – at least we were supposed to!

The typing course lasted one month and at the end of it we were not very fast: I suppose we did about thirty words a minute, but our instructor seemed satisfied, though he told us that some improvement would be required in the final stages of our training; all we had learned was only a beginning.

We then received a number of severe lessons, and I mean 'severe' because although the work was basically translating from or into English it included typing and the pace was forced. It became very hard to keep up and I decided I needed extra work if I was to master this new vocation. The thought of failure had come to me and I was quite terrified that I might be sent away in disgrace into some bad kind of job that I did not want. When I told my room mate she said that her man friend worked in a Berlin office where there were lots of typewriters, and she might be able to arrange for me to do some practice in off-duty hours – preferably at weekends. I would have to wear civilian clothes but I was quite happy with this.

We met her man friend late one Saturday afternoon and I was surprised to see that he was a lot older than she was; in fact he said we must hurry as he must get home to his family. This was a surprise but my friend explained that he was a widower with several children and an old mother to care for.

He let us into his office in the business district and, having brought some paper, I got on with my practising while my room mate went off with her man for some kissing and cuddling, I believe; I didn't care so long as I could improve my work. After about half an hour they returned and said it was time to go but I could come again by arrangement.

Two weeks later the course was over. I had made another visit to that office while my friend went off somewhere with her man for an hour or so. Our tutor told us that tests would now begin to assess our standard, so he switched on a gramophone record and told us to type out what we heard; it was one of the BBC recordings and we began typing at our best speeds with the volume of the gramophone turned up loud. Our papers were called in and at once the same man in civilian clothes came into the room and delivered another lecture, this time on military matters, and this too we had to type out as he spoke. He did not rush which was a blessing, and I believe I did quite well.

All that happened in the morning. In the afternoon came more tests and an oral examination by the instructor, who fired questions at us in one language so that we had to answer him in the other – German and English. Then he had us out in front of the class one at a time and without warning told us to speak for thirty minutes on any subject – in English. For my own effort I chose the selling of foodstuffs to the public based on what I knew from my experience in the family shop. The class were very interested and I think my instructor was rather surprised as he applauded me at the end. Some of the others gave lectures on things like astronomy or politics or nautical subjects. It was all a very interesting experience and I believe we gained a lot of confidence.

These self-lectures were spread over a day or two and were obviously designed to improve our knowledge and ability in spoken English. Then at a final lesson we had to take down a lecture on military affairs given at some conference or other. This was very long and hard and involved a number of technical phrases we were not familiar with. This ended the course. Our tutor told us we were due for one week's leave, after which we must return to learn our fate. So I went home relieved that it was over to enjoy a very good leave. This was early in 1941 and I had not heard from Heinz for some months. Unless we met by chance on leave I was unlikely to see him and did not really know his parents.

I reported back to the school at the end of my leave to find the students talking of their experiences and how they thought they had done in the tests. Then at last our tutor came in to tell us the worst. He announced that all but one pupil had passed the course but that further training would be given 'on the job'. So we looked about us and wondered who the unlucky one could be; I had a terrible feeling that it would be me, but I was wrong. Our instructor said that a short report on our test results would be given for us to study with a view to improvement and that our orders would soon follow.

We left the room holding our reports and when I glanced over mine I found some glowing remarks as well as criticisms, and that I must try to improve myself. I was overjoyed and returned to my barrack room. Later that day I heard from another student that he had failed; he was very dejected but said he had another trade and hoped to get into that with less bother.

About three days later we received orders to report to the orderly room where we were told to pack up and set off for the destinations named on written orders. On opening my envelope I found that I was posted to a Luftwaffe intelligence centre in West Germany near the Dutch border, though at that time I did not know it was an intelligence unit as the orders stated 'signals'. I was very excited and discovered that only I was posted from our class to that unit. We all left together by truck and I travelled by train with two others to Hamm, changed trains for Münster, thence by truck to the destination. It was a long ride and we did not arrive until after dark, so all I saw was a sentry box before reaching the orderly room. A male sergeant-major sent me with a corporal to a billet where I found three more girls who made me welcome.

I asked them about their work and they told me we had to listen in on the

British air force radio frequencies so that everything heard could be taken down and used as intelligence. The work went on continually so we were one of two shifts which meant that we would be working by night at times. They had not been there all that long and had not come through the same course as I had, but had been tested. In fact two of the girls spoke perfect English; I believe they had lived in England and knew it well. One knew a lot of English as she had an English relative, and had been to a language school in Berlin.

I went to bed in some excitement wondering what sort of life it would be.

Next morning we were up and ready for work after breakfast by eight o'clock and I had to report to the radio room with the three other girls. The camp was not very large, with the radio room near its edge and near some brick buildings where I learned officers assessed the intelligence gathered. Outside the huts were aerials while inside the radio room itself I found an NCO in charge with tables on which were set typewriters and radio sets. There was no question of anyone operating these sets as they were all tuned in to set frequencies. All we had to do was put on earphones and type down everything we heard.

When we arrived that morning four girls had just completed a shift and my colleagues took over while the NCO gave me my instructions. She said that as I was new I should not worry if I missed a few words or got flustered: 'It will come in time, but in a week you should have mastered all this without any difficulties.' She was more like a school teacher and I liked her; she was very different to the red-faced NCO at recruit camp.

I sat down at my place and put on the earphones, but heard nothing at all for some time, so tried to adjust my seat to get the feel of the typewriter. One or two of the girls began typing very rapidly in short bursts and then stopped suddenly. I sat there feeling rather foolish while our NCO went off to write out reports. I hoped that someone would bring me some coffee before long. It must have continued like that for an hour or more before I suddenly heard a crackling noise and a whistling as if the frequency was coming to life and I sat up very expectantly. But nothing happened and I waited and waited so that when I did finally hear a voice it took me by surprise. It was very weak at first but then I heard it quite clearly – 'Willco-Roger'. This was new to me but I typed it out as heard and the NCO came over to me at once and explained the significance of the words and I grasped what it meant. Our own airmen always called 'Ende' after a message, so 'Roger' seemed rather a novelty and amusing.

After that I felt much more alert and felt sure that I would hear something very important and secret. But the morning went by and all I heard was more crackling and not one word. I was very disappointed when at one o'clock we finished our shift for lunch. The NCO gave me a little pamphlet to study while in the mess. It was a glossary of RAF slang terms and radio call signs such as

'T-Tommy', 'I-India' etc, and I found this very interesting. In fact I kept this little booklet for many years. The NCO also warned me not to speak of my work to anyone: it was a very serious offence, she said, to tell anyone what we were doing. The most I could tell my family was that I was a translator of technical publications, certainly not that I was listening in to the enemy.

About two o'clock we returned to the radio room and I began my listening watch again. This time to my surprise and excitement things were much more lively, as if the English had just got out of bed; the crackling and messages were almost continuous, though some I just could not understand at all, but I told myself not to worry, I was doing my best and got some of them. They went like this:

'Hallo A-Apple, Apple pancake. I say again – Apple pancake. Over.'

'A-Apple, A-Apple, Roger-Roger.'

Then one ended, 'This is a dicey one, can't we let down?' And I heard someone say, 'Sod it – we're going in the drink if we're not careful!'

Not long after that there were a lot of calls and I got the impression that a plane had come down and the airmen were in trouble. There was a certain amount of bad language which I could not follow or understand and I heard strange accents; it was impossible to get through it all. The men's voices sounded very ordinary: there were very few 'posh' accents and I thought of all those young men caught up in the war and perhaps even losing their lives even as I listened in.

I heard one man who I assumed was a commander and he used a few words I could not understand; he said something like this: 'Brown, you're a clot, you'd better get down in one piece so that I can bloody well court-martial you!' This was so funny that I burst out laughing and this brought our NCO running to my side to remove the paper. Her job was to keep all this material flowing so we had a messenger continually removing trays full of it to the assessment centre. I was finding it extremely interesting and instructional. I can remember listening to the almost continuous tap-tap of the typewriters in our room as we were kept busy all of the time. Every time a message ended we made a stroke mark and began the next; it was not our job to sort it all out into meaningful patterns.

The day went very quickly after that and we left at five for a meal and the other shift took over. We had to report back at nine o'clock so I assumed we would not be getting much sleep; I had yet to find out how these shifts really worked.

That four-hour night I did was really illuminating. I settled down just after nine and at once heard traffic in a continuous stream, and will give a few examples of what was going on. It seemed that a lot of planes were taking off and assembling over England; it was easy to hear the airmen giving brief messages:

'P-Peter, airborne and in circuit.'

'B-Baker, we have a small problem, may we pancake?'

'B-Baker – wait. I say again – wait.'

'I-India to H-Harry – get down old thing will you? You're holding up the whole bloody show!'

A certain amount of swearing, a lot of indecipherable words and interference, then after about an hour it started to get quieter so I assumed that if the bombers were coming they were on their way. It was a very odd feeling to hear it all happening over England long before most on our side knew anything about it. It was strange too how close some of these young Englishmen seemed to me on my radio. Then there were the different regional accents and some Americans or Canadians, New Zealanders or Australians, and others who could have been European.

I did not hear very much later on and assumed that my radio was tuned in only to a bomber frequency and that all the chatter would start up again when they got back to England. But I was back in my bed after my four hours' duty and was told to report back at nine a.m. I believe there were shifts taken by NCOs from elsewhere who I never saw, but I do know that those radios were manned twenty-four hours a day.

My next morning's duty was much as before, with little happening till afternoon during which I had my time off and back to duty again before evening, when it was again all hustle and bustle in the air over England and I did hear some extraordinary events – at least, they were for me as a newcomer; I expect my work colleagues found it normal.

One excited Britisher called that he had an engine on fire and would have to ditch; the controller assured him that he was pinpointed and would alert the air-sea rescue. This sounded like a potential tragedy and I was amazed that this drama was coming to me over the headphones. Then I heard a few more snatches from the same voice and concluded that they had managed to land safely after all. Then there was another emergency and a lot of voices calling at once so that the controller told them to shut up. One high voice called 'Mayday, Mayday! We are about twenty miles out and going in now. I'll leave my key down so you can get a fix!' Some radio operator was about to jump or crash with it into the sea. I was very excited and in somewhat of a state as I listened in to this drama; I had had no idea at all that I would be involved in such things.

A little later I heard several calls of pilots wanting to 'pancake' and the controller becoming very irritable. I must say they were usually very patient but much less so when the controller was a woman of the WAAF. I was very surprised when I first heard a well spoken woman's voice over the radio; I had not expected this at all. She was calling up a certain aircraft that was overdue, and although it was obviously an anxious time she sounded extremely matter-of-fact and calm. I was amazed to be listening in to an enemy female, but the I suddenly realised that there must be Waafs listening in to our people in exactly the same way!

Our routine never varied, but at the end of these duty hours I felt rather tired and had backache. Then I found I was in the middle of the night shift and it was even busier so that I was typing continuously and began to make errors. We had a different NCO on duty and she noticed this but said nothing, for which I was grateful.

A few weeks went by and I was granted leave. By then the air raids were becoming a nuisance and interrupted the train services, for when enemy bombers were overhead the trains stopped. I told my parents I was on secret work involving what I had learned so they asked no questions but were glad to hear I was happy and interested in my work. I never heard from Heinz again and was told by a friend that he had been sent to the Russian Front and had had a bad time.

Back at work I found that two more girls had joined us so we were very well staffed. One of the newcomers was called Lisa and also from Berlin, so we became firm friends and often went for walks together in the country when we had the time. She was a well educated, sensitive girl and I believe a little upset by some of the things she heard over the radio. One did tend to become rather involved in a sense, after all; even though one was listening in to the enemy they were young men and human beings and we could not help feeling sorry for them when they were in trouble, and they often were.

Our work was continuous and rather a strain mentally and physically, and I found it a good idea to snatch sleep whenever I could, as did the other girls. But it continued to prove very interesting to me as we got through 1942 and the war did not look like ending in our favour, especially as America had come into it. It was in that summer of '42 that we received special instructions to listen out for Yankee bomber crews and anything that sounded like American air operations. Our radio sets were recalibrated and we did our best and one or two girls did begin to receive a lot of American chatter which was on another frequency and very voluble. It was not easy to follow, I believe, because of the new accents, but once attuned to it we began to get results.

Then one day we received a visit from a high ranking officer connected with intelligence matters; he was accompanied by other officers including a woman and they told us how important our work was as everything we heard and recorded helped them to piece together a great deal concerning the enemy's order of battle, of units and personnel which could be especially useful in PoW interrogation. He made quite a speech and seemed to really appreciate what we were doing.

I myself continued to listen to the RAF frequencies and now received another girl tuned to a similar wavelength. Great care was taken to see that we did not duplicate messages; that would have been wasteful. Over the next few months into 1943 a big increase occurred in the air war which kept us all very busy indeed; I must have taken down thousands of messages.

One evening I heard a lot of chatter as the RAF bombers were taking off and circling over eastern England before setting out over the sea for Germany, and there were the usual difficulties with some crews calling that they had problems. I heard one pilot call, 'Can't you see I'm bloody well on fire you clot – get us down will you?' I don't know what happened to him.

Another time a Canadian was in a panic as his undercarriage would not go up or something, and he had a full bomb load. He called out, 'I'm not coming in again with all this f— —-g lot on board you bastards. I'm gonna drop this lot in the drink!' Another voice began singing the popular song called 'Marta', and in fact we often heard the men singing which was very amusing, and I did not know at first whether to type all this down or not, and the NCO said of course not but try to learn the words, you might learn from it! Some of the songs were not of the BBC variety, shall we say, although we did hear a lot of the latest popular tunes as the airmen sang or hummed them and forgot to switch off their transmitters which would bring them a lot of 'flak' from other airmen all over the place. They sang dirty songs at times just as troops do everywhere, including our own people, and all this came over the air. Of course these RAF men had I'm sure been warned that the Germans were listening in and should have been much more careful than they were. But on the whole it was fairly harmless, though our intelligence people may have got a lot more out of it than we did.

I remember hearing one boy calling out that he was lost and could not see the beacon; could they give him a fix? He called several times and the controller told him to wait as he had more urgent business. I wondered what became of that lad. Then I heard an extraordinary encounter which our NCO had told us especially to listen out for.

It was a German voice butting in on the RAF transmissions giving them counter-orders, and this was very startling. Unfortunately the German's accent was not very good and I think they soon 'rumbled' him, but he must have caused a little confusion at first. I know the RAF became rather expert at this radio game, but I was not involved in the night fighter frequencies.

One day I was listening when it was fairly quiet as there was a lot of bad weather about; then the set came alive and I heard a very faint voice calling 'Mayday! Mayday!', but the rest was indecipherable. The call was repeated many times and then faded away. It was very eerie and I wondered how many had lost their lives.

Sometimes we heard other airmen on the wrong wavelength, and even German air crew whose sets were 'out of line', and this brought problems as it interfered with our watch and could not at once be rectified. When the voice was in English we took it all down, as it could be a fighter pilot and it was all useful. But sometimes the transmissions were so brief that it was impossible to catch and interpret them, almost as if a fault was cutting the words short. I remember one night when there was a lot of this and I asked for my set to be checked while the NCO used my earphones, but there was nothing we could do. Then on other occasions owing to weather conditions we heard voices that had nothing to do with air operations speaking on various topics, and this too was diverting and annoying as they were not the kind of things we wanted to hear.

In 1944 the volume of traffic became so great that our staff was doubled, but not all the newcomers were good enough and the NCOs became angry at the inexplicable drivel that sometimes resulted. Some of the new girls had been hurriedly trained and just could not cope with the rapidity and volume of the transmissions. In fact they sometimes just gave up, slumping over their tables with their heads in their hands; but most were very efficient and carried on in a very tiring job.

When the Allies advanced across France to our border we had to pack everything up and move back a little way, and by then we were picking up extra transmissions from much closer at hand and it all began to get very difficult. In fact we were now receiving interference from ground stations based in France and Belgium which blanketed out a lot of our reception. We had to do something to improve matters, and were just beginning to have some success when we had to pack up and move again across the Ruhr. By then I was feeling rather worn out and sick of the war, as I suspect many of us were; but we carried on to the end, though the whole effort had become rather futile.

I can remember the last day we operated as a radio listening post. It was in April 1945 and we were still watching the enemy's bomber transmissions, but to little effect as the whole system was collapsing about us. All our intelligence files were being destroyed or removed to secret locations and we felt the end was near. Then we heard of Hitler's death and someone, I'm not sure who, gave a cheer. No one said anything at all.

Then we were ordered to pack up everything and some Luftwaffe men came in and smashed up all the radios. Then we ate a good meal and paraded outside the camp just in time to see the American tanks coming into sight. I was put into a PoW camp with the rest until the females were moved to a barracks and locked up. Much later we were released and dressed in oddments. I tried to get home. My parents had remained in a shelter in Berlin but I had no wish to try and enter the Russian zone. So I stayed for some months at various addresses using odd rooms in old barracks, doing odd jobs and living on small rations before I finally obtained a permit to enter the Soviet zone to look for my home and parents.

When I arrived back in Berlin I was surprised at how much was still standing, but our shop had been smashed and looted. I found a neighbour who told me that my parents were safe but living with a relative. It took me a while to find them for a brief reunion as I had no pass to stay on in East Berlin. It took some years to get my parents into West Germany. Until then I worked as a typist and managed to send them food parcels and other goodies.**

CHAPTER 12

Reinhardt Fuschler

A generation of air-minded youth was again rekindled in Germany in the late 1920s, but especially came to life in the succeeding decade when Hitler removed all the stops to building a new air force.

The Nationalsozialistisches Flieger Korps, or NSFK, had its origins in the so-called 'aviator storm units' prior to 1933 when certain SA and SS men began their paramilitary activities and managed to acquire both airfields and equipment. Yet despite this early start there came no formal building of these units into a larger national structure until 1937, which is perhaps surprising in view of the great zeal of those Nazis and enthusiastic aviation officials whose sole desire was to create a powerful new air arm. Not only guidance and training but the need to infuse and indoctrinate a new generation of German youth into nationalistic air-mindedness had to be realised, yet the official birth of the Luftwaffe in 1935 does not appear to have been matched by the setting up of a really comprehensive air cadet organisation. In passing it can be mentioned that in Britain such a need was not to be fulfilled until well after war began with the setting up of the Air Training Corps in February 1941.

It is perfectly possible to have a deep interest in aviation, or, to be more specific, flying machines, and yet evince little desire to fly them. If this were not so then many fine designers and engineers would never have come to the fore as they did in sufficient numbers over fifty years ago. And by 1940 thousands of boys across the world, but especially among the warring nations, had taken up the hobby of building model aircraft, which for many was the first step towards enrolling in a junior air organisation and learning how to maintain or fly the real thing.

In Germany the NSFK make a late start and first came to the fore in the 'Round Germany Air Race' of 1938 when 390 of its planes containing 780 of its members took part, a number of them air force veterans and even World War I aces. Some mystery attends this event, as one report suggests that it was begun with a fanfare by Göring who was Reichsminister for Aviation but ended in silence before the full course was flown.

The NSFK was a rather exclusive organisation since its voluntary members were not permitted to belong to any other Nazi group, even though they were permitted to recruit 'aiding members', anyone who was willing to promote air-mindedness and could contribute one Reichsmark or more per month as subscription. The Korps promoted everything to do with aviation including gliding and other air sports, model making, the building and flying of planes and ballooning. Like the other Nazi organisations it had its own distinctive uniform and rank system, and awarded badges for achievement in gliding and ballooning. Similarly, its structure was based on groups, 'standards' and 'storms', each unit corresponding with the various Party districts as well as the territories of the Hitler Youth, which came to rely heavily on the NSFK for all aviation activities. The NSFK introduced Reich schools for every facet of air training and indoctrination. By 1938 80,000 boys of the Hitler Youth were receiving such training, including instruction at the 4,000 glider schools in Germany. Naturally, when war came its services were in even greater demand.

The Luftwaffe was primarily a tactical air force, which meant that it was very much tied to the Army, and since that force was trained in mobile warfare its air arm had likewise to be capable of a rapid change of bases. This mobility was fully tested during the campaign in the west in 1940 when the air force units were obliged to keep moving forward in the wake of the advancing troops.

Following the collapse in France and a rather idyllic interval the air fleets were regrouped to deploy for the Kanalkampf (Channel battle), as the Germans called it. But flying continued even during the respite between combat and this always entailed work for the ground crews, many employed in the maintenance of the Messerschmitt 109E fighters, with a lesser number cosseting the larger, more cumbersome Me 110 which was soon to be discredited in the battle.

The Messerschmitt 109 always enjoyed a superiority over the Hurricane in terms of speed and weight of fire, yet in the right hands the rugged British fighter could and did destroy its opponent. The Messerschmitt was a quality production, well designed and manufactured with a proven engine by the renowned firm of Daimler Benz. Yet, surprisingly, production of the type was comparatively slow, its assembly at Augsburg being based almost on 'family firm' methods which relied on craftsmanship and quality rather than mass production methods. It was well into the war before a shake-up produced a leap in turn-out. It had been Herman Göring's task as economic supremo to boost war production, and in this he proved a failure. It is extraordinary that in Albert Speer, ostensibly Hitler's only favourite architect, that a genius emerged capable of pushing German aircraft and all other production to far greater heights than before.

The Luftwaffe ground crews were dubbed 'schwarze männer' ('black men') on account of the regulation black overalls they were issued with, though these were often superseded by work clothes of other hues, or even far more informal wear when in hot climates. Inevitably, over the years the ground teams got to know many young fighter pilots whose machines they watched over, and in most cases would see many come and go, killed, wounded or missing. By 1944 the American P-51 Mustang had begun to spell the death knell of the Luftwaffe's fighter arm as it ranged far and wide over the Reich. The attrition caused in air combat drained away the average German pilots so that towards the end there were only a small handful of experts left poorly aided by a few hundred learners, all of them increasingly grounded by lack of fuel.

Men like Reinhardt Fuschler enjoyed a comparatively easy war in the West, until, that is, the eruption of constant Allied air attack on the Luftwaffe's bases. The Me 109 'Emils' and 'Gustavs' (109E and G models) were comparatively easy planes to maintain, the ground crew work falling into three categories: engine, airframe and armament. There were no complex electronics as in modern-day aircraft. An increasing weight of armour plate was compensated for by uprating the Daimler Benz motor, and changing this would have been the only lengthy operation, while the simplest was perhaps painting victory bars on the tail fin. The learning of new modifications was done 'on site', but some units converted to the more formidable Focke-Wulf 190, so this involved lengthier instruction.

"I can remember the end of the first war. I was a small boy of three and my father came home from the factory in Essen in a black mood. It was all over, he told us, a terrible war had been fought and lost. What would become of us? Over the next months and years we suffered a great lack of nourishment as the food was so hard to find and the money no good. We had been one of the leading manufacturers in the world, and now we were, it seemed, destitute.

When I was a little older I saw some French troops marching about and some of our youths making rude faces at them, so the Frenchmen grew very angry and chased them. This was a fairly common event, and later on we saw the first Nazis in their grey and brown suits waving flags and shouting slogans. I did not understand at all as I was too young.

I had two sisters and one brother who was just younger than myself and called Lothar; my sisters were Magda and Gerti, as we called her. My parents were good, hard working people, my father engaged in the armaments industry, I'm sorry to say, but at least he was never out of work for long! Some factories were dismantled and taken away by the French, but most firms in Essen survived and when the war ended they went over to making other things. But when the economic situation grew worse some were obliged to close down. This was a very bad time though my father was lucky as his firm stayed open though some men lost their jobs. The factory went over to making saucepans and that kind of thing.

At school I was always hungry. But things improved and my brother was able to learn a little running errands all over the town while I went on to high school. I had a great interest in technical subjects in general. My mother was not very well; it had been very hard on the women in those years of the war and afterwards. My sisters grew up and eventually found jobs in the factories as they reopened and took on staff. I became very interested in aeronautical engineering but could only advance myself in this subject by leaving home and attending a college elsewhere, and I did not want to do this. So I went into a routine office job with dull paper work connected with accounts and records.

The depression was very bad and another blow, but it was then that my big chance came as I sought to further my ambitions. It looked like a golden opportunity. I had heard that the new and vociferous Nazis were looking for young men of suitable qualification to join technical units including aviation. A friend told me that if I went to the local Nazi Party offices I could find out more. So I did this and was told yes, I could enrol as a technical assistant in the Party's new air arm, such as it was, and learn all about the maintenance of aircraft. I was very excited, though a little puzzled as to how this could be possible as at the time, around 1930, Germany had no air force, though there were civil planes flying as airliners and mail carriers in a small way; there were also some glider clubs. But these Nazis were a political party who had already failed badly in Bavaria, so I had heard, and were not in charge of the nation's affairs, so naturally I wondered how they could have any kind of 'air arm'. In fact, when I asked about this I was told that it was a kind of non-military club of some kind. You must understand that in those days the laws were very lax and the various political parties were allowed to wear uniforms if they wished, and in the Nazis' case they also had arms and the government, Army and police turned a blind eye to it, and in fact saw the Nazis as a kind of buffer against the Reds.

I was told to report back later in the week for an interview and to take a suitcase as it would mean going away to school. I told them I did not want to go away but they replied that it was the only way. So I went home and discussed it with my parents and they wanted to know about wages and I told them I had forgotten to ask! They told me I was silly and I should go back and find out so I did. At the Party office they laughed at me and told me that I would be well looked after with food and board. I was satisfied and a few days later returned to the Party offices with my bag packed and ready for the great adventure. I joined some others and we were taken by car out of town to an aerodrome where we found some planes carrying civil registrations. There were huts and people about and one of these was introduced to us as our instructor. He was in fact, like all of them, a member of the NSFK. I had never heard of these people before but I learned later that it was early days for them and that their whole aim was to create a national socialist air force and we few were, shall we say, in on the ground floor. I was soon to learn that there existed a widespread organisation with officers and men, many of whom had been in the old Flieger Abteilungen of the great war.

I was not given any uniform, only a stickpin badge – NSFK. I was shown into a room in a hut with another boy and told that we would be required to attend lectures on aircraft as well as receive practical instruction on plane maintenance. There was a mess for meals and we would also have to undertake a small amount of military training to get us used to discipline, though no arms would be issued. I found there were about twenty youths in this 'course', which was very interesting. I learned a very great deal and was able to go home to see my parents at weekends.

During the following weeks we were shown various small aircraft and given certain tasks and test to assess our progress. I seemed to have a natural aptitude for all this and did very well. And then one day we received a big surprise – a visit from Göring himself. He was not actually in command of the NSFK but having been an airman and air ace in the war we were very impressed, though not by his appearance I may say: he was like a big, fat, overgrown schoolboy, but full of enthusiasm with strong words of encouragement and you could not help liking the man. He inspected the school, ourselves and the planes and told us of his experiences in the war and how he had loved it all.

I am not sure how long that course lasted but it was very thorough as the people in charge were professionals and knew their stuff. The Nazi Party was now in the ascendant and eventually Hitler came to power by which time I had long finished my course and passed out with flying colours. I had also at last received a very smart uniform complete with pillbox cap and swastika armband. I was not too happy about the last part but it was part of the uniform and I had to wear it on occasions, though when at home I wore civilian clothes. I was now an NCO, though in those Nazi organisations they had their own rank systems which were very confusing.

Not long after the Nazis came to power we were called together and told that a regular air force was being organised and had been for some time and that all who wished could transfer to it, though it would be a little time before it became official. In other words, the new 'Luftwaffe' was still secret and we now had the chance to get into it as officers if we wished. It was a little confusing as we knew so little about it or the equipment we would be given. I was quite happy to enter this clandestine air force owing to my great passion for the flying machines, though I had no great desire to pilot them, even though by then we had all taken a few flights in small aircraft which I had enjoyed, though I was still more interested in them on the technical side.

I was one of those who agreed to go over to the air force, even though the NSFK would continue to provide a grounding for the air-minded youth and especially the Hitlerjugend on the gliding side of things. I was especially interested in the design of aircraft and their engines, though the latter were not my forte, so to speak.

It was in the summer of 1934 that our CO sent for several of the men including myself; he told us that we would be transferred into a Luftwaffe unit as from that day. In fact, we *were* the unit! We were given fresh uniforms which had only just been made and flown off to another aerodrome where we met the man who was to command us as a unit of the new air force. He told us that we were a fledgling unit of the new fighter arm, we had no staff or planes but these would be forthcoming, and that in the meantime we must work hard to try and get things organised. From that day I was no longer a part-time airman but a member of a regular air force yet to become known to the outside world. We were all rather excited at the responsibility of it all; we had no real military experience so did not quite know how to begin. But our CO was a war veteran and had drawn up a table of organisation which I suppose had been approved as standard. We would receive three fighter squadrons in due course, but not until we were ready for them. It meant having to organise their accommodation and messes etc, but we had no experience of such things to help us; but there were two very good NCOs who had, it seemed, been through it all, so with their help we began to make progress.

All the equipment for this venture and many others was of course funded by the Nazi Party, which had taken over the Government and Treasury, so there were no problems in that direction. Göring himself was our enthusiastic mentor so anything we needed he saw to it that we received – we had only to ask.

But it took some weeks before we were in any way recognisable as a military airfield, and then the planes, pilots, and other personnel began to arrive. The machines were Heinkel 51 biplanes plus a few other types, and within a few months (in 1935) we began to receive recruits who knew nothing whatsoever about planes but were keen to learn. I was now a sergeant, which was the equivalent of my old NSFK rank, and made an instructor and obliged to try and teach all the newcomers all I had learnt about aircraft design and maintenance. In fact I was still learning myself, especially on some of the aircraft which were quite unfamiliar to me. We had no proper technical school in the Luftwaffe at that time, so we had to improvise and learn our trades as we went along. I was not by profession a tutor so I had to do my best, and I must say I found it very interesting.

My parents were full of questions but I think quite proud of their son, as were the rest of the family. I was quite passionate about planes and had no time for anything else; even when I was not actually instructing I was thinking about the subject and how best to formulate my lessons. We were inspected by our CO regularly and he seemed well satisfied with our progress.

As more pilots came to us from the training schools we were able to form our squadrons, but it was not until 1936 that we were fully up to our planned strength of three complete fighter units. In those days, when the organisation was new, the rules of air safety had not been properly formulated so inevitably there were some crashes, some on our field and some elsewhere. Planes would go missing and eventually we would receive a call from the police or someone that there was a wreck to be collected. I myself had to take charge of this business of wreck recovery on occasions; we had been provided with a truck fitted with a small crane for the work and I had four men to assist me. I was not of course the only NCO assigned to such duties; there were others and we had a rota system. I recall one of those jobs very well.

We received word concerning one of our planes that had come down near a farmhouse not far away in the country. We had trouble finding the location but did so eventually. The farmer was very angry because the biplane had smashed his chicken houses, but I was more concerned for the pilot, a young man with a broken neck. He had already been taken to hospital but died later. Our job was to try and dismantle the wreck and remove it from the farmer's premises, but our truck was too small. In those days we were not properly equipped for such work so all we could do was remove the wings and wait for a larger vehicle to remove the pieces later.

There were many crashes both slight and bad on the field as our pilots trained, and some were very distressing, though we did become used to it. I saw one small plane crash into a fighter on the ground, a fire followed and a pilot was killed. I was not on duty but there came other occasions when I was on the spot and was obliged to try and help rescue the pilot.

One fighter came in too fast and tipped over its nose so that the pilot hung upside down in his cockpit. The plane caught fire at once and he was burnt alive. That, I'm afraid, was one of my duty days and I was sick afterwards. We had no proper fire fighting equipment at first so had to improvise in that too, but I'm glad to say that things improved a great deal later on.

By 1938 we were a fully-fledged unit and I suppose ready for war, though looking back on those days it all seemed to come about in a terrible and inevitable way and not at all as I had hoped. Keen as I was on those machines, I never thought of it in terms of preparation for war. It may sound crazy but it's true. I was mad about planes, and especially warplanes, yet not interested in fighting and killing; something of a paradox, yet I'm sure others were the same.

When things became serious on the international scene we could see that some of our young pilots might be killed. We were training continuously and had lost the biplanes which were replaced by the very much faster Messerschmitt 109s, though they were tricky to fly. A rota system was introduced with all the NCOs having to go away to a new technical school to learn about this new plane. For this course we were instructed by technicians from the Messerschmitt firm who knew their stuff. Interesting as it was, I preferred the old biplanes.

I saw a lot more crashes before the war started, but it was something we grew used to with such machines and young men who at times were just high spirited and liked to show off in various ways. I remember one young officer who should have known better: he came in low with his wheels up just to show off his flying skill, crashed and ended up hanging from a tree, stone dead, his plane a wreck. The CO was very angry about such things and threatened to court-martial the next pilot who contravened his orders.

When the war came we were sent east into Prussia to an improvised, temporary airfield for operations against the Poles. Our pilots flew continuously but saw very little in the way of enemy aircraft, though one or two were met and quickly shot down as they were very obsolete. Our Messerschmitts were mostly engaged in escorting Stukas and larger bombers. We were kept very busy maintaining the fighters, but there were very few problems as the type was very sound mechanically as well as from the design point of view.

When the campaign ended we were all very jubilant and returned to Germany and some leave. It had been our first experience of war and we had not lost a single pilot so felt very relieved and pleased with ourselves. My parents were also relieved and did not seem to realise that I was never in any danger. We were dismayed when the war went on, but by then I had woken up to what sort of government we had. They were rude in their speeches and dealings with other nations, though I have to say we did not think much of the Poles either.

That winter of 1939–40 was very bad, but we did not suffer too much and I was able to get home every few weeks. In that period we had a kind of rotation system and moved from one airfield to another in West Germany and not far behind the Western Front line. During those winter months we did not see a single enemy aircraft, but things soon hotted up in May when our offensive began. We had been carefully briefed in our role and were organised to move forward at very short notice. So after the attack began we had a few days before our first move, which was across the border into Belgium for a short stay on an airfield, while each day our boys were flying like mad and claiming their first victims in the West. We had one pilot go missing but he soon returned to continue flying. Our next move was to Brussels airport, before we went on again over the border into the French countryside.

When we moved all our trucks were lined up full of men and equipment, which by that time included everything we needed; we even had an armoured car for protection. We also had our fuel wagons, trucks full of spare parts and a control truck with an Army liaison officer. Sometimes we drove for hours through the heat with no idea where we were going, to be suddenly told to turn off into a suitable field to make camp or set up in a French barn. In these weeks I saw the first Tommy prisoners, airmen of the RAF who had not retreated fast enough. We fed them and showed them over our machines before they were taken away. I remember one young fellow, a Hurricane pilot from London, who was very sorry to become a prisoner, but we told him that he would soon be able to return home again!

Those weeks were very hectic and we had our first casualties. One pilot went missing and was never found; another crashed not far from us, and two more were injured in accidents. But overall it was a very great victory, and when at last peace came we were able to relax on the grass of the French countryside for a while. Everyone thought the war was over. The English army had fled back to England and lost all its equipment and we could not see how the war could continue. Hitler visited the troops, though we did not see him ourselves, then he returned to Berlin for the great victory parade so we wondered when we too could go home again. Meantime life was very good to us. I borrowed a bike and went all around the countryside and found a farmer happy to let us have eggs and vegetables in barter, so all was well with us.

Then to our disappointment we were ordered north. We had been in a field near Arras but now moved to another airfield nearer the coast where our CO told us that as the 'stupid English' had refused to give up the war they would be pursued until they saw sense. He said that they could have had an honourable settlement with us but preferred to engineer their own destruction, which was now certain as they were alone without allies. I had to admit that his opinions did not seem unreasonable. Our new base was at Calais-Marck and we got busy preparing it for operations over the Channel. I realised later that the great day of our air offensive turned into a fiasco, but on 'Adler Tag' we did not know this. I remember that first day seeing the bombers going over and disappearing into the clouds which were rather heavy, but it was a while before things began to really hot up, and we received a steady stream of casualties.

Those summer days of 1940 are a hazy memory; they were all very much the same. Exceptions came when the weather turned bad, but mostly it was fine. We would rise at dawn to begin work in trying to ensure that every available machine was in flying condition, and they mostly were. I remember the young faces of the pilots: they were brimming with confidence and eager to get into the fight with the RAF. Day after day they flew off into the morning sunlight to escort the bombers, and day after day we watched anxiously for their return. On the first day of combat there were strained faces on the ground as we counted them back – there were two missing; one was a sergeant I knew, the other a fairly new youngster and no one knew what had become of them. One or two more Messerschmitts returned holed, but nothing serious.

Around this time we received some reinforcements, three more flights and a new commander, Adolf Galland, whom we had heard of. I had never seen such a character; his cigar was always clamped between his teeth, though I'm sure he was forced to remove it when on oxygen. I never had a chance to speak to him but saw him often and we all knew he was a great leader and an ace of aces. We saw several other young pilots whose scores were climbing, but not all survived.

One day we were waiting for our boys to return when we were raided by RAF Blenheim bombers and we had to run for our lives as the bombs and bullets came down. But since our planes were not there little damage was done. No one was killed but it gave us a big shock, and I know that one or two of those brave Tommies were shot down and many more later. Also in this period we met one or two English pilots who had incautiously chased our Messerschmitts back across the Channel and been shot down. One I recall was a dark haired, short lad who we allowed to sit in the cockpit of one of our Messerschmitts. He seemed very interested but insisted that his Spitfire was better. I had no way of disproving his case, but I know that our boys thought our Me much better.

As the weeks passed it became obvious that the battle could not be won. We lost about half our boys in air combat and more in accidents, and I believe the bomber losses were very heavy. Then the autumn weather came bringing low cloud and rain and we knew that we had reached a stalemate. I had not had any leave at all during the Kanalkampf but was finally able to return to Essen in mid-October to a great homecoming. But as the winter came we wondered what would happen next as the invasion of England was not on. I had more leaves to my home and a really grand Christmas, the last good celebration of the war, a good, festive time with many friends calling but with much uncertainty for the future.

Our unit was then switched back to West Germany and I did not see Galland again as he was promoted to chief of the fighter force. We had a fairly quiet time until the spring of 1941 when the war flared up in Africa and the Balkans, but we did not become involved in the great assault in Russia and felt especially glad about this later on, though we felt that sooner or later we would be sucked into it. In fact we were sent back to Calais-Marck and I saw the first Focke-Wulf fighters, which were very good. But we stayed with our faithful Messerschmitts and moved on west to yet another base; they were all much the same. We seemed to get a lot of windy days along the Channel, and by then the Tommies were coming over regularly and I saw a lot of combats and planes going down – Spitfires, Hurricanes, Blenheims, Bostons, all sorts. We took a few prisoners ourselves because if the enemy planes crashed in our area then we would race to reach the sites before the Army. We were not always successful, but the soldiers had orders to turn over all RAF men to us and they did so. Our usual procedure was to bring survivors back to our base for a meal and sometimes show them around, though on other occasions we did not have the time. They were mostly grand fellows just like our own air crew, and relieved to be alive though not looking forward to the PoW camp. In fact I think they would have preferred to stay with us!

Inevitably some boys of the RAF and later the Allied air forces found their last resting place in France, and occasionally we had the grim and sad task of removing bodies or bits of bodies from the wreckage. The machines themselves had to be salvaged, intact if possible, though quite often there were bits and pieces scattered over a wide area and at times with pieces of bodies still in them. I remember a Wellington bomber that came down one night; we found it the next morning in the rain. The fuselage was mostly intact but the wings and engines torn off. We looked into the cockpit and were surprised to find the pilot, I believe, still sitting in his seat. His eyes were still open and his hands on the controls, but when we climbed inside we found he had been shot dead before coming down. He was the only man in the plane; the rest of the crew had baled out.

We gave them military funerals. Due to conditions later on these sometimes took place on the airfield, otherwise in the nearest village cemetery where we knew the French people put flowers on the graves.

As the war in Russia grew worse and worse, we were very surprised and relieved to be left out of it. Owing to the great losses in the east we always expected to be sent as replacements. But the Allies in the west maintained a heavy pressure which increased by the month so we needed all the planes we could get in France and Belgium, and things became more serious when the Americans began their attacks, though at the start they were quite weak.

I saw some of the first American Forts come over, only a few. They dropped their bombs and the flak caught some of them. We had heard stories of their great firepower and I believe our pilots were a little wary of them at first, but soon began to get the measure of them. So it was not long before we saw the first B-17 on the ground: it was full of bullet holes and some of the engines had been knocked out. We swarmed all over it in great interest and could see that it was very well designed and made. In fact we were amazed at the amount of room in the cockpit. Our technical experts made a very thorough examination and were especially interested in the bombsight, which was undamaged and removed for a closer inspection.

The crew had baled out and miraculously the bomber had landed itself in near intact condition. I did not see these Americans but did meet many later on. In fact it was only a week or two later that the Army brought us the first Yankee prisoners and we fed them briefly and interrogated them before they were sent back to Germany. They looked a little sorry for themselves but quite interested in all they saw. They had a long wait for liberation.

The air war hotted up very considerably, especially by night, and I grew very worried for my family in Essen which was a big target for the RAF. Although the city was full of factories and it was hard to miss all of them, the target was itself, I assume, not easy to find; at least, the bombs fell all over the place. I cannot blame the RAF boys, who were doing their best and doubtless had in mind what our Luftwaffe had done to their own cities. But my parents were right in the middle of a plum war target and I only wished I could get them away. The raids grew steadily worse and the damage in Germany was terrible, but still my parents refused to leave Essen. Both my sisters worked in factories while my brother had entered the Navy and served on a minesweeper. I always listened anxiously to the news bulletins but there seemed nothing I could do.

The big raids on Cologne and later Hamburg shook us terribly. Despite all the Nazi propaganda we knew that catastrophe had fallen on Germany so that all I wished for was an end to it all.

When the invasion finally came we had been reduced by terrible losses, but most of all by shortage of petrol, to a shadow of our former strength. We had been shuttled about over the various bases in northern France, bombed and strafed continuously, never knowing where we would go next. Our families had either been killed or were in great danger, some of our personnel had lost their homes in Germany and relatives, and morale was low. What's more, men were being transferred to the infantry and even the Russian Front. After June 1944 we had trouble getting even ten planes into the air. Our latest Messerschmitts were not much use against the hordes of Allied planes, and a lot of the time the air-fields were unusable.

Until that time I and my comrades had had no trouble with the local popula-tion, who were in the main quite friendly. Of course we knew about the Resistance, but that was a problem that did not usually concern us; nobody attacked us or spat at us. But following the invasion things changed and we could no longer go about outside the bases at all. Everyone had to remain on the field, ready to move at a moment's notice, which of course we did as soon as the

Allies advanced. In fact we retreated right back into Germany and lost more men on the way including, I'm sorry to say, deserters and of course air attack. It was very difficult to move at all by day because of the 'Jabos'* which always seemed to be hovering somewhere in the sky and waiting to pounce on us. I recall one day when we had just crossed over the frontier from Belgium when we were spotted and attacked by Mustangs who shot us up badly. Our CO was killed and most of the vehicles put out of action, and I lay cowering in a ditch until it was safe to emerge. I don't know how we managed to continue as most of us were on foot until we could find some transport.

In any case, it was almost the end for us; our planes were fairly useless, and only the new jets stood a chance of combating the hordes of enemy bombers, but we had none at our new base. It reached the stage where we daily expected to be transferred into the infantry or even the Volkssturm as officers. But the day never came as Germany surrendered, and I became a prisoner of the British.**

*Jagdbomben – fighter-bombers.

CHAPTER 13

Betti Brockhaus

t is an inevitable fact that the most memorable or traumatic events in the lives of my generation took place in World War II, and this is certainly true of Fraulein Betti Brockhaus, whose personal climacteric occurred in the early summer of 1942 when the RAF mounted its first 'thousand-bomber' raid.

Until early 1942 RAF Bomber Command had been attacking Germany with comparatively small forces of bombers, inflicting little more than pinpricks and achieving far less than they or the public at home realised. The fatuous tales concerning Germany's imminent collapse through lack of food and raw materials that were current during the early months of the war had been replaced by Air Ministry propaganda asserting widespread and serious damage to Hitler's Reich through night bombing. The truth was that the secret Butt Report of the summer of 1941 had revealed bombshell findings which stated that most RAF air crews were depositing their bomb loads miles from their target areas: only about one in five crews were scoring damage anywhere near their objectives, even in optimum conditions, which usually meant moonlight; in worse weather the ratio dropped disastrously to one in fifteen. These findings had been carefully arrived at by analysis of reconnaissance photographs, despite the fact that the bomber chiefs through the Air Ministry's publicity machine in London's Kingsway had been claiming by similar pictures quite opposite results. Propaganda photos usually appeared to show bomb strikes on target, or acres of 'de-roofed' buildings.

The shake-up that followed produced Air Marshal Arthur T. Harris, who had been a Bomber Group commander and took over Bomber Command in February 1942. A South African by birth, Harris was a firm believer in the heavy bomber as a war-winning weapon, or at least was an advocate of bombing on such a massive scale by thousands of bombers that the Germans would be forced to negotiate and thus make a bloody invasion of the Continent by Britain unnecessary. In other words, he saw the heavy bomber as a way of saving thousands of lives – in the long run. He knew, as Churchill did, that Britain alone was not strong enough to defeat the Wehrmacht on the Continent. The Americans had come in but were committing much of their power in the Pacific, while in Russia, despite the fact that the German drive had been temporarily checked, the Soviets were in dire trouble.

There were other factors which compounded Britain's great difficulties, and Harris's.

For a start the war of the Atlantic lifelines against the U-boats was a desperate one and, as one admiral said, could cost us the war. The Sea Lords demanded long-range aircraft to help defeat the German 'grey wolves', but these were hard to prise from the Air Ministry in sufficient numbers. Harris was under pressure from this direction, but Britain's position was invidious. In the Middle East German intervention brought crisis after crisis which threatened our vital oil supplies; that theatre was draining off much of our war supplies even though the forces committed by Hitler under General Rommel were comparatively small. Most of our tank production was being shipped to the desert and to Russia. In the Far East British prestige had been shattered by the Japanese invasion and would never be recovered; there the commanders were crying out for men and planes and supplies, all this while the War Cabinet at home felt obliged to maintain a large army, air force and navy against the hugely diminished German threat across the Channel. In fact the desert commanders were starved of modern fighters while hundreds were unemployed in Britain.

Yet ever since the war began it had been Bomber Command that carried the war to the enemy, even if its efforts did seem so puny to the Germans. But now Air Marshal Harris saw only one course open to him if he was to ensure renewed belief and effort in his weapon: he must convince the growing number of doubters that he was right – the RAF had the power and the will to smash Germany, more specifically to destroy every town and city containing some vestige of war industry.

But the slow arrival of scientific aids to help air crew find and pinpoint targets meant that 'area' bombing was forced on Harris in his night operations, and his decision in this had full Air Ministry and War Cabinet backing. After two and a half years of war he still had only a small force of heavy bombers, though his Command included a few squadrons of the new four-engined types, the Stirlings, Halifaxes, and some Lancasters. Above all Harris needed to prove to Prime Minister Churchill that his men could do the job. So within a short time of his taking over the chief's desk at Bomber Command HQ at High Wycombe with his right-hand man Air Vice-Marshal Robert Saundby, he had organised and carried out two raids on Germany which were by far the most telling blows yet struck on Hitler's Third Reich, and heralded a new kind of assault on German cities.

The old and fire-vulnerable town of Lübeck in north-east Germany was razed, the raid swiftly followed by a similar attack on Rostock which housed the Heinkel aircraft works. Both targets had been easy to find as they rested on the northern coastal fringes of Germany. The Germans were shaken by these attacks, yet they were to Harris no more than a token; he needed something really big to achieve his aim, and so the sensational notion of the world's first 'thousand-bomber' raid was born. Yet initially neither Harris nor his deputies could see how such a huge number of bombers could be mustered, so they were forced to try and drum up support from other RAF Commands – Flying Training, Coastal and Army Co-operation. In the event 1,134 planes were assembled to mount the biggest air attack in history, but this included only aircraft from his own units of the Bomber and Flying Training Commands.

Although not in terms of population, Cologne (Köln) was considered Germany's second city, its citizens numbering some 765,000 as compared to Berlin's 4,299,000 and Hamburg's 1,677,000, these figures remaining correct until the cities were disrupted and ruined by air attack, at which time thousands would flee into the safety of the countryside or safer towns and villages throughout Germany. Like many old European cities Cologne contained its old section where the houses were based on wood, and also of course its famous cathedral which was almost one thousand years old. But like many built-up areas it contained its quota of military objectives.

Harris was known to his intimates as 'Bert', later as 'Butch' to his crews, and could be seen as the ideal commander in war who is given an objective and carries through his task with admirable efficiency and with an apparent disregard for casualties. In fact Harris had no such disregard, but like any leader in war felt obliged to stifle his humanistic tendencies and get on with the job since he firmly believed that the sacrifices made would help shorten the war and thus save lives. Now, in May 1942, having gone a long way towards assembling a force large enough, the problem of which target to attack presented itself. Obviously the accentuated problems of navigation brought about (so it seemed) by the inclusion of freshman crews in the force precluded the choice of targets deep inside enemy territory; it had to be a city easily indentifiable, and as often the first and obvious choice lay in Hamburg which could easily be picked out by the few new Pathfinder crews using some of the brand new Gee radar sets. The great seaport lay just across the North Sea in the mouth of the river Elbe.

Yet, as was so often the case, the fate of hundreds, maybe thousands, was decided by the weather, for on Saturday, 30 May, heavy, thunderous clouds extended right across northern Germany and hid Hamburg from view. But there was a good chance that the secondary target, Cologne, would be clear by midnight. So the die was cast, and following his usual morning conference and deliberations Harris stabbed his forefinger on the map and said: 'Thousand planes tonight. Target Cologne.'

It had been a mild, overcast but not unpleasant day in Cologne while by late evening in England the same inclement weather affecting much of northern Germany was causing problems for the RAF bomber bases in the eastern counties. As the bombers took off and climbed away to altitude thick icing forced some crews to turn back, but the great majority made sufficient height and set course for Germany.

The raid has been well documented elsewhere, so only a few general facts need repeating here.

According to the Cologne Police President, the first yellow air raid alert came at 2353 hours, this being followed six minutes later by the red warning, though the city's sirens did not sound until 0017. The first bombs fell at 0047 in what the police report referred to as Cologne's 105th air raid, but which the RAF saw as its 107th. None of the previous attacks had caused any serious damage and life in the city had remained constant. But this warm May night was to prove very different.

By the time the 'all clear' sirens sounded at 0335 hours, a great number of high explosive and incendiary bombs had fallen on the city, recorded by the police as: '864 HE, twenty air mines, around 110,000 incendiaries, causing some 12,000 fires which completely destroyed 3,330 residential buildings, badly damaged 2,090, caused slight damage to 7,420. About 1,505 industrial and commercial firms were put completely out of action, 630 were badly damaged and 425 slightly so, the loss of industrial production varying from fifty to one hundred per cent. A total of 469 people were killed including eighty-five Wehrmacht, Police and civil defence personnel, 5,027 civilians being injured. Over 45,000 people lost their homes.' The Police report stated that no particular aiming point for the raid had been noted as damage was spread right across the city, with some bombers flying over at low level in moonlight, despite the flak barrage, described as 'intense at times'. After a week all tramcar services were still at an almost complete stop, and this fact was noted by some RAF prisoners. Inevitably, water, gas and electricity mains were severed in many places.

During the raid the RAF crews dropped leaflets over the city which compared the gloating of the Nazi Press and radio following the Luftwaffe's attacks on British cities, and in particular the heavy raid on Coventry which destroyed its cathedral, as well as Hitler's threat to erase British cities. And over the following weeks further leaflets were distributed over the Reich assuring the population that over one thousand RAF bombers had indeed attacked Cologne; as Winston Churchill said publicly on 31 May, the raid heralded a new era of air attack on enemy cities. Perhaps surprisingly, the 'Führer communiqué' issued oñ Sunday, 31 May admitted 'great damage', churches, hospitals etc and the civilian population being hit, but claiming that thirty-six bombers had been shot down. In fact, a total of forty-four RAF planes were lost from all the night's operations, or 3.9 per cent of the forces employed.

But within a few days the Germans, noting the world headlines achieved by the great British raid, had begun to issue denials, and to ridicule that any such number of bombers had attacked Cologne (about 910 had actually arrived over the target and bombed). It was claimed that at least half of the attackers had been shot down, but the nervousness, contradictions and lack of co-ordination of the German counter-claims was clear. The evidence was there, not only from the police and citizens of Cologne but also neutral observers, and when, after three days, the Cologne *Times* was able to recommence publishing, it said that those who survived could say farewell to the old city, to 'their Cologne'; the damage was enormous, the traditions and character of the city had gone for ever, which were remarkable admissions in a country dominated by heavy censorship. Yet the Nazi Propaganda Minister himself assessed the German claim of only seventy planes taking part as 'absurd'; he had before him his own city Gauleiter and Police reports which spoke of 'wave after wave' of bombers overflying the city for nearly two hours. Yet Goebbels refused to admit that the British could possibly have mustered as many as a thousand planes, or that it was any more than an isolated attack. But he knew there was no way the Luftwaffe could match such raids, and delivered the opinion that only reprisal attacks on British cultural centres would hurt the enemy. Which is precisely what happened: small terror raids were made on Canterbury and other 'Baedeker' cities.

RAF Bomber Command had put in a great effort to mount the raid; on some stations around two hundred ground crew had worked eighteen-hour days for a week to get every plane possible into the air. In the target area crews saw the great twin spires of Cologne cathedral silhouetted against the great red glow of three huge fires that were visible sixty miles away.

'With the searchlights rising from the fires, it seemed that we were leaving behind us a huge representation of the Japanese banner. Within nine minutes of the coast, we circled to take a last look. The fires then resembled distant volcanoes.' That was how one RAF bomber pilot reported on returning to base, and soon after the Air Ministry claimed that nearly three million square yards of Cologne had been destroyed. This estimate was measured from photographs obtained five days after the raid; the pictures had been impossible to obtain earlier owing to smoke over the city. The Air Ministry also claimed that the photographs also showed that 'there is no absolutely no transport visible: no trains, trams, buses or motor cars.'

The effects of such a raid would soon be spread by word of mouth and letter across Germany; the authorities knew this and took special measures to try and curb the damage to morale with face-saving propaganda. Everyone leaving the city was obliged to sign a declaration to maintain tight lips on what they had seen, but it was a futile gesture.

"I was born in Cologne and had one sister called Carla, but she died young from pneumonia. Then after a few years my father died from a heart condition, an ailment that I also suffered from. My mother was frail and heartbroken.

After I left school, and not being very bright, I found a job in a small draper's shop on the outskirts of the city and this wage helped us to live; my mother was receiving some social welfare payment as a widow. Our home was small and my mother really wanted to move to Düsseldorf where my aunt lived in a large villa, but for various reasons this never happened, partly because the aunt had a husband and two children and I suspect did not really want us there.

Then Hitler came to power and at first nothing much changed. We had seen all the street parades and speechmaking and knew the threat of a Red takeover; I suppose we were relieved that the issue had at last been settled. I had now moved into a better job in a store in Cologne which was a large and beautiful city and I was quite happy there. I had a man friend called Ernst who had been in the SA brownshirts, but he had left the organisation as he no longer cared for them. He had a job as a salesman in the boot and shoe trade and seemed to be doing well.

When the war came in 1939 I was still working in the store and in no danger of being called up for the forces; it would be a long time before women were conscripted in Germany. We were very disappointed by the outbreak of war as we had expected some sort of settlement; I had seen English and French tourists and thought they were very good people. But Hitler had decided otherwise.

The store I worked in sold all sorts of clothing which was good for I was able to buy dresses at a discount, but our imports from France and England had of course been stopped by the war. Then my mother passed away and left me alone in our home, so I felt it perhaps a good idea to get married. I was still young and had a house vacant. But although I liked Ernst very much I did not feel passionate about him so was undecided.

The situation then changed as Ernst was called away into the Army and I saw a lot less of him; in fact he rather left me in the lurch for another woman elsewhere, and we lost touch. I then found I was becoming bored with my life, so I suddenly volunteered for military service. This was rather drastic, and in any case there were very few females in the Wehrmacht at the time, though of course it all changed later. I did not want to join one of the Party organisations as they would have kept me in Cologne, and I longed for a change of scene.

I first visited the Wehrmacht offices in Cologne in about spring 1940, and they seemed surprised as I was perhaps a little older than the usual recruit. In fact they told me that only younger girls with suitable qualifications were being considered and advised me to try the Party offices as they knew I would be accepted. So I was rather disappointed. But I had not left my store job and stayed on working there but kept in mind that I must try to get out into something else. For some reason I was attracted to a life in the military.

But the months went by and after the great news of our victories in France I could see that I had no chance of getting into the forces as the war seemed to be over and we expected thousands to return to civilian life. By 1941 I had grown even more restless and decided to save up for a little holiday. The war had not ended as expected, far from it, and our future looked very uncertain. But I did not take my planned vacation as early in that summer I met a man while out walking by the river who seemed my ideal: he was tall as I was, fair, and in the uniform of an Army captain; he had fought in France and been decorated, and I fell in love with him. It all happened very quickly, and then he was snatched away from me to fight in the invasion of Russia. I received some letters from him and then they stopped and I assumed he must have been killed. He came from the Ruhr but I did not know his family. This was a very sad time for me but I tried to get on with a new life.

The months went by and despite great victories in Russia the war did not end, so I felt it must surely be time for me to try and get into the Wehrmacht again. This time when I visited the offices the officer told me that I could go back later if the situation worsened, or else be given work with the forces but not as a member of them. This puzzled me so I assumed they meant some kind of civilian occupation in the welfare branch. I was in the dark, but interested, so asked them to explain. I learned that it was possible to be employed by the Wehrmacht in that capacity and helping to feed the troops; in other words, as it turned out, helping the cooks in messes and canteens. This, they told me, could mean being directed elsewhere, though it was possible I might get a job locally at one of the bases around Cologne. So I went home to think about it and then decided I would give it a try. But I had my house so decided to let this to a tenant or family, and in fact did so by placing an advertisement in a Cologne newspaper.

I returned to the Wehrmacht offices in the city carrying my packed suitcase as directed and was told that if I returned in an hour or two I would be sent to a post. It was as easy as that. I would of course be fed and given some kind of work clothes, a wage, and, I assumed, accommodation. Although the German forces had their own cooks they also employed some civilian staff who sometimes lived out in their own homes, but some working elsewhere were accommodated in billets.

So I went for a walk and returned later to learn that I would be sent to a Luftwaffe base outside the city at Wahn. I knew of Wahn village near the other side of the river so there was no problem in finding my way there; I had only to take a bus or taxi across the bridge. So they gave me a pass and form to show at Wahn barracks and off I went, excited and wondering what the life would be like. But before I arrived I realised that I need not have rented out my house at all, and wondered if I was making a mistake. However, all turned out for the best.

At Wahn I showed my pass to a soldier on the gate and was shown to the guard room or orderly office where I was told that all civilian workers lived off the camp in billets and that it would not be difficult to find accommodation.

I was told I could leave my bag in the office and was shown to a mess with an NCO in charge; I believe he was a sergeant-major. He was a very jolly man and said he was glad to have me there; in fact he was rather forward and remarked that he liked tall blondes, so I decided I would have to be careful. He explained that he had two messes or canteens to run with about three civilians plus his own men in each. It was, as I said, a Luftwaffe base complete with airfield.

The NCO told me that if I was found competent I could help cook the meals, but that in any case there was always plenty of work to do in preparing it and cleaning up etc. Well, this was a drastic change from my shop job and I did wonder what I had taken on. But I remained quite cheerful and asked where I would live, so he took me to an office and gave me several addresses as well as introducing me to a woman who he said could direct me to a boarding house where some of the workers lived.

Some of the addresses were in Wahn itself, so I decided to try them; I would be expected to start work at 6.30 the next morning, which was very early for me but I didn't complain. When I walked round the addresses there was nobody at home so I had no idea if there were beds vacant or not. Then I went into a little shop opposite the base and got talking to the proprietor who told me that he owned a little cottage which was at the other end of the avenue from the camp in the main part of Wahn village. He told me to take the key, look it over, and if I liked it I could rent it and even take another girl in with me if I cared to. This sounded fine, so off I went into the village and when I found the cottage it turned out to be exactly what I needed as it had all I required – a small living room and bedroom alongside, with a cooker and furniture, though the toilet was in the back garden. I decided to accept it, but perhaps look out for something better later on.

I returned to the base, collected my bag and went to pay some rent to the owner of the cottage, but he told me to leave it for a week to see how I liked it. He was very kind and offered to drop by that evening to see how I had fitted in. I could, he said, buy things I needed in the village and he would be glad to help me in any way. So I felt very pleased, and that evening tried to settle in. It was very quiet in the cottage and I had no radio. But I slept well and was up early next morning to present myself at the base. My new landlord had called and had even brought me some items including a new kettle for the electric stove.

I was at the base promptly at 6.30 and found my new boss at the mess with the rest of the staff who were already preparing breakfast. I was introduced to them all, handed an overall, and my work began. All I had to do as a start was cut a large number of bread slices, and when this was done I was able to sit down and take coffee and a sausage sandwich with the rest of the staff. My boss was from Hanover and a great talker; his name was Karl-Ernst and he claimed to have six children, though he had been away in the air force for many years. He was a jolly type and I enjoyed his company but he was a little too familiar. He liked to put his arms around me and place a kiss on my cheek, and I soon found that he did this to the other women, though everyone seemed to find it good fun.

About an hour after my arrival I saw the men coming in for their breakfast, and soon an officer came in to inspect us and give his approval. Then we had clearing up to do and then another coffee break followed by the main work of the day preparing vegetables and meat for lunch. There were huge sacks and boxes to be emptied, and this work took us all the rest of the morning. I was amazed at the constant gossip and laughter that went on continually among the staff, much of which I could not understand. Most of the staff of civilians I met then and later were 'Colognese'; that means they spoke in local dialects which were not always easy to follow. This may seem strange as I was born in that city, but it was true, I did have trouble understanding them at times, apart from which these simple folk had their own private jokes and business which were not my concern. Even so, I quite enjoyed this drastic change of life and had no regrets.

When we had prepared all the food the cooking began, and my boss showed me which of the ovens and vats were used for the different items, and when dinner time came I was shown how to serve the meals over the counter to the men who came in to queue up, unlike the officers who had their own mess and waiters. As soon as the men had finished we had to clean up the tables and could then eat our own meal in the mess just vacated, and this I enjoyed. We then spent an hour or so washing dishes, after which it was time for a cup of tea during which my boss asked me all sorts of questions about my life. I didn't mind telling him, but not in front of the others; they all sat around listening as if we were all one big happy family. I did not care for this as I felt my affairs were private. This became especially embarrassing when my boss began making jokes about not being married 'at your age'. I grew very red in the face and stammered something about my man friend being an Army officer who had gone missing. This quietened them down at a bit, but the NCO soon began making saucy remarks again, that with my kind of figure I should have no trouble finding a husband, or a man.

But apart from that sort of thing it had not been a bad day and I did not regret the change. We had completed our duties by five o'clock though the boss and his airmen remained of course, so I walked back to my new billet and was glad of a rest. My landlord had brought me a little radio, so that evening I relaxed and listened to it and decided that when the weekend came I would go into Cologne to see one or two friends.

The days that followed were very similar. I heard the planes on the airfield but saw nothing of them as it was not visible from our place of work. Then I received a surprise: I was told by my boss that for the time being I was being transferred to the other airmen's mess not too far away, and a man showed me how to find it. I had to report to the sergeant in charge there and found him a very different fellow, stiff and correct and saying little apart from 'Hallo, you know what to do?', and letting me get on with it. There were two more civilian staff, females, plus an airman cook. The whole atmosphere was different in that kitchen and dictated by the sergeant, who discouraged gossip and laughter. I felt quite happy about this as the other place was a little too easy-going and the sergeant-major much too familiar for me. His staff had all been younger than myself and had a different attitude; in fact at some moments I felt a little old!

So my days were now a little different, though the work was identical, preparing, cooking food and cleaning up. We had one or two air raid alarms as there was a siren on the base but these did not come to anything; though we heard distant gunfire, nothing happened in our area. All this was of course to change greatly.

A few months later in the earlier half of 1942 and after the Russian Front war had come to a stop, we had the terrible big air raid on Cologne. I will not easily forget that night.

I had returned to my cottage as usual after work and had arranged to meet an old friend in Cologne for an evening out. I had changed my clothes and was almost ready to leave when I had a strange feeling; I cannot explain this at all, but it was as if something was telling me to stay home that evening. Or perhaps I should try to put it in ordinary terms: I suddenly felt I could not be bothered to go out, even though I had looked forward to seeing my friend as she was an old colleague from the store and I was anxious to hear all the latest news from her.

It was still fairly early so I sat down to have a cup of tea. There was still plenty of time, and as I had been on my feet all day I thought I needed a rest before going out again. I still had plenty of time in hand before catching the bus into the city.

It is very strange in view of all that happened to me later, but after I had drunk my tea I still did not feel like making the effort to go out, and I was rather puzzled and wondered what my friend would think if I did not turn up. I had arranged to call on her so that we could go out for a drink and a long chat. She was divorced with a little boy, her mother watched over him in the evenings if she went out. I had no telephone so could not contact her, so I remained puzzled as to my best course. Eventually I decided I was being silly so got up to leave, but then another surprising thing happened: my landlord called to see how I was getting on, so I had to let him in and offer him some tea and we sat down to talk. I told him I was quite happy at the base and he said he would call now and then. I could always pay the rent at his shop whenever I felt like it, and if I ever felt lonely I could rely on him to keep me company. He was in fact, I learned, a widower and a very pleasant sort of man but I had no wish to become involved with him. I could see that he was rather lonely and this was embarrassing as I had no wish to offend him as my landlord in case he gave me notice to quit. So I felt rather awkward, but stood up staying I was going into Cologne to meet an old dear friend I had worked with. So my landlord stood up rather quickly to excuse himself, saying that he hoped I would enjoy myself and he would see me again soon.

I then found it was after eight o'clock and suddenly I felt too tired to do anything else at all, but though I had still not decided about my outing I went into the bedroom to lie down for a few moments. I took my shoes off and lay on the bed and must have fallen asleep as I next realised it was quite dark and the air raid sirens were sounding. I got up at once and went into the back garden and saw searchlights and the thud of distant gunfire. So I went indoors to get my coat; I had no air raid shelter but was not worried. When I went outside again I heard people in the street at the front and planes coming over and the guns were now very loud. I knew there were some guns on the airfield and many more around the city, and suddenly the sky was lit up like daylight by huge flashes and the noise grew a lot worse. I went back into my cottage and sat on the little sofa and wondered what I should do. I felt very vulnerable and worried as the noise got worse and worse. I switched off the light to look out of the window and saw lots of twinkling stars which were the shells bursting. The searchlights were all over the sky and the bangs were continuous.

I pulled the curtains again and switched on the light and put the radio on. There seemed to be no programmes that I could get from our own stations, but by twiddling the knob I found some good music from a foreign station so I left it on while I made some coffee. When I had drunk this I tried to lie on the sofa to get some sleep, but my nerves were in such a state that it was impossible. The noise went on and on and I realised it was a very big raid on our city.

I had no idea how long the raid lasted and was just beginning to fall asleep with the radio on when I suddenly realised it had gone much quieter and at last I heard the all-clear sirens. I went outside into the back garden and was amazed at the great glow in the sky and realised that Cologne was on fire. I heard noises in the street, vehicles racing past and men shouting so I went through to the street and saw some policemen riding past on bicycles, and then soldiers and others in vehicles all flying past on their way into the city. My neighbours came out too and remarked how terrible it was that this should happen to their beautiful city and how awful the English were and all sorts of things about our useless air raid defences. I then went inside again for a wash and it became light, and when I went outside again I saw lots of smoke from the city and wondered if I could go into the place to see if my home had been hit. Then I thought of my friend and realised what an amazing escape I had had. This realisation hit me like a bolt from the blue and I sat down at the table in my little kitchen-living room in amazement. I might easily have been killed – and why was it I had not gone out? Was it God stopping me? I was nobody of importance.

I ate some toast and got ready for work, and when I arrived at the base things seemed rather different. Only the sergeant-major was at the first mess and without his staff. He looked rather glum and said that the English swines had ruined the city. He told me that the staff had been delayed and that men had been sent from the base to help clean up the mess, and that I should report to the other mess as usual. There I found the sergeant was not about, but a corporal was at work with one woman helper so I began work. All that day men were coming and going by road and air. We heard all sorts of rumours and the radio bulletins told us that English airmen had laid waste a great city to no good purpose and that reprisals would follow. The corporal was very talkative and told me that he had been out in the city to see his girlfriend and that the damage was terrible. In fact he had been with his lady friend in the city during the raid but, though reluctant to leave her, had been forced to return to duty at Wahn. I was worried about my home so the corporal said I could leave early that afternoon but that he doubted if I would be allowed into the city without special permission. Later on his officer told me that military squads were being rushed in from all over Germany to assist in clearing the ruins, and he did not think I would even be allowed over the river, but changed his tune when he heard my home was in the city. Then he told me that he had to go into Cologne with some men to assist so I was welcome to go along with them, so I simply stayed in his car as we crossed the Hohenzollern bridge, and then I had to get out.

I saw all sorts of gaps beside the river where previously buildings had stood and there was a terrible smell everywhere though the fires, I believe, were almost out. But as soon as I got out of the officer's car I saw an appalling mess. There were lots of people trying to make their way through the streets, which in some cases were just rubble. There were lots of men in uniform and civilians helping to clear paths in all directions, and of course police everywhere. There were fire engines and Army vehicles and some from the Air Force, ambulances, and all of the walls still standing were blackened by fire. There were people standing about outside some of the houses and buildings while others were searching in the rubble.

I tried to make my way along a well known street but it was blocked by debris and police and it took many diversions before I could finally reach the area of my home. And when I arrived I found the street mostly in ruins. There were people going about with carts and vehicles full of possessions, and as I walked along the road I began to think that perhaps my house was intact, but as I drew nearer I was shocked to find that it was almost totally destroyed. It is a horrible feeling to see the house you know so well in ruins. All your private memories are shattered, they seem broken open to the whole world and I felt I wanted to rush into the ruins to cover it all up; I was always like that about my privacy. I could not see how it could have happened to me, as if I had suddenly been spot-lighted in front of everyone. It sounds very silly, but that is how I felt.

No one took any notice of me; they all had their own private grief and worries as most of the street was in ruins and some of the houses had simply vanished. I was so shaken I did not know what to do, but I finally forced myself to climb into the ruins. I could hardly believe that these walls had once been part of my home. Of course then I wondered what had happened to my tenants, and I must admit that for a while I had almost forgotten them, which seems very callous. I had no idea where to look for these people, a small family, the husband with his work in the city, his wife and two small sons. I became terrified in case they were lying in the ruins so I walked around and over the heaps of debris looking for clues. There was so little to be seen, just bricks and dust and plaster, a few broken pictures and bits of furniture, glass, but no sign of fire. I thought, is it possible they are under all this?

I wanted to ask the police and ARP people if they knew anything, but could see no one about in authority. I walked up and down the street as far as I could but saw no one I recognised. I saw people crying and being consoled or getting into cars and trucks and leaving with small possessions. The only thing I could think of was to try and telephone my tenant at his work, but with so much damage it was impossible to find a telephone and his work place was probably in ruins anyway. Although I had the address the city was in such chaos I never thought I would find it. Then I suddenly realised that I had yet to find my friend to see if she was safe, so I set off at once as best I could towards her address.

I decided to try and find the store in case my friend had managed to get to work, but had great difficulty in crossing the city at all because of streets blocked off and police controls. But after a lot of walking and stumbling about I at last managed to find my old place of work – it was partly intact but had been burned. There was no one about but one policeman, and he knew nothing so I decided to try and find a telephone. But the policeman said this was impossible at the moment and told me that if I wanted to return home across the river then I had better do so before it got dark. I felt this was good advice, and also felt my landlord might be able to help as he had a telephone.

So I started off back to Wahn, and this journey, which would normally have taken only a few minutes, took me three hours. There was no transport at all and the ruins and police blocks made progress very slow. But at last I had reached the bridge, and once over the river started walking to the village. I had some luck, however, as a truck full of Luftwaffe men gave me a lift, but I felt very embarrassed climbing up into the back with all of the men cheering and laughing at me. I soon arrived back at Wahn where I found my landlord had closed up his shop for the day; he soon opened up to my knocking and agreed to let me use his telephone. But though I tried several times to get through to my friend and also my tenant I failed, so at last I returned to my cottage and went to bed feeling very worried.

Over the next few days I carried on working at the base but had some time off at the weekend and went into the city again and found things rather easier as the streets had been cleared of rubble. I found my old street but there was no one about, so I went to the store again but saw only a sign that it was closed until further notice. I next decided to try to reach my friend's house and on doing so was relieved to find it intact; her mother was there and told me that all was well: her daughter was out trying to trace some of her own friends but had left a note that she was safe.

I then went back into the city centre to try and find my tenant's work place, but found the area cordoned off because of dangerous buildings or unexploded bombs, so I was again frustrated. I thought I had better go to the police to try and find out something, and when I reached police headquarters I found it too was heavily damaged and they were using only part of the building. Eventually I found a man who would look through the casualty lists and those missing for me and I was very relieved when he returned to say he could find no trace of my tenants. But I was still puzzled as to what could have happened to them, and I returned to Wahn.

But about two days later I received quite a long letter from the tenant telling me he was very sorry the house had been destroyed but that in the circumstances he could not pay me any more rent! He had in fact written from the home of a relative in Düsseldorf where he had taken his family in a great hurry as the raid began. He considered them to be very lucky. But his new address was hit by a fire bomb a year later and burnt out; I believe the family survived, but I never heard from them again.

I had lost my home and did not receive any compensation so was quite poor as a result; the house had been my insurance. I was very depressed but carried on working at the Wahn base, and in 1943 the war news got worse and worse as did the air raids. There were so many on Cologne, but by some miracle my friend survived them all though one of my distant relatives died in one of them. Yet the famous old cathedral survived, and this seemed a miracle as it was surrounded by ruins.

A very great sadness came over everyone after the Stalingrad disaster, and I don't think anyone thought the war could possibly be won. I had never taken an interest in politics until it began to affect my life, and of course by 1943 everyone was in the war, so to speak, what with the rationing, air raids and terrible casualties. Then all the younger women had to join the Wehrmacht or do something for the war effort. I was registered but considered well employed in the service of our country, so it seemed I would not be sent into the forces, for which I was a little old, even in my early thirties.

The mess sergeant was sent elsewhere but the sergeant-major remained but became a lot less jolly as the war became worse, though he was never short of opinions as to what should be done. The sergeant in my mess was replaced by his corporal, and the women replaced by older staff. Things became very scarce as the quantity and quality of supplies became worse; all we seemed to get was potatoes, bread, sausage and cabbage, but the troops never went hungry, though we ourselves did not do too well. The inspections became a lot more rigorous as there was constant drive to prevent black marketeering and the siphoning off of military supplies for civilian use. We even had the Cologne Gestapo visit us one day concerning some profiteering scandal, but though we were questioned we knew nothing.

By 1944 we knew the war was lost and it was only a matter of time before the Allies entered Germany. But after our big offensive in Christmas 1944 we hoped that some miracle might save us from occupation. Everyone began taking a lot more interest in the war maps to see how far the Allies and Russians had advanced. We never thought the Reds would get as far as our city, and the very idea of it terrified me.

During all this time my landlord had continued to be very nice to me but had realised that I was not 'available' for him other than as a tenant. I had met a junior Luftwaffe officer at Wahn, which was quite convenient as he was able to take me home in his little car and even call now and again, and we became very friendly. His home was in the Ruhr and his parents were bombed out so they now lived in the country. I liked him quite a lot though without any romantic attachment; in fact he had an English name – John. I think he was just glad to get some female company, so he used to pick me up at the cottage in his car and we would go into the city for a drink and a meal, but this became increasingly difficult because of the air raids churning up what little remained of the place. In fact it became pointless to go into Cologne at all, so we began taking small meals at my cottage and listening to the radio to try and cheer ourselves up. We used to sit and talk and talk over a glass of schnapps and wonder what things would be like under occupation.

Then came the day when the ground fighting reached Cologne. We were very worried and were told to stay away from Wahn base. This only happened at the very last minute when shells began arriving from the west, and we heard all sorts of firing. I stayed in my cottage and hoped for the best and at last knew that it was all over. There had been a lot of heavy firing and explosions from the city and I wondered how much longer it could last. A lot of American planes flew over at a very low level, and every time I looked out of the window I could see them.

Then it grew very quiet and I heard a lot of noisy vehicles rushing past, and when I glanced out of my bedroom window at the side of the cottage I saw American soldiers standing about in the street and tanks and all sorts of other vehicles passing by.

I had discovered earlier that I had a weak heart. This happened when I went to the doctor concerning some small sickness and he advised me not to get over-excited or to exert myself. Well, these were not only exciting times for us but very stressful. I tried to remain calm and expected a knock at the door or even shots but nothing happened; no soldiers came and I then thought of one close neighbour who had been in the SS. Would they come for him?

Then I put my coat on as it seemed very quiet again. I went into the street and looked up towards the centre of the village and saw an American tank with some soldiers on guard, but looking the other way I saw nothing. So I went indoors again and tried to make some coffee, but there was no electricity so I made do with cold milk. I was not sure what to do as I had been used to eating meals at the base. I had very little food in the cottage but did not care to go out because of the American soldiers in the village.

Then I heard a knock at the door and felt terrified, but when I dared to open it I found the landlord there and was very glad to see him. He came inside and told me that he had been very worried about me and had brought me some things to eat. I was very grateful and asked him about the situation.

He said the Americans had taken over the base and were everywhere but seemed quite friendly so I was not to worry. He advised me to visit the base to see if any food was available, or at least to find out the situation. I was worried about this but he said he would be glad to go with me; he had some supplies in his shop and would be happy to share them with me.

Well, we walked into the village centre and right past the Americans who took little notice of us, then on up the long straight road to the base where we saw more Americans with cars. My landlord took my arm and walked us right up to them. I was very nervous and a sergeant asked us what we wanted in bad German and my landlord said: 'This lady worked on the base and would like to see if she can get some food.' The sergeant said he did not think so but went off into the guardroom and then returned to ask me a few questions which I did not really understand properly. But he sent us inside to my place of work and warned us to get out quickly afterwards.

So we went into the mess and there was the sergeant-major looking very unhappy with Americans sitting around drinking coffee and smoking. When they saw me they started calling and laughing and even threw me some chocolate and cigarettes. I believe some also made suggestive remarks. I asked the sergeant-major if he had any food so he told me to help myself: 'I'm no longer in charge here.' There were the usual sacks of vegetables and some stale bread, so I made up a parcel in a bag and left at once.

Somehow I managed to live with my landlord's help, but they were very difficult days. I had a surprise visit from my friend in Cologne and she brought me a few things but told me it was very hard to get anything in the city, though the Americans were bringing in supplies and things were expected to improve. This situation went on for a while, but eventually the Americans left as it was to become part of the British zone, and I remember the day they came.

I was taking a walk in Wahn village when some strange vehicles came by which I knew were not American as they had the RAF roundels on them with airmen and airwomen in trucks and cars. I had never seen any Allied servicewomen before and was very interested. I walked up to the base and at the gates saw an RAF man dressed like a soldier with a rifle; he wore a blue-grey beret and gaiters and looked smart. I went into my landlord's shop to see if he knew anything, and he told me that he had already spoken to the gate guard and that the RAF had taken over the base but that there were very few troops left in Cologne itself.

I then had the crazy idea that I might be able to return to my old job – even with the enemy! But I did not know what to do about it. There was no work in the city, which seemed full of wandering people and ex-soldiers and black marketeers. A lot of people now walked or stood around in dark places trying to sell or barter all the time, but I myself had nothing to use in that fashion to try and raise money. My landlord said that some sort of official rationing system was being organised, but meantime it was up to us to try and get on our feet again.

I told the landlord that I would like to work on the base again; if the English were going to remain there they would need meals, and though they must have their own cooks they might need some help. He said yes, and why not. And right there and then he took me outside across the road up to this young RAF guard and told him we wanted to see his officer! I was so nervous and thought he was being very silly. The guard just jerked his thumb towards the guardroom, which of course I knew well enough, so we went to the window and saw men inide with white caps who asked us what we wanted. So my friend told them that I used to work on the camp as a cook; was it possible for me to return? I thought he had a terrible nerve, and in any case the policemen did not seem to know what he was talking about. They went away and came back with an older woman who I recognised as from the village, so I supposed she was doing the cleaning or something. When she heard what we wanted she said 'Ach so!', and was able to my surprise to translate into English. I knew a little of the language but could not really understand what the men were saying, but they said it was too early to say who they would need but I could try again later.

Some weeks went by and one morning my landlord called again to tell me he had good news. The RAF were taking on a few German workers but they had to be vetted, but if 'OK' (as he put it) then they were taken on at a reasonable wage. A few Germans had already started work doing odd jobs such as tending to the boilers etc; all I had to do was ask again at the guardroom and fill in an application. I did so the next day, and when I called back a week later they told me I could start work at the mess under RAF supervision. This I learned from a German who had been taken on as boss of German labour. They had set up a labour office and were employing various people to help in the airfield and base.

Within a few days I was back in the first mess and helping in exactly the same way as before, but now my bosses were two RAF men, a sergeant and a corporal who seemed very nice; there were also two German women and a boy who ran errands. The food was plentiful and I found the men generous in handing out cigarettes and occasionally chocolate. So began my new 'career' with the Allies which lasted about three years when they said that all German kitchen staff must go as they were not needed. I was very disappointed as I had enjoyed it on the camp and made good friends there including an RAF man who visited me at my cottage and gave me various welcome items such as soap powder and washing soap which were in short supply in Germany at that time.**

Betti Brockhaus was unlucky in losing her job at RAF Wahn as German help was still in vogue when I reached the base, men being employed as workers on the airfield, to tend the boilers, and there was a camp barber, who had his cubby-hole behind the guardroom. Germans were also employed as mess staff at other RAF bases and probably by the British Army, from my experience at Wahn most of the RAF and WAAF personnel used No 2 Mess. The NAAFI canteen rations of cigarettes, sweets or chocolate were collected fortnightly, and in Germany supplemented with washing powder and soap to enable one to make one's own arrangements regarding laundry if the camp system was not used.

There were two or three little shops opposite the camp gates; one sold pastries, the other, run by a man (possibly Fraulein Brockhaus's landlord), was a photographic shop though with practically nothing on display.

The Wahn base could boast a squadron of Spitfires and one of Mosquito fighter-bombers, plus an RAF regiment company including armoured cars.

Betti Brockhaus eventually achieved her ambition to move to Düsseldorf and live with her aunt, but has since succumbed to her heart condition.